$ 19.95

F

$ 19.95

the behind-the-scenes story
exclusive interviews with the writers and directors
a complete guide to every episode ever aired

The longest running network television drama ever!

GUNSMOKE

EDITED AND DESIGNED BY HAL SCHUSTER

the behind-the-scenes story
exclusive interviews with the writers and directors
a complete guide to every episode ever aired

The longest running network television drama ever!

GUNSMOKE

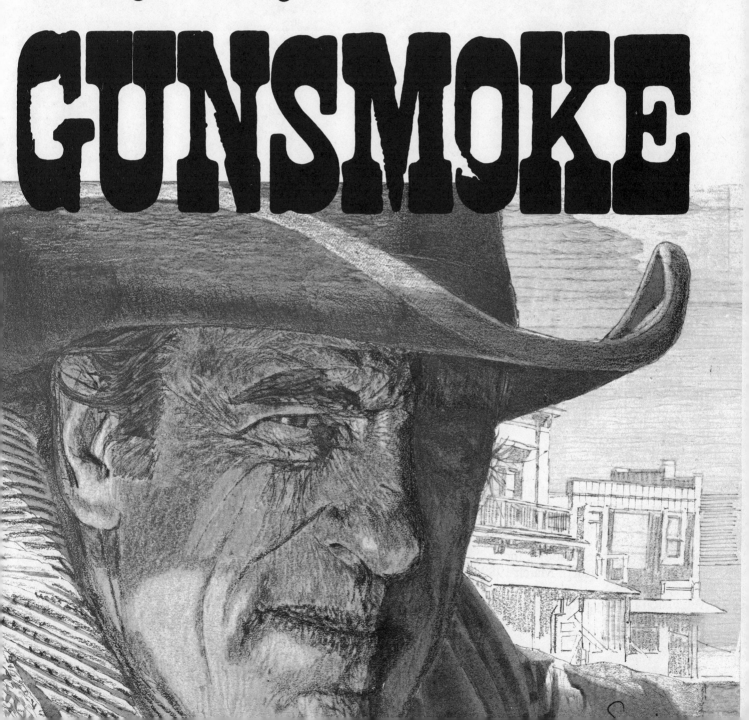

The Gunsmoke Years is published by Pioneer Books, Inc. All rights reserved...reproduction by any means is strictly prohibited without prior written permission. All photos are copyright (c) 1989 Viacom Pictures, Inc. and used only for illustrative purpose in this reference work. All other material and design copyright (c) 1989 Pioneer Books, Inc. All correspondence: 5715 N. Balsam, Las Vegas, NV 89130.

Published by Pioneer Books, Inc.
First Edition: Published: March 1989

Television History, Popular Culture, Americana, Mass Communications

10 9 8 7 6 5 4 3 2 1

DEDICATED TO MATT AND KITTY, MAY THEY FIND PEACE...

GUNSMOKE

CONTENTS:

GUNSMOKE

INTRODUCTION:

It began in 1955, when television was finally coming of age. It grew into the Sixties, when some of the very best television of all time was born. It finally died in the mid-Seventies, along with much that remained of the original energy that formed television's early years. It resurfaced once as a tv movie, and plans are underway to revive it as a series of such films.

Lasting from 1955 to 1975, **Gunsmoke**'s twenty years of production make it the all-time winner on American television for a drama series with continuing characters. **Death Valley Days** lasted twenty-three years in syndication, but never had continuing characters. The English science fiction series **Doctor Who** is in its twenty-sixth year now, but the original cast and crew have changed numerous times. Yet, in twenty years, **Gunsmoke** had but four producers, and two of the cast (James Arness and Milburn Stone) stayed the whole time. Amanda Russell remained 19 years; Dennis Weaver lasted nine, and Ken Curtis eleven.

Whichever way you cut it, this is a terrific record, never likely to be equalled again. Clearly, there was something very special about **Gunsmoke**. And there still is. Though Westerns are currently out of style, **Gunsmoke** is one of the handful that has been continually rerun. As this is written, it is currently being shown by both CBN, The Family Channel (the hour-long black and white episodes) and TBS (the color). Its only rival there is **Bonanza**, itself a 17 year veteran of the small screen.

The reasons why **Gunsmoke** lasted so long and did so well are many: fine casting, high production standards and some superb scripting. In 640 episodes, there are so few that don't work, it seems almost magical. Most shows suffer a "failure" rate of around a third of their episodes — stories rushed through, squeezed in when others fell out; ones that were done despite a lot of reservations. **Gunsmoke** has very few of these; almost every episode is worth the viewer's time. It is one of those rare items in life whose quality lies beyond dispute.

A fine roster of actors marched across the screen for the series. Charles Bronson, Robert Redford, Bette Davis, Jon Voigt, Harrison Ford, Betty Hutton, Buddy Ebsen and many, many more graced the show adding their own unique but significant contributions. Many future film stars made their acting debuts on **Gunsmoke**. The producers of Gunsmoke, safely at the helm of a winner, disregarded star reputation to choose the finest talents they could find. In doing so they discovered many of the stars that would illuminate Hollywood for decades to come.

The regular cast worked so well together, and achieved such believability that the era of Dodge City's violent days seems fresh and alive. The show ensnares the viewer, and never lets them forget it.

—John Peel

GUNSMOKE

Chapter One:
From Radio To The Silver Screen

Like many shows of the early days of television, **Gunsmoke** is rooted in radio. During the Thirties and Forties radio became a fixture in every home. And it brought much more than just music into every kitchen and living room. Families eagerly tuned in favorite comedy and drama series as they gathered about the set, ready for their shows. The scene would be repeated at the turn of the Fifties with the novelty of television. Today, with the blander fare of music and disc jockeys, few imagine the excitement listening to weekly radio broadcasts brought to huge audiences throughout the country.

Many radio series became legendary — "The Shadow," "Lights Out," "Sherlock Holmes," "The Green Hornet," and especially "The Lone Ranger." This last made one of the earliest transitions to the filmed medium, but not alone. Curiously, "Gunsmoke" began later than most of the classic radio shows, and in the end lasted only nine years in that medium — as opposed to the twenty years of the television series.

The various Western shows heard on the radio prior to "Gunsmoke" were mostly family or juvenile fare, like "The Lone Ranger." Good was good, bad was bad, and everything worked out neatly in the end.

"Gunsmoke" began life as a reaction against that simplistic sort of radio drama. It was the brainchild of Norman Macdonnell, at 35 already a solid professional in the field of radio. Macdonnell brought in writer John Meston, and the pair fleshed out the entire concept; the key-note of the show: realism.

Setting the stories in the real-life town of Dodge City began to create the air of reality. Dodge, a cattle town formed to service cowboys moving up the Santa Fe trail that ran up from Texas into Kansas, had been named for nearby Fort Dodge, five miles downriver from the town. Fort Dodge (named for Colonel Henry I. Dodge) had been founded in 1864, and Dodge City around 1872. Incorporated in 1875 as something of a boom town, Dodge found growth fueled by the money brought by the Texas drovers. While bringing the needed money to run a town this raised many problems. The drovers, after weeks on the trail driving their "beeves," arrived in a mood to drink as much as possible and generally raise a ruckus. The townsfolk needed the cattle (over eight million passed through the town in 1884 alone), but they didn't need the trouble that they caused. Once a railway line met with the city, the town founded by drinking, supplying and whoring became the seat of Ford County, and the townfolk wanted to become respectable. The town needed a city marshal.

Dodge, already divided into sides, notoriously grouped about the rail head. "The other side of the tracks" found real meaning in Dodge. The most famous lawmen in Dodge were Wyatt Earp and Bat Masterson. They enforced strictly the law of checking in guns when visitors came to town on the right side of the tracks. On the other side, however, such enforcement appeared virtually impossible. Gambling, prostitution and beer halls abounded in the town in such great numbers that it became known as "the Gommorrah of the plains" (which Matt Dillon mentions in the first story of the series). Trying to keep a lid on such corruption and potential violence presented a difficult job in the best of times. At one time, the fastest-growing section of town was the notorious Boot Hill cemetery.

Dodge needed law enforcement, but it could not be too rigorous or the cattlemen would take their trade to a more obliging town. The town needed a lawman, but no one wanted one. Added to this, the lawmen employed tended to be former gunslingers and troublemakers themselves, men who decided to become respectable and get paid for their killing.

"Gunsmoke" soaked all of this in. Though fictional, the marshal's problems and profile appeared very real. Matt Dillon, straight, sober and hard-working, found himself intensely disliked by most of the "decent folks" in town. He did what he was paid to do. He kept the peace to the best of his ability, despite the fact that he received a low salary and very little backing at all. Matt was a quiet man, a loner, and very introspective. The show allowed listeners to tune in to his cynical and weary thoughts.

They cast actor William Conrad for the pivotal role. His dry, raspy voice sounded perfect in the part, his Matt Dillon projected the image of a credible, dog-tired enforcer of the peace. "I'm that man," he announced at the start of the show. "Matt Dillon, US Marshal. The first man they look for and the last they want to meet. It's a chancy job, but it makes a man watchful... and a little lonely."

The opening narration for the stories underlined the brutal nature of the job. George Walsh, briefly spelled by George Fenneman, delivered these narrations over the years. In the earliest days, Roy Rowan did the job. "Around Dodge City and the territory out west there's just one way to handle all the killers and the spoilers, and that's with a US Marshal and the power of... gunsmoke." Actually, the title engendered something of a double meaning, one an oblique reference to the sponsors, Chesterfields and L & M. As with many radio shows, the star came on to plug the sponsor at various points during the story. Conrad extoled the praises of smoking. Other shows pushed different products, perhaps the least likely being Sherlock Holmes selling cheap wine!

GUNSMOKE

Conrad's Matt Dillon offered a classic performance, but he never rose to stardom until he cast as the overweight detective Cannon in the Seventies. Later, he appeared as television's Nero Wolfe and currently works in his large capacity on **Jake And The Fatman**. Though he never appeared in the television incarnation **Gunsmoke**, he did actually turn his hand to directing that show. The never considered Conrad for the lead role because of his portly stature. The Network wanted someone they felt television audience's would believe looked the part, this despite the fact that the real West was populated with some quite portly lawmen. Despite this, it's impossible to forget the wonderfully weary tones of Conrad's Dillon.

Matt was a lonely man, but not totally alone. Solace of different types appeared in the guise of three supporting characters of the radio show. Pride of place went to his deputy, Chester Proudfoot (for the television series, the name changed to Chester Goode). Like Matt, Chester's radio character was a far cry from the television version. Although still chatty, nosey and inclined to get things wrong, he became a definite shade more obsequious. The vocal inflections were completely different and he lacked the famous limp! Parley Baer played the radio Chester and appeared for guest spots on the television series, but not in the Chester role. None of the radio cast carried over.

Chester served as Matt's deputy, but Matt treated him with a kind of good-natured contempt that occasionally could turn quite sharp. Matt would apologize for his strong words, but you gained the impression that Chester suffered a great deal of verbal abuse that he never did on television.

Howard McNear voiced the role of Doc Adams, a man with a secret past and a tendency towards drunkenness. Definitely something of a ghoul, Doc enjoyed his work as coroner in order to pick up extra autopsy fees! This carried on to the television show in only one episode ("No Indians"). And then the television series made it clear that Doc was joking. On the radio, Doc was perfectly serious. McNear assayed the part as something of a likable rogue, rather than the crusty physician of television.

Kitty Russell, the final pivotal character played by Georgia Ellis, brought sex appeal to the show. Not yet the saloon owner that she became for television, Kitty was one of the girls that persuaded lonely cowboys to take another drink — and then perhaps pay for other favors. Kitty clearly acts as Matt's refuge after the rigors of the job. It wasn't love, but simple sexual release. Kitty, when you come down to it, was a whore. Though on radio Amanda Blake gleefully announced that Kitty really ran a frontier brothel, this never happened on the television show.

The strong cast ran through amazingly realistic tales. The sound effects of Dodge gave credibility to the show. You hear Matt walking across the boards; in the back-

ground, a dog howling, the wind rustling, and the cowboys making fun. Everything sounded perfect, courtesy of excellent work by technicians Tom Hanley, Ray Kemper and Bill James. Rex Koury provided the music for each story. He also composed the familiar theme that continued on the television series.

Macdonnell explained his philosophy behind the characters to *TV Guide* (December 6th, 1958): "Half the time the town-tamers were worse than the gunmen they were hired to tame. They were constantly suspect, no matter what good guys they were. And Matt Dillon is no exception. If you look closely, you will see that there are only three in the world who care at all whether Matt lives or dies. One is Doc, who digs the bullets out of him; another is Chester, who admires him and calls him Muster Dellon; and the other is Kitty, the dance hall girl who loves him."

Tough and often depressing, the show featured a multitude of murders and deaths. Matt deals out his own brand of justice and upholding the law. When the television series mined the radio shows for material, it toned it down for the screen! A pervasive violence, true to the times, saturated the radio series.

On the other hand, the cast didn't take everything entirely seriously. Once, while Vic Perrin (who played many of the villains) read his lines, Conrad yanked Perrin's pants down. On another occasion, whilst Matt and Chester talked in the Long Branch, the sound effects team portrayed a stranger coming in, asking for Miss Kitty, climbing the stairs, closing the door to a room, and then making love. Both occurred in rehearsals – when the show taped for the air, it was all business.

"Gunsmoke" actually fudged the facts a little. If Matt served as a U.S. Marshal, then his jurisdiction lay outside of Dodge. He would never be allowed to operate within the city limits. Historically, Dodge hired a sheriff for such duties. When Wyatt Earp served as the U.S. Marshal, for example, the sheriff of Dodge was John Behan. The two men didn't get along at all, and whenever Earp used his powers within the city, Behan would be furious. Such historical complexities were ignored (and no doubt wisely so) by the show, which gave Matt authority within and about Dodge City.

As television extended its influence, "Gunsmoke" seemed a fine possibility for adaption to the new medium. Extremely popular, with a hard-core of viewers, CBS felt that "Gunsmoke" listeners would become viewers. They proved right.

Naturally, John Meston and Norman Macdonnell involved themselves in the television set-up. Neither carried a record of experience in the young art-form, so the Network brought in a supervising producer for the first season: Charles Marquis Warren.

Born in 1912, Warren specialized in the West. After writing novels and film screenplays that included **Streets Of Laredo** (1949), **Springfield Rifle** (1952) and **Pony Express** (1953), he directed a few films, and worked in television production. Brought in by CBS, Warren brought the skills needed to help Macdonnell and Meston through their initial year of transforming the radio show into television.

Along with him came then-writer Sam Peckinpah, then noted as a writer of gritty, realistic western shows. He worked on **Gunsmoke** for a while before drifting on to many of the other television series in production. He eventually found his niche as a director of violent western films like **Ride The High Country** (1962), **The Wild Bunch** (1969) and **Pat Garrett And Billy The Kid** (1973).

The group brought in further craftsmen and began assembling the series. The Network decided from the start to go with a fresh cast, despite objections from both Macdonnell and Meston. Macdonnell told *TV Guide* (February 21st, 1976): "John Meston and I thought Bill would have made a hell of an impact, but the Network didn't see it that way." They wanted an tall actor, who looked commanding on screen. Someone, they said, like John Wayne.

Among the many myths swirling about **Gunsmoke** lies the story that they offered the lead role to John Wayne, who turned it down. Like so many stories, it possesses no basis in fact. At this point in his career, Wayne held great box office power. The Network could never afford to create a tele-

vision vehicle with Wayne as the star. Actually the Network sought Wayne's opinion in casting the part. Wayne looked over the project, and instantly named James Arness. Wayne knew Arness from films they made together. Further, in a gesture of typically Waynesian generosity, he offered to narrate a special introduction to the first show. They snapped up the offer immediately!

Twenty-six actors auditioned for Matt before they cast the man Wayne reccomended. Failed hopefuls included Raymond Burr and John Pickard. After Arness signed, he asked Wayne to get him out of his contract! Wayne advised him to change his mind.

Arness's Matt Dillon differed from the radio version, but the first story seemed much like the radio show. After the Wayne introduction to the new show, Matt walks on Boot Hill, looking back at Dodge City on the plains below. Matt's voice gave us a short introduction to the idea, then the tale proper began. The first episode has Matt lose a gunfight to a faster gun, and almost die. Dillon might represent the law, but, from the start, he possesses human fallibilities. Could you imagine the Lone Ranger getting shot down in action? Matt appears vulnerable, and that made his character appealing.

A fine trio of character actors rounded out the show. Milburn Stone played a mild romantic lead in the late Forties in various films, but never quite seemed right in those parts. He did far better honing his idiosyncrasies and playing the part of Doc Adams.

Amanda Blake intended to become one of a stable of pretty stars in the cinema, but never found her niche. She was perfect as the rather more than tarnished Kitty Russell, always wanting to be more important to Matt.

The role of Chester served as the proving ground for a young actor by the name of Dennis Weaver. Weaver, excellent in the part, became one of the very earliest of the television superstars. Women adored his character, and he soon became established as a firm television favorite. He portrayed Chester as well-intentioned, but a trifle slow, and always unlucky with women. As the show began to take shape, Weaver and Charles Warren realized they had to explain why Chester always hung around Matt, aside his obvious hero-worship. They gave Chester a limp, and thus rendered him not quite suitable for anything else.

Curiously enough, nothing ever explained why Chester should limp. He simply did. Many people assumed that because Chester was lame, so was Dennis Weaver. Nothing could have been further from the truth; Weaver had been something of a track star at school. The accent that Chester sported, too, was put on, borrowed from a classmate that Weaver recalled. The limp gained much attention, especially from the one episode in which Weaver forgot to do it. Warren recalled: "None of us noticed it in the filming or editing, but about a million viewers spotted it. Many letters simply said, 'Thank God, Chester is cured.'" They must have been terribly disappointed when he came uncured in the following story!

When **Gunsmoke** hit the air, it became the first of the adult Westerns. At the same time, the only other adult western hit the airwaves, too: **The Life And Legend Of Wyatt Earp**, starring Hugh O'Brien. That series lasted six years, also set in Dodge City for part of its run.

When **Gunsmoke** finally left the air, it had not merely outlasted all of the other Western shows, it brought down the curtain on an era. In 1975, it was the only Western series left on television. The two decades during which the Western ruled supreme on television were over. More recent attempts made to restart the genre failed.

The reasons **Gunsmoke** outlasted the rest are many, but some are easy to note. An excellent cast portrayed natives of Dodge City, creating the illusion that the town was in some way real. The show always had the best writers in television working for it. Guest stars included the top names in entertainment of the time. Many minor guest players on the series went on to become superstars, and one — Burt Reynolds — played a regular for a while.

GUNSMOKE

Chapter Two:
The Gunsmoke Television Era (1955-75)

Gunsmoke planted itself in the public eye so firmly that to many people it was not merely a Western, but *the* Western. The first six years worth of half-hour black and white stories were rapidly repackaged in a syndicated version called **Marshal Dillon**. The show then went to an hour format, then finally to color.

It proved a very viable overseas seller, as well. Dubbed into numerous languages, **Gunsmoke** drew huge audiences in Germany and Japan. In England, they renamed the half-hour stories **Gun Law**, which they deemed to have a better ring to it. When the series went to an hour format, they restored the original title, **Gunsmoke**, confusing everybody. (This sort of thing happened from time to time on English television. **Sugarfoot**, for example, became **Tenderfoot**, since the first title was meaningless in England. Unfortunately, the title song kept the original lyrics, which generated some confusion!) Under the title **Gun Law** a superb daily newspaper strip ran in England for a number of years.

The show made stars of the four main characters, somewhat to their embarrassment and pleasure. A number of spoofs based about the show came out. A record by The George Garbedian Players called "Mr.

Grillon" scored big, with Walker Edmiston playing "Fester." (A prophetic combination of Chester and the still-to-come Festus!) Walker Edmiston did such a fine parody that he spent several years doing similar ones. His best one appeared on an episode of **Maverick** called "Gun-Shy."

"Gun-Shy" is the best of the parodies because it keeps close to the real thing. The Kitty look-alike says nothing for the whole show but "Be careful, Mort." Mort Dooley is the Marshal, played by Ben Gage. Gage would later be Jim Arness's double in the **Gunsmoke** shows when Arness's leg bothered him rather badly. He and Doc would spend long, pointless minutes discussing things totally irrelevant to the story. The funniest of these appeared when Mort ruminated upon the strange characters passing through town. One of them had been a gunslinger with a business card — a sideswipe at **Have Gun, Will Travel**. There was even a pastiche of the opening credits of **Gunsmoke**, with the camera shooting between Mort's legs as he draws and fires at Bret Maverick... The whole thing is hysterical, especially for fans of the real thing.

James Arness didn't find it quite so funny, however. "It's poor taste and poor busi ness for one show to rap another," he complained. Everyone else loved the take-off.

Though everyone in the cast and on the production side of things got along well, there were some problems. After the first three years of the series, Arness complained about his share of the profits. Things soon settled, and the Arness Company took over production of the series, allowing him a larger say in running the show. Arness never insisted he be the only star. Completely unselfish in this matter, Arness always wanted Milburn Stone, Amanda Blake and Dennis Weaver to get their fair share of both plots and action.

The only one to constantly voice contrary opinions was the late Milburn Stone. When the unexpected announcement of Dennis Weaver leaving the show hit the air, Stone grumbled. Tired of **Gunsmoke**, Weaver wanted to move on to other things. He tried taking outside acting jobs — such as on **The Twilight Zone** — but always returned. Eventually, with **Kentucky Jones** snapped up, he left the show after nine years. "We had about nine funerals over him," Stone complained, before Weaver finally left.

Then the job of replacing Chester began. Oddly, the initial person chosen for the job proved too adept! Burt Reynolds — just half a decade away from his eventual film stardom — simply didn't work out. His role, as half-breed Comanche Quint Asper, was a fine part, but Quint was no Chester. Brood-ing, strong, capable and solitary by nature, he never caught on. After three years of intermittent appearances, his part disappeared.

The second try eventually succeeded, lasting longer on the show than Chester had: Festus Haggen. Festus while not simply a clone of Chester, did have many of Chester's qualities. He possessed a strange, twangy accent (again not real, but adopted for the show). Very unconventional, scruffy, unshaven and inclined not to be terribly interested in being all that civilized, Festus won the hearts of viewers. He managed the much needed trick of being adaptable either to comedy or drama.

Like Chester, Festus endured lots of problems with his family and women. Playing Festus was Ken Curtis, one of John Ford's stable of character actors. Curtis appeared in **The Searchers** and other films. Noted for his vocal prowess, Curtis started as a very occasional guest-star. He gained his permanent spot when the production team changed.

After eight years, **Gunsmoke** slipped badly in the ratings. CBS worried. They eventually decided to remove Norman Macdonnell from his position as producer, a move that didn't initially sit very well with the cast. Macdonnell had, after all, created the show and been its guiding light for eight years. CBS, however, remained insistent on

19

the change for the show to survive. Their choice for his replacement: British-born Philip Leacock.

Leacock directed several films in England before moving to Hollywood in the late Fifties. There he directed films like **Let No Man Write My Epitaph** (1960) and **The War Lover** (1962). He also worked in television, directing shows like **The Defenders** and **Route 66**. Pleased with his abilities, CBS brought him in as a first-time producer to revitalize **Gunsmoke**. With him, Leacock brought John Mantley as his story editor.

Mantley toiled in television from its inception, and the two men worked well together. They started to make the changes needed in the show. The decline in the ratings halted for a time.

Stone, cantankerous as ever, complained to *TV Guide* about their changes (June 12th, 1965): "We were all stunned," he recalled about the firing of Macdonnell. "They called Norm over to CBS at six o'clock one evening and told him the news." The changes didn't sit well with Stone: "The scripts coming through now are written by people who don't understand the show at all. We're also getting into something else I certainly don't agree with. They're bringing in guest stars."

Unfair criticism, but understandable. Stone liked Macdonnell and respected him. In fact, the new writers included some of the best talents available in Hollywood, and they produced some superb scripts. Leacock, naturally, disagreed with the judgment about guest stars: "It's awfully good for us to have a good outside actor give us a breath of fresh air occasionally." Stone did eventually calm down — though he would explode from time to time if offered a script he didn't like. He eventually came to appreciate the new production team.

By the end of that initial season, CBS agreed to renewal, and the format switched to color. The show still ranked lower in the ratings than CBS liked, though. At the end of the year, the Network cancelled **Gunsmoke**. This move had been expected for the past four or five years. It still came as something of a shock to all concerned, especially CBS chief William Paley. Leacock took a job producing a new show, **Cimmaron Strip**, and that seemed to be that. Then the unexpected happened: Paley returned from his vacation in Bermuda. He insisted on his favorite show being reinstated, and so it was. By then the Saturday slot belonged to **Mannix**, so **Gunsmoke** moved to the only available slot: Monday evening, against the worst possible competition, **The Monkees** and **The Man From UNCLE**. Already at work on his new show, Leacock made way for John Mantley, suddenly elevated to producer of **Gunsmoke**.

Incredibly, the publicity over the dramatic cancellation and reinstatement and the switch in night worked brilliantly for the

21

show. **Gunsmoke** annihilated the competition, and returned to the top of the ratings. It remained there for the rest of the run. Nothing, it seemed, could stop the revitalized series. It proved that the original estimation that it had run its course was completely incorrect.

By this point, Festus rated a firm viewer favorite. Many did still wish they could have Chester back, though. They tried two more attempts to add to the cast of the show.

First they tried Thaddeus (Thad) Greenwood, played by Roger Ewing. He lasted two seasons without making much of an impact (1965-67), and simply faded away. With the renewal of the show, a new character, aptly named Newly O'Brien, arrived in Dodge. A gunsmith, who later studied medicine with Doc, Newly became one of Matt's deputies. Played by Buck Taylor, he proved popular enough to last from 1967 to 1975, when the show finally ended its run. He even returned in the television movie as Dodge's Marshal after Matt left.

For a while in 1971, a new Doc, John Hingle, appeared played by Pat Chapman. This lasted a couple of months while Milburn Stone recovered from a heart attack. As soon as Stone was certified fit again for "active duty," Hingle left. The only other major change took place when Amanda Blake left the show. Fran Ryan (as Miss Hannah) replaced her for the final season . Fran played a regular part on **Green Acres** and more recently appeared on **The Wizard**.

Dodge City itself pulled in lots of the viewers. Reality was forged by the various townsfolk who stayed for many years, enabling viewers to come to know them.

Glenn Strange played Sam, the bartender. Strange had been a bit actor for years, one best known for playing Frankenstein's monster in several Fifties films, or for playing Butch Cavendish, the villain of the first episodes of **The Lone Ranger**. But for more than a generation, he was the bartender.

Dabbs Greer, a true veteran of television breathed life into Jonas, the owner of the general store. For several years, a viewer believed this man a storekeeper. His clerk, Howie, was played by Howard Culver.

James Nusser gave us his Louie Pheeters, the town drunk, and the viewer cared. Sarah Selby played Ma Smalley, who ran the quiet, respectable rooming house. Hank Patterson assayed Hank, the stableman. Other regulars included Charles Seel as Barney; Tom Brown as rancher Ed O'Connor; John Harper as Percy Crump; Ted Jordan as Nathan Burke; Ted Jordan as Mr. Bodkin, the banker; Woody Chambliss as Lathrop; and Charles Wagenheim as Halligan. None appeared in every show, but each of them appeared often enough for us to care about them. This gave the show a strong air of believability. The viewer knew Dodge City as a real town they had visited.

It seems appropriate to allow Macdonnell the last words on what made **Gunsmoke**

popular. In *TV Guide* (December 5th, 1968), he explained: "We try to capture some of the real feeling of the West. As well as something real in the people. As soon as your lead becomes a hero, you're in trouble. Sometimes we sit down and say to ourselves, 'You know, this fellow Dillon is just getting too noble. Let's fix him.' So we do. John [Meston] writes a script where poor old Matt gets out-drawn and out-gunned and pulls every dumb trick in the book. It makes him, and us, human."

ACADEMY AWARD WINNERS

Jack Albertson
Ed Begley
Bette Davis
Eileen Heckert
Kim Hunter
Ben Johnson
George Kennedy
Cloris Leachman
Mercedes McCambridge
Ellen Burstyn

GUNSMOKE

TOWN CHARACTERS

Dodge City itself pulled in lots of the viewers. Reality was forged by the various townsfolk who stayed for many years, enabling viewers to come to know them.

Nathan Burke (Ted Jordan) was in his 40's. He was the town gossip, as well as it's freight agent. Irritating if not actually unpleasant, he could say the things the regulars couldn't.

Barney (Charles Seel) was in his 60's. The telegrapher, he always spoke his fiesty, crusty oldster mind. He had the habit of announcing telegrams before the recipients got to read them.

Lathrop (Woodrow Chambliss) was in his 60's, and a genuine middle-of-the-roader. As storekeeper he could get involved in just about anything, and no one knew just where he would stand.

Hank (Hank Patterson) was in his 70's, still a lank, wiry, capable man, a fascinating salt of the earth.

Halligan (Charles Wagenheim) was in his 50's. He was the typical busybody, small in stature but large on opinions. He was a professional "me-too'er" but amusing.

Ma Smalley (Sarah Selby) was in her 60's and quite motherly. She ran the boarding house.

Louie Pheeters (James Nusser) was in his 50's was the town drunk that always saw the most interesting events.

Howie (Howard Culver) was in his 50's. He was the hotel clerk; slight, bespectacled and quite nervous. He was a bigot filled with righteous indignation, often for the wrong reasons, but he always meant well.

Percy Crump (John Harper) was in his 40's. He was a tall, thin undertaker.

Mr. Brodkin (Roy Roberts) was in his 50's. He was the typical, pompous banker.

Judge Brooker (Herb Vigran) was quite soft-spoken and reasonable in his 60's or 70's.

Ed O'Connor (Tom Brown) was a local rancher and in his 50's.

Occassional Characters included **Dump Hart** (Lane Bradford), a farmer, **Mr. Dofeny** (Charles Macauley), the banker, **Hank** (Hank Wise) a waiter, and **Bull** (Victor Izay), the Bull Head's bartender

GUNSMOKE

Chapter Three:
Producer John Mantley on Gunsmoke

As told to John Peel

[John Mantley was born in Toronto, Canada, in 1920.] My mother and father met on the stage in a play directed by Maurice Costello and Mary Pickford, who was also born in Toronto. She was a cousin of mine, so I was naturally interested in the theatre and motion pictures. Television didn't exist at that time, of course!

All they had in my high school was a singing group, and I couldn't sing, so I got them to found a dramatic society. I was the president of that society, and when I went on to the University of Toronto Victoria College, I became the president of the dramatic society there.

I joined the Royal Canadian Air Force in the last major international misunderstanding. I was a fighter pilot, but by the time I got to London, England, fighter pilots were a dime a dozen, so they sent me to India by sea. In the 38 days it took to get to India, I produced troop shows on the ship. Then, when the war was over, I went to the Pasadena Playhouse. I was the first undergraduate student ever to play a lead on the stage there, in 'The Hasty Heart.' I also played Cecil to Jane Cowl's Elizabeth. She was one of the great stars of the legitimate theatre. She still, posthumously, holds the record for the most Shakespearean performances on Broadway, as Juliet in 1920. I played cross-country with her in 'Elizabeth The Queen.' Then I went to New York and did a lot of live television, and I became a producer/director of live television in New York.

At one time, I had three shows on the air live each week. One of those shows was called **Mr. & Mrs. Mystery**. That show was written by John Gay, who got the Academy Award for his wonderful motion picture **Separate Tables** (1958). John played Mr. Mystery, and his wife Bobby played Mrs. Mystery. I think for their combined performances and an original script every week, they got a grand total of a hundred dollars! And people like Harry Townes and other fine actors were working for me in those days for ten dollars and a meal! I had two other shows on the air each week at that time, and I was directing them, designing the sets, bringing the props and doing the casting — and all three shows together made me $118 a week. But they were interesting days, in the sense that no one knew anything about television in those days. We were all learning.

One of the television shows I had was called **Peracho Televisione**, which was the first foreign language television show in American history. It was not looped or lip-synched or anything, it went out in Italian. The sponsors were the Delarosa Macaroni Company, and it made them into a big company. It was very successful, and got great reviews. One of the stories I did was this wonderful script in Italian, a sort of Jack the Ripper story in the London fog. I was shooting in this little studio, the Mutual Network studio, on 69th Street, and they had no big expensive technical facilities. I didn't have any fog-producing machines, and I didn't have any money. So in desperation I got a terrarium, and I put dry ice in the bottom of it. I was given permission to put an uncapped camera against the glass. I was only allowed two cameras and two camera operators. So I had this camera focused on the tank, and a technician standing over the top, wafting away with a newspaper. Because you can do anything electronically, we got the most beautiful fog effects you ever saw! Everyone was calling me, asking how we'd made them, but I wouldn't tell anybody.

I lived on Benzedrine in those days. There wasn't much time for sleep. With **Peracho Televisione**, I went to Italy with the executive producer, who was a brilliant man called Andre Delrocco. We made the pilot here in America, then I went to Italy, where we made 39 half-hour anthology drama shows for American television. I think those were the first 39 film shows ever in the can for television. They played here in over a hundred markets, and it was a great learning experience for me. When I got to Italy, they had never shot lip-synched sound. I had to teach them that. All they could do was print films, too; they couldn't do any special effects like fades or dissolves. We fell in love with Italy and stayed for four years. My first son was born there. Nobody had heard of me by the time I came back!

[Instead of doing television work, he turned to writing novels. His first was **The 27th Day**, and his second **The Snow Bridge**.]

That was made into a movie for 20th Century Fox. It was directed by Henry Hathaway, starring Susan Hayworth and Stephen Boyd. It was retitled **Woman Obsessed**, which I thought was a terrible title for my book. I was granted an interview with the producer, Spiros Scouros, which lasted for about forty seconds! I was very nervous in this huge office, and I told him who I was, and that I didn't think **Woman Obsessed** was a very good title. He looked at me and said: 'Is good title. Pig you!' That was the end of that interview. The other book was filmed by Columbia, and from that I began to write television. No one would hire me as a director, and nobody remembered me as an actor. By this time, I had decided I really didn't like acting, anyway.

27

GUNSMOKE

I wrote for all of the usual shows. I did two **Playhouse 90** episodes, but unfortunately that was the year that the show was canceled and neither of them was made. I wrote about twenty **Untouchables**, five or six **Desilu Playhouses, Outer Limits** and **Kraft Theatre** and all those things that the freelancers did in those days. Then I became the story editor on **The Great Adventure**, and after that became the story editor on **Gunsmoke**. Executive story consultant they call it now, a very pretentious title. The next year I was made producer, and when the executive producer — a splendid man called Philip Leacock — was picked to produce what should have been the greatest western ever, a two hour western called **Cimmaron Strip**, he left **Gunsmoke**. I was left to do the show alone. I remained on **Gunsmoke** for eleven years. Apart from the lead actors, no one was with the show as long as I was. Maybe one or two of the craft people were. The late Tiny Nichols began as Jim's stand-in and later became an assistant. He was one of the first people, too. I was there for eleven years, and enjoyed every minute of it. Then I went on to do **How The West Was Won** for four years.

[The show at this point was in something of a slump. Dennis Weaver had left, and color would be introduced the following year. The show had been upgraded from a half-hour to a full hour series.]

Ken Curtis was an intermittent regular. Philip and I made him a regular on the show. When we took over, **Gunsmoke** was in the middle of the ratings and slipping. I think the reason was that Norman Macdonnell — who had produced the show for eight years — got into the same kind of problem that all producers do with this kind of show. **Gunsmoke** in the early days was almost a no-drama show. There was a shorthand: 'I'm going to kill you, because you killed my brother;' 'We've got to cut 'em off at the pass;' and there was a necessary shoot-out at the end of each show. Towards the end of Norman's reign, he became so frustrated with this sort of format that he began experimenting with somewhat unusual forms of shows. The audience didn't want that. They wanted the traditional no-drama. I suspect that's why the ratings were slipping. The cast was the same, and very polished by this time, and very, very good together.

Philip Leacock and I came in together. We had met on **The Great Adventure**, on which he was the director and I was the story editor. He was a splendid man and a great pal. He directed two of my favorite pictures, **The Little Kidnappers** (1953) and **Hand In Hand** (1960). After a year, he went off to do **Cimmaron Strip**, but that show just didn't work for a lot of reasons. I was left alone to do **Gunsmoke**, and to do one thing in addition. We were sent over to try to rescue **The Wild, Wild West**. This was in trouble financially, and they had no scripts ready. Philip, for various reasons, was never allowed to see the scripts or come into the offices because the man who owned the show, the executive producer, did not want to share the credit. So I had to do the work alone. I only remained long enough to get the show back on track, but for a time I was doing two shows at once, **Gunsmoke** and **The Wild, Wild West**.

At that point, **Gunsmoke** was beginning to pick up. At least, it was stabilized and no longer slipping.

[The show then went through an amazing period. Having slipped in the ratings, **Gunsmoke** was canceled by CBS in 1967. It was returned to the air, according to most reports, because William Paley — the head of CBS — loved it so much. It returned on Monday night, against strong competition.]

No one will ever convince me that the powers-that-be did not put **Gunsmoke** on on Monday nights except to prove to Mr. Paley that they were right in having canceled it. **Gunsmoke** had been on Saturday night since its inception and had been very successful there. There wasn't any question though that the ratings were slipping, for the reasons that I explained earlier. So the show was canceled. Mr. Paley was very upset when he returned from his vacation, for it was always one of his favorite shows. There was also a tremendous outcry. I still have the Congressional Record for the day that a senator castigated the Network for removing a classic. I think, though, that one of our most powerful allies in our defense was that several Midwestern stations refused to carry any CBS programs if they did not include **Gunsmoke**.

Whatever the reasons — and many have been put forward — **Gunsmoke** was reinstated. By that time, the Saturday night slot had been filled [With **Mannix**]. So it was scheduled for Monday night, as I said, to prove to Mr. Paley that they had been right in canceling the show. You can imagine why, for we were on the air against **The Monkees**, which was the second or third highest-rated program on the air at that time. That faced our first half-hour. The second half-hour faced **The Man From UNCLE**, which was also in the top of the ratings. On the opposite side, on ABC, was coming in the show that everybody thought was going to be the hit of the decade. The Network had already proved what Chuck Connors could do with a little boy and a rifle in **The Rifleman**. That had been enormously successful, so someone had the bright idea to put Chuck Connors with a boy and a gun in Africa with lots of animals. It had to be the hit of the century!

At the end of that year, **Cowboy In Africa** was gone; **The Man From UNCLE** was gone and **The Monkees** was gone. [**Gunsmoke** also made it back to #4 in the ratings.] In the following years **Gunsmoke** destroyed nine other shows: **Red Skelton, My World And Welcome To It, I Dream Of Jeannie**, and so on." For its remaining years on television, **Gunsmoke** beat all its opposition, and remained a firm ratings favorite.

GUNSMOKE

After about five years, I started doing what Norman had done. I was getting restless, and wanted to try new things. I was getting a little frustrated by the format itself, and I found myself unknowingly and unwittingly doing what Norman had done. At least, I assume that this is what Norman did; we never spoke about that, and he's gone now so we can't tell. I wanted to resign, but Jim Arness talked me out of it. Not too long after that, Robert Kennedy and Martin Luther King were assassinated. This nation reeled in righteous wrath at these dreadful events, and television became the scapegoat. There was a tremendous revulsion against violence, and television took the brunt of it. The producers of all action and adventure shows spent an entire summer in the cutting rooms deleting violence from shows that had already been aired. So, in the reruns they were taking out the violence that the audience had already seen! It seemed rather silly to me and everybody else, but we did it.

What happened then was really quite incredible because no one knew what to do with an action/adventure show if you couldn't have violence. Everyone stayed entirely away from me, and I did *exactly* what I wanted. I began by making my biggest single mistake in my history as a producer! I was delighted when this edict against violence came out because I thought to myself that I was one producer who didn't have a problem. I had four of the best actors around, who were great together, having played in an ensemble for all these years. I

could build any number of shows about these people, without any problem. I could not have been more wrong.

Conflict is the essence of drama. And I couldn't create conflict between these people! They felt so much alike, they had so much faith in one another, they loved one another so much. They understood one another so much within the context of that show that I don't think that in the ensuing five years or so that I was able to make more than one or two shows in which I could create realistic conflict between them. Then I had to do what I had done on **The Untouchables**. My **Untouchables** were always built about innocent individuals who somehow got sucked into the conflict between Ness and the gangs. Those people became rich characters, when I did them well, which wasn't always! It gave the show a different texture. And that's what I did with **Gunsmoke**. I brought in guest stars, who gave outstanding performances. People like Ed Asner, and Richard Kiley and many many, others. All of these really splendid people.

We had one show, for example, where we couldn't find the right actor for a second son, and an unknown actor came in and read it absolutely brilliantly. This was the first lead for a man no one had ever heard of. His name was Richard Dreyfuss. Another time, we were looking for a Swedish boy, and a young man came in who couldn't do a Swedish accent. He didn't know that was what we wanted. He asked us to give him ten minutes, came back and did a brilliant reading. He had never had a credit before in his life. His name was John Voigt. I wrote a long scene for a prostitute in a two-part show; we must have read sixty women, and I finally threw up my hands and was convinced I'd written an impossible scene, a lousy scene, that we should dump. Still, there was one more girl to see, and she came in and put us right out of our minds. That was Ellen Burstyn. Nobody had ever heard of her, either. There was also Loretta Swit... the list goes on and on and on.

Everyone went away and left me alone. The story with Richard Dreyfuss was about a Jewish patriarch and his dedication to the Torah. Now, can you conceive of any network allowing a producer to make a show about a Jewish patriarch as a Western? It couldn't have been done. We won two awards from the President's Council on Mental Retardation for things we did. We got all kinds of accolades from educational associations, one for a show called 'The Fires Of Ignorance.' That was about the need for compulsory education for children. In the years prior to the anti-violence trend on television, I think **Gunsmoke** won maybe three major awards. From that point to the last show of the twentieth season, we won eighty three awards. We won nine consecutive Best Script Awards from the Western Writers Of America. We won five Western Heritage Awards. We won the Cody Award. We won the Brotherhood Award from the National Conference of Christians

and Jews, and citations from the National Education Association. The awards just piled up, and over the years we got a staff of splendid writers. Bill Kelly and Earl Wallace won the Oscar two years ago for **Witness**. They both came out of **Gunsmoke**. Jim Byrnes, the predominant Western writer in America today, came out of that time. So did the late Ron Bishop. A brilliant writer and a splendid man. Jack Miller, who unfortunately took his own life. Paul Edwards... They were all splendid.

We did have some clunkers. Sometimes there are clunkers because you just can't get the actors. For instance, we had a purely delightful show which had a ridiculous premise, because with **Gunsmoke** you could do anything from the most intense melodrama to the wildest farce. We did one story about two ancient brothers who brought their hundred-year old father in because there was an outstanding warrant on him that was sixty years old! We did lots of nonsense shows, but we did one of them about a midget who swore he was going to turn into an elephant on New Year's Eve! The problem was that we couldn't get the only really good little people actor, who would have been wonderful in the part. We had to settle for second best, because we obviously couldn't play it with anything but a midget. That actor didn't work in the part at all. We had our share of failures — everyone did — but we had such wonderful writers. They competed with one another. They were off and running. Kelly, for example, had never written anything but novels when he came to us. Earl Wallace had been the assistant editor of a Thousand Oaks newspaper! Jim Byrnes had never sold anything before he came to us. He sent me a script about a trek, which was no good for **Gunsmoke**, but five pages in I could see he was a wonderful writer. All of these talents came together to make what was the most exciting period of my life. I've only named a few of the actors and writers who went on to greatness who were a part of **Gunsmoke** in those years.

One thing I had always wanted to do, but was unable to was after **Gunsmoke** had gone two or three years, I suggested doing a retrospective. We had it almost put together, and during the show we aged Jim Arness backwards in time to match the clips. We had **Gunsmoke** in Italian, in German and in Japanese — the same scene, cutting between them. We had the most exciting dramatic footage we had shot, racing down wild rivers, going over cliffs and all of that sort of thing. We were going to air it opposite the return of the Smothers Brothers in the late Seventies, not the recent one. We never did get it on the air because there were so many stars in the show that we simply couldn't get clearances on all of them. They started too late, and there were something like 130 stars. Bette Davis, Jean Arthur, Robert Redford, Betty Hutton, to say nothing of the other stars. So we never did do that retrospective. I guess it's a little too late now.

ACADEMY AWARD NOMINEES

Jean Arthur
Lew Ayres
Ralph Bellamy
Theodore Bikel
Beulah Bondi
Ellen Burstyn
Dyan Cannon
Lynn Carlin
Jack Cassidy
Stanley Clements
Lee J. Cobb
Ellen Corby
Nina Foch
Vincent Gardenia
Thomas Gomez
Arthur Hunnicutt
John Ireland
Richard Jaeckel
John Kerr
John Marley
Ron Moody
J. Carroll Naish
Nancy Olson
Katherine Ross
Alfred Ryder
Cicely Tyson
John Voight
James Whitmore
Chill Wills

We may be making another [**Gunsmoke** television movie similar to the one made under Mantley's supervision in Alberta]. It was not, in my opinion, the **Gunsmoke** it could have been. I think it had some good moments. The main thing is that it got very nice ratings and the Network was very happy with it. It got some good reviews, and a lot of people liked it. I just thought we could have done better, but we had a lot of problems. The show did do very well, and on account of that there may be some more.

I've had a lot of time to think about it [what made **Gunsmoke** so uniquely successful for so many years]. One main reason is that I think that the characters were brilliantly created. If you think about it, there's sort of a cross-section of mankind. First, you've got the benevolent dictator, with the power of life and death in his gun. That's Marshal Dillon. Then you've got the man who has the power of life and death with his scalpel, with knowledge. The Doctor. Originally, he was a drunk [in the radio series] and had a very shady past. He'd obviously been thrown out of the East for something nobody really knew. Milburn never played him that way. He played a different kind of character, and brilliantly so. So you have the benevolent dictator, and the man of science and learning. Then you have Miss Kitty, who was the Earth-mother to all men. Then you have the court jester. First was the charming court jester, willing and able but not too bright, played so finely by Dennis Weaver. Later, it was Ken Curtis as Festus.

The only thing we tried to do, and which I think we succeeded in at the end, after trying three people, was to add the one element that seemed to be missing from that cross-section. That was the young man who learned from the older. So we brought in Buck Taylor as Newly O'Brien, who was a gunsmith and then began to read medicine under Doc. Eventually, in the two-hour show, he turned out to be the Marshal.

I think the creation of the characters themselves was the number one thing. The second thing was the brilliant casting of the show. The third thing that contributed to its longevity was the absolutely wonderful feeling among all of these characters of contributing to the show without concerning themselves about how much they had in the show. I did that show for eleven years, and I never had any of the actors come to me and complain about the size of their part, or that someone else had more lines than they had. Nobody! You could walk on that set and hear Milburn saying, 'Why doesn't Kenny take this line? He'll get a much bigger laugh with it than I will.' Or Amanda would say, 'Wouldn't this scene play better if it were slanted to Doc?' Or Jim would say: [adopts deep, gruff voice] 'I don't need all of these words! Why don't I just say 'Hold it!'?' They were absolutely so unselfish in the way that they conducted themselves on that set. Everything was for the good of the show. You must realize that in the early days, those people spent more time on the **Gunsmoke** set than they did in their own private lives. They were, in every sense of the word, a family. I think that the love that they felt for each other as characters and in real life was reflected on the screen.

Buddy Ebsen was another example of an actor who has that kind of a relationship with an audience. On **Barnaby Jones**, the writing was not great, the plots were not wonderful, but that show survived all of those years because he had such a following, he was such a warm human being. Whenever I put him on **Gunsmoke**, the ratings went up by two points. It never happened with anybody else.

Jim, as you know, was wounded by machine-gun bullets in the landing at Anzio. His leg troubled him after that all his life. Towards the end of the series, it was even more so, and we got a lot of letters on it. Several times, I tried to write in a scene to explain why he should limp, but they never got filmed. Then I did it in **How The West Was Won**. I put in a whole scene where he was torn up by a bear. That was never used, either. I just got a double for him, Ben Gage, so that the letters would stop, and Jim wouldn't limp so much in crucial areas.

There isn't any question that those **Gunsmoke** years were the happiest of my career in television. The world today is a far, far different place. I used to wake up back then and think, 'My God, they're going to pay me to do this again!' It really was exciting.

There was an unholy magic that had caught all of us — the writers and the actors and the producers and the directors. Just look at the talent involved. Leonard Katzman, who was my line producer on **Gunsmoke** for about five years is now the executive producer on **Dallas**, and one of the outstanding producers of television in this nation. There was Joe Dackow, a wonderful man, who died of a heart attack. John Stephens, who was my line producer on **Gunsmoke**, **How The West Was Won** and **Buck Rogers**. He's now an executive producer in his own right, and has been doing **Simon & Simon** so brilliantly for the last five or six years. Everyone who came out of that show seems to have done extremely well. In eleven years, you have the time to nurture the talent that you find. I had Cal Clements with me on the show, and he's written more drama than any human being in the history of the world! He wrote over a hundred **Gunsmoke**s alone, and he's been on almost every other show in the business. I'm the only man for whom he ever worked as a story editor. He would come for a couple of years, then go off, then come back. But we're still great friends, and I think he's a great writer. There were so many great writers around in those days.

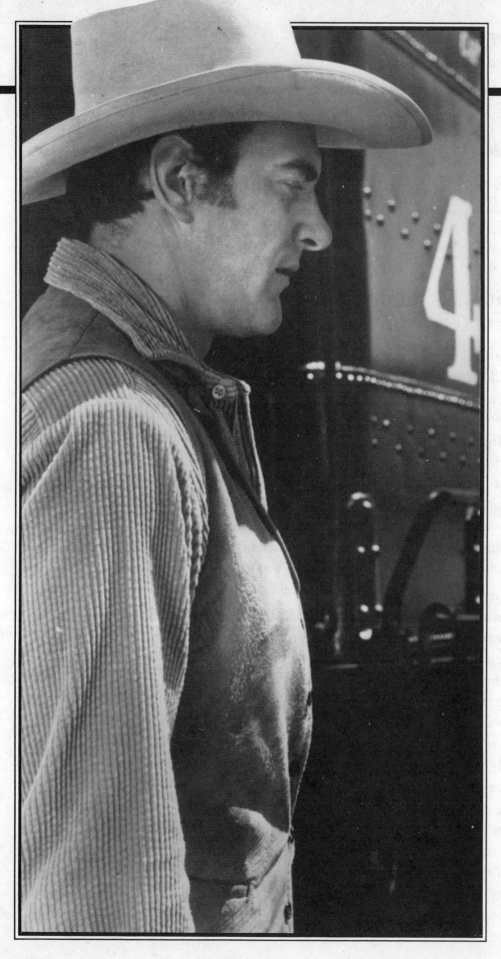

GUNSMOKE

Chapter Four:
An Interview with Story Editor Paul Savage

Interview by John Peel

Paul Savage worked on **Gunsmoke** for two years as the story editor, under both Philip Leacock and John Mantley. He is currently writing for series like **Murder, She Wrote** and **High Mountain Rangers**, and was the writer of the TV movie **Bonanza: The Next Generation**. His career, however, began as an actor, in 1946. He had been wounded in the Second World War, and sent through various hospitals, the last of which was on Long Island.

"Shortly after I was discharged, I went to Florida as an actor," he recounted. "This was for an independent movie. I was told I would be in their next picture that would be shot in Alaska from the headquarters here in California if I could be in California by February. So I moved, and did some radio and some stage — which I had done in summer stock from High School. For five or six years, I did very little work; hat in hand stuff out here, as an actor. So I began to write. I sold a story to a program called **The Millionaire**, and from that got my first credit and my first agent. About six months later, he got me another job, and little by little I left the acting profession. Now, for

some thirty-odd years, I've been a writer.

"I've had two agents in that time. The first agent left the field to become a producer, so I went with the office that he had been with at the time. The head of the agency had seen my work, and liked it enough that he wanted to work for me. I wrote for **The Big Valley**, **The Restless Gun**, **McKenzie's Raiders**, **Laramie** and **A Man Called Shenandoah**, for example.

"Norman Macdonnell is very important to the history of one of the top shows ever, **Gunsmoke**. Norman was the godfather and guider of the series. When it was a sustaining radio program — before Chesterfields first sponsored it — Norman gave me a handful of jobs doing off-mike ad-lib head-nods, and they literally fed me. Thirty five dollars a show. When I started writing, after I had gotten enough credits, I went to Norman and because of his great kindness and goodness, I ended up doing eight episodes for him. That was for the television show."

It was shortly after this that CBS fired Macdonnell from the show, and replaced him with Philip Leacock. Many of the regular writers for the series refused to work with Leacock, feeling that Macdonnell had

EMMY AWARDS

Jack Albertson
Ed Asner
Ellen Corby
James Daly
Cloris Leachman
Michael Learned
Kathleen Nolan
Carroll O'Connor
Milburn Stone
Frank Sutton

TONY AWARDS

Ed Begley
Ralph Bellamy
Vincent Gardenia
Harry Jones
Richard Kiley
David Wayne
Fritz Weaver
Ellen Burstyn

been treated very badly. These included John Meston and Kathy Hite. "Philip Leacock was given the producer's job," Paul recalled, "and John Mantley came in as his story editor. They had never had anything to do with **Gunsmoke**, and the old hands on the show did not want to go in with this new regime. I was sort of the nexus between the old and the new. I was called in because of the episodes that I had done for Norman. John Mantley left the show briefly, and became producer of **The Wild, Wild West**. I moved in to **Gunsmoke** as story consultant. When John came back, he came back as producer, having come off **The Wild, Wild West** as producer. Philip Leacock became executive producer, and I was their story consultant. After about a year or so, Mantley took over as executive producer. I stayed on another couple of years, then left for Disney. This was in the days when we were doing 39 episodes per season, and I was the only one in story at the time. Today, they have four, five or six people on story — and do 22 episodes a season!

"It was a well-done show, and we were left pretty much alone. There was obviously some Network input, but they wisely didn't interfere too much with that which was successful. We did it as we felt we should. Later, Joe Dackow came in as associate producer. When I left, Mantley continued on, and Dackow died. They had a series of other story editors: Jack Miller and Calvin Clements, with assistants." Paul believes that **Gunsmoke** lasted so long for a single reason: "Honesty! It was as true a depiction of the West as was possible to make. The Western is the one, true, original American story form. It was, if you will, the day of the individual, when Matt Dillon could stand up, stradle-legged, with his hand hanging next to his gun and tell somebody to 'get out of *my* town.' Peace ruled, with him as the leader. Times have changed — the ACLU would come down on you like a ton of bricks if a man said 'get out of *my* town" today! As a consequence, we have all of the negative elements that now exist. Sure, we have lots of freedoms, but... They were telling stories of the old days, where the strong protected the weak, where the strong led the way, and where I suppose you might say that the weak were willing to follow, because they recognized the strength that they didn't have. Today, everybody thinks they're strong.

"We had excellent writers, for openers. Understand, also that Norman and John Meston set the tone. When a change was made, it still followed the spine that they laid down, that they had created. It was too good to mess with! So we left it alone. We told honest and true stories. There was always some dickeying with the scripts that I did, and those that followed did. There were nuances that were only really understood by those who were as close to the show as we who were on staff were. There was also such a love for the realities of history. I'm sitting in my den right now, and it's filled with bits of the West, the early West. When I was a boy, I wanted to be a cowboy.

When I grew a little older and realized that there were no more cowboys, I wanted to be a rancher. It was all the West, and what the West meant. I was lucky, because I got into a field that let me vicariously live that life for a long, long time.

"Sadly, there are no Westerns any more. No real Westerns, because of the elements that made them. As I said, the one lone man who stood up against 'evil.' You had a clearly defined bad man. The Indian — misread — was seen as the evil one; the bloodthirsty redskin. The outlook on the Indian has totally changed today. Where he was seen once as a roadblock against advancing civilization, he is now seen as a stalwart who was protecting his own. You can't do that story element any more as you once did. With attitudes expounded by the liberal bent today, you can't have the one man, the one leader. The recent attempts at reviving Westerns were not true Westerns. They wanted the Western genre, but they wouldn't stay true to the original lines. So they did a little joke, they used little gimmicks. They did it funny. Along came **Bret Maverick**, and **The Over-The-Hill Gang**, and even today, they are doing caricatures. Even Clint Eastwood, who could very well have been the catalyst to bring back the Western with his **Pale Rider** did a caricature, and an old story — it was just **Shane**, all over again. Again, **Silverado** was more of a spoof."

"You can't compare even the best of **Bonanza** against the best of **Gunsmoke**. Even though **Bonanza** ran as many years as it did, I think to the Western aficionado, **Gunsmoke** stands out, head and shoulders. We weren't afraid, for example, to let Matt kill the wrong man. Matt was as human a person as you could wish to write. He was human, and had foibles. The sex, if you will, between him and Kitty, was one of the most adult pieces of business that was ever on the air. You never had to use the devices that are used today. We never had to get dirty, or show them getting in or out of bed together. **Gunsmoke** was honest!

"I can speak for when I was on the show, and when I knew Norman: a point of view was always the start of our stories. A character with a problem; a character with a point of view. It was never a plot, per se, that was approached. It was a character with a problem that was approached and developed. **Bonanza** is being more heavily syndicated than **Gunsmoke**, and I'm a little disappointed. I think it should be the other way 'round! **Gunsmoke** is more visceral. I don't want it to sound like I'm putting down **Bonanza** or any other show, because they all went into it. As Hitchcock said, 'Nobody sets out to make a bad picture.' They were all as honest as their point of view let them be, or made them be. I just think that as established by Norman Macdonnell and John Meston, **Gunsmoke** was the best. They set the path, and it was a clearly defined path, lovingly followed by those who came after."

GUNSMOKE

GUNSMOKE'S DIRECTORS AND WRITERS

*Much of the success of **Gunsmoke** was based on the talent of the actors that the viewers became accustomed to seeing every week, like old friends.. Much of the success was based on talent the viewers never saw at all. These were the writers and directors that brought the characters to life, that put the words in their mouths and made sure the stories worked. Many of these talented people went on to success in other vehicles. Some went on to direct or write hit movies while others made their mark in other television series.*

MARK RYDELL directed **The Cowboys, Cinderella Liberty, The Reivers** and **The Fox**

BERNARD KOWALSKI directed **Krakatos-East of Java, Macho Callahan, SSSSS** and **Stilletto**

ROBERT BUTLER directed **Scandalous John, The Barefoot Executive, The Computer Wore Tennis Shoes** and **Now You See Him-Now You Don't**

BERNARD McEVEETY directed **Ride Beyond Vengeance, The Brotherhood of Satan, One Little Indian** and **Napoleon and Samantha**

RICHARD COLLA directed **The Man Who Loved Cat Dancing, Fuzz, Zig Zag** and **Lolly Madonna XXX**

RICHARD SARAFIAN directed **Vanishing Point, Fragment of Fear** and **Man in the Wilderness**

VINCENT McEVEETY directed **Firecreek, The Biscuit Eater, The $1,000,000 Duck** and **Charley and the Angel**

PAUL STANLEY directed **The Virginian, Mission Impossible, The Untouchables, Hawaii Five-O, Dr. Kildare** and **Combat**

ALEN REISNER directed **Kojak, Hawaii Five-O, Cannon, Mannix, Ironside, Marcus Welby** and **Kung Fu**

HERSCHEL DAUGHERTY directed **Bonanza, The Virginian, Alfred Hitchcock Presents, High Chaparral, Star Trek** and **Winchester 73**

DAVID ALEXANDER directed **Emergency, Get Smart, Marcus Welby, The Man from U.N.C.L.E., F Troop** and **The Ghost and Mrs. Muir**

ROBERT TOTTEN directed episodes for **Kung Fu, The Cowboys** and **Doc Elliot** as well as the films, **The Red Pony, The Wild Country** and **The Quick and the Dead**

GUNNAR HELLSTROM directed episodes for **Bonanza, The F.B.I., Cimarron Strip** and **The Wild Wild West**

ARNOLD LAVEN directed episodes for **The Plainsman** and **The Rifleman** as well as the films, **Geronimo, Rough Night at Jericho** and **Sam Whiskey**

JOHN RICH won the Emmy for directing **All in the Family**, but was also involved with **The Dick Van Dyke Show** and directed the films, **Roustabout, The New Interns, Wives and Lovers** and **Easy Come, Easy Go**

THOMAS THOMPSON won Western Writers of America Golden Spur Award 1953-1954 and served as President of the Western Writers of America in 1957 and 1966; he has 500 magazine stories and a couple of novels to his credit along with the screenplays for **Cattle King** and **Saddle the Wind**

JOHN MANTLEY wrote **The Parson and the Outlaw, My Blood Runs Cold, The 27th Day** and **Woman Obsessed**

MICHAEL FISHER wrote **Buckskin, The Savage Seven** and **Killers Three**

ANTHONY ELLIS wrote **The Ride Back**

CALVIN CLEMENTS wrote **Firecreek**

SIMON WINCELBERG won the Writers Guild of America Award for television twice and the wrote **Fighter Attack, On the Threshold of Space** and episodes of **Lost in Space**

WARREN DOUGLAS wrote **Night of the Grizzly, Cry Vengeance, Sierra Passage** and **Northern Patrol**

RICHARD FIELDER wrote **A Distant Trumpet** and **Return of the Boomerang** and won the Western Heritage Award for television

FRANK COCKRELL wrote **Inferno, Darl Waters** and **On the Threshold of Space**

DONALD S. SANFORD won two nominations for the Writers Guild of America television award and wrote **The 1,000 Plane Raid** and **Submarine X-1**

RICHARD CARR wrote **Heaven with a Gun, Too Late Blues** and **Hell Is for Heroes**

20 years of GUNSMOKE EPISODES

"Good evening. My name's Wayne. Some of you may have seen me before. I hope so — I've been kickin' around Hollywood a long time. I've made a lot of pictures out here, all kinds. Some of 'em have been Westerns, and that's what I'm here to tell you about tonight — a Western. A new television show called **Gunsmoke***. When I first heard about the show* **Gunsmoke***, I knew there was only one man to play in it — James Arness. He's a young fella, and maybe new to some of you, but I've worked with him, and I predict he'll be a big star. And now I'm proud to present* **Gunsmok***."*

—Introduction to the first episode, by John Wayne

GUNSMOKE

Season One
September 10th, 1955 through August 25th, 1956
Produced by Charles Marquis Warren
Associate Producer: Norman MacDonnell
Production Supervisor: Glen Cook
Director of Photography: Fleet Southcott, Ernest Miller, ACE
Art Director: Nicoli Remisoff
Property Master: Robert Easton, Mike Gordon
Supervising Editor: Fred W. Berger, ACE
Makeup: Glen Alden
Hairdresser: Pat Whiffing
Wardrobe: John E. Dowsing, Jr
Script Supervisor: Mary Chaffee
Special Photographic Effects: Jack Rabin, Louis DeWitt
Sound: Roderic Sound, Inc
Casting: Lynn Stalmaster

Cast
Matt Dillon: James Arness
Chester Goode: Dennis Weaver
Doc Galen Adams: Milburn Stone
Kitty Russell: Amanda Blake
Louie Pheeters: James Nusser
Barney: Charles Seel
Howie: Howard Culver
Ed O'Connor: Tom Brown
Percy Crump: John Harper
Mr. Jones: Dabbs Greer

1) Matt Gets It
September 10th, 1955
Written by Charles Marquis Warren, Story by John Meston, Directed by Charles Marquis Warren, Assistant Director: Glenn Cook
Guest Cast: Paul Richards, Robert Anderson, Malcolm Atterbury
Sheriff Jim Hill from Amarillo arrives in Dodge City, looking for Dan Grat. Grat is trouble, a bully who provokes people to draw, then guns them down. He shot an unarmed man in Amarillo, and Hill is here to take him back. Matt realizes that Hill wants to beat Grat in a gunfight, and is warned by Hill to stay out of it. Matt visits the Long Branch, where Kitty tries to get romantic with him. Grat is there, and informs Matt that he doesn't want any trouble if he gets involved in any killings. He knows about Hill being here, and aims to kill him. Matt warns him that this will be resisting arrest, and asking for trouble. Grat doesn't care, and he and Hill face off. Hill loses, and is shot dead. Matt has to try and take Grat, but Grat is even faster than he is, and Matt is gunned down.
 He's in bad shape, but alive. Chester is furious, and promises to go after Grat with a shotgun if Matt dies. Matt recovers, however, and in the week he's laid up, Grat kills two more people, both from close up. Matt begins exercising, to be able to take Grat on again, and after another week, he feels confident enough to try it. He goes to the Dodge House, where Grat is staying, and calls him out. He realizes that Grat relies on his fast draw, and doesn't take time to aim. Matt's only chance is to provoke the draw before Grat gets in range. Grat knows what Matt is doing, and keeps trying to get closer. Once he thinks he's close enough, he goes

for his gun. He outdraws Matt, but misses. Matt is a fraction slower, but kills Grat.

The first story gave us the theme: Matt stands virtually alone against lawlessness. Grat is the fastest there is, but Matt takes that extra second to fire, and wins. The opening credits for the show reflect this same slight slowness on the draw.

Matt's Colt Peacemaker has an extended barrel, giving him the extra accuracy. (There's one delicious outtake of the opening sequence where the draw takes place, and Matt falls over "dead" instead of the villain!)

2) Hot Spell
September 17th, 1955
Written by E. Jack Neuman, Directed by Charles Marquis Warren
Guest Cas: John Dehner
When a gunfighter is released from jail, Matt is forced to defend him from a lynch mob.

3) Word Of Honor
October 1st, 1955
Written by Charles Marquis Warren, Story by John Meston, Directed by Charles Marquis Warren
Guest Cast: Robert Middleton, Claude Akins, Ray Boyle, Will Wright
Doc witnesses a murder, and the killers aim to silence him permanently.

4) Home Surgery
October 8th, 1955
Written by John Meston, Directed by Charles Marquis Warren
Guest Cast: Joe De Santis, Gloria Talbot, Wright King
Matt and Chester discover a man dying, supposedly of an accident.

5) Obie Tater
October 15th, 1955
Written by Charles Marquis Warren, Story by John Meston, Directed by Charles Marquis Warren
Guest Cast: Royal Dano, Kathy Adams
Obie Tater is an old prospector who has struck it rich. This attracts a gang, wanting his money.

6) Night Incident
October 29th, 1955
Written and Directed by Charles Marquis Warren
Guest Cast: Peter Votrian, Jeanne Bates
The boy who cried wolf — an imaginative youngster isn't believed when he overhears plans for a robbery.

7) Smoking Out The Nolans
November 5th, 1955
Written by Charles Marquis Warren, Story by John Meston, Directed by Charles Marquis Warren
Guest Cast: Ainslie Pryor, Jeanne Bates, John Larch
An old friend of Matt's has witnessed a murder, and is now hunted by the killers and the friends of the dead man.

GUNSMOKE

8) Kite's Reward
November 12th, 1955
Written by John Meston, Directed by Charles Marquis Warren
Guest Cast: Adam Kennedy, James Griffith
A reformed outlaw comes to Dodge, and Matt tries to help him get a job. Then a bounty hunter turns up, looking for the man.

9) The Hunter
November 26th, 1955
Written by John Dunkel, Directed by Charles Marquis Warren
Guest Cast: Peter Whitney, Richard Gilden
A buffalo hunter ignores Matt's advice and hunts the animals on the sacred grounds of a local Indian tribe.

10) The Queue
December 3rd, 1955
Written by Sam Peckinpah, Story by John Meston, Directed by Charles Marquis Warren
Guest Cast: Keye Luke, Sebastian Cabot
A Chinese cook becomes the target of hatred and prejudice.

11) General Parsley Smith
December 10th, 1955
Written by John Dunkel, Story by John Meston, Directed by Charles Marquis Warren
Guest Cast: Raymond Bailey, James O'Rear, John Alderson, Wilfred Knapp
"General" Parsley Smith is an eccentric teller of tall tales, whom no one believes. Then he makes friends with an infamous gunman.

12) Magnus
December 24th, 1955
Written by David Victor & Herbert Little, Story by John Meston, Directed by Charles Marquis Warren
Guest Cast: Robert Easton, James Anderson

Chester's brother, Magnus, arrives in Dodge for Christmas. Determined to show him up, Chester tries to introduce him to "civilized" living.

13) Yorky
December 31st, 1955
Written by Les Crutchfield, Directed by Charles Marquis Warren
Guest Cast: Lola Albright, John Carradine, James Drury

Dancehall girl Lucy marries older Ephraim Hunt for his money, planning to kill him and run off with drifter Booth Rider.

14) Professor Lute Bone
January 7th, 1956
Written by David Victor & Herbert Little, Story by John Meston, Directed by Charles Marquis Warren
Guest Cast: John Abbott Jester Hairston
Lute Bone is a travelling medicine showman, whose "medicine" has proven fatal to some of his patients.

15) No Handcuffs
January 21st, 1956
Written by Les Crutchfield, Story by John Meston, Directed by Charles Marquis Warren
Guest Cast: Vic Perrin, Charles Gray, Mort Mills

A crooked sheriff arrests an innocent man to cover up his own dealings. Matt is forced to face off against the sheriff to stop Hank being railroaded.

16) Reward For Matt
January 28th, 1956
Written by David Victor & Herbert Little, Story by John Meston, Directed by Charles Marquis Warren
Guest Cast: Paul Newlan, Helen Wallace, Val Dufour, Jean Inness
When Matt is forced to shoot and kill a crook, the man's widow offers a bounty for anyone who in their turn will kill Matt Dillon.

17) Robin Hood
February 4th, 1956
Written by Dan Ullman, Story by John Meston, Directed by Charles Marquis Warren
Guest Cast: James McCallion, Nora Marlowe, Barry Atwater, Wilfred Knapp

A daring robber is protected by the people of Dodge, since they believe that he is robbing the rich and helping the poor. Faced with a distinct lack of cooperation, Matt has to prove that this "Robin Hood of the West" is not what he appears to be.

18) The Reed Survives
February 18th, 1956
Written by Sam Peckinpah, Story by John Meston, Directed by Charles Marquis Warren
Guest Cast: Jeff Silver, Mary Gregory, Howard Petrie, Dennis Cross
A white boy who has been raised by Indians has his own way of looking for horse thieves — and then stopping them permanently.

19) 20-20
February 25th, 1956
Written by David Victor & Herbert Little, Story by John Meston, Directed by Charles Marquis Warren
Guest Cast:Wilton Graff, Martin Kingsley, Pitt Herbert,

An old gunfighter and lawman is losing his eyesight. A younger man looking for a reputation knows this, and plans a gunfight.

20) Reunion '78
March 3rd, 1956
Written by Harold Swanton, Directed by Charles Marquis Warren
Guest Cast:Val Dufour, Marion Brash, Maurice Manson
A cowboy claims to have shot and killed an outlaw in self-defence. Yet he had an excellent motive for having really murdered the man.

GUNSMOKE

21) Helping Hand
March 10th, 1956
Written by John Meston, Directed by Charles Marquis Warren
Guest Cast: Ken L. Smith
An old prospector gets a new assistant — but the man is only helping to try and learn where the prospector's finds are hidden. Then he plans murder and theft.

22) Tap Day For Kitty
March 17th, 1956
Written by John Dunkel, Story by John Meston, Directed by Charles Marquis Warren
Guest Cast:John Dehner, Mary Adams
A rich miner wants to marry Kitty, who doesn't like him. When he is shot, he blames Kitty for the deed.

23) Indian Scout
March 24th, 1956
Written by John Dunkel, Directed by Charles Marquis Warren
Guest Cast:Eduard Franz, DeForest Kelley, William Vaughan, Pat Hogan
A man whose brother was a cavalryman who was killed by Comanches accuses the troop's Indian scout of having betrayed the patrol.

24) The Pest Hole
April 14th, 1956
Written by David Victor & Herbert Little, Directed by Charles Marquis Warren
Guest Cast: Patrick O'Moore, Howard McNear, Norbert Schiller, Evelyn Scott
Typhoid has broken out in Dodge, and Doc is sure he knows the source — a German cook.

25) Big Broad
April 21st, 1956
Written by David Victor & Herbert Little, Story by John Meston, Directed by Charles Marquis Warren
Guest Cast:Dee J. Thompson, Joel Ashley, Terry Becker
Lena Wave is a huge woman who arrives in Dodge with her husband. They begin a gambling game, and when Chester accuses her of cheating, she beats him up. Later, she kills a cowboy she claims was making advances at her.

26) Hack Prine
May 12th, 1956
Written by John Meston, Directed by Charles Marquis Warren
Guest Cast:Leo Gordon
Hack Prine is an old friend of Matt's, but when he visits the Marshal in Dodge, it's with the purpose of killing him.

27) Cooter
May 19th, 1956
Written by Sam Peckinpah, Story by John Meston, Directed by Robert Stevenson
Guest Cast:Brett King, Robert Vaughn, Strother Martin, Vinton Hayworth
Cooter is a retarded young man, who is used as part of a scheme to make Matt look bad.

28) The Killer
May 26th
Written by John Dunkel, Story by John Meston, Directed by Robert Stevenson.
Guest Cast: , Charles Bronson
Crego is a rancher who only shoots in self-defence — but provokes people into drawing on him in order to remain within the letter of the law.

29) Doc's Revenge
June 9th, 1956
Written by John Dunkel, Directed by Ted Post
Guest Cast: Ainslie Pryor, Harry Bartell, Chris Alcaide
A man who threatened Doc in public is found murdered, and Doc is accused of the killing.

30) The Preacher
June 16th, 1956
Written by John Dunkel, Story by John Meston, Directed by Robert Stevenson
Guest Cast:Chuck Connors, Royal Dano, Paul Dubov
A newcomer in town becomes the target for a cruel man. To avoid the innocent man's death, Matt resolves to settle the issue himself.

31) How To Die For Nothing
June 23rd, 1956
Written by Sam Peckinpah, Story by John Meston, Directed by Ted Post, Assistant Director Robert Farfan
Guest Cast:Mort Mills, Maurice Manson, Lawrence Dobkin, James Nolan, Bill White, Jr, Herbert Lytton
Zack and Ned, two Texas trailhands, ride into Dodge, determined to whoop it up. Matt warns them to behave whilst in town, and asks for their guns. Zack starts to draw, but Matt pistol-whips him. Ned fires, and Matt is forced to kill him. Zack warns Matt that there will be trouble from Ned's brother, Howard Bulow. Bulow is the sort to shoot Matt in the back, and won't face him in a fight. Matt starts getting edgy, constantly checking the shadows. When Chester wonders how Matt will recognize Bulow, Matt suggests that "he'll probably be the first man who tries to shoot me in the back." Outside, Matt sees a man hiding in the shadows, and asks him his name. The man won't tell him, and Matt is about to arrest him when Riesling, owner of the Dodge House, tells Matt that the man is Roberts. The real Bulow arrives, and jeers at Matt for making a fool of himself. Bulow threatens Matt with a bullet one day in the back, and Matt throws him in jail for it. The following morning, Will Jacklin, the trail boss, turns up and demands that Matt set Bulow free. When Matt refuses, Jacklin returns with fourteen of his hands, threatening to tear the town apart if they don't get Bulow. Riesling urges Matt to do it, but Matt threatens to kill Jacklin if he tries anything. Jacklin isn't afraid to die, and Matt is forced to give in and set Bulow free. He warns the man to stay out of Dodge. The next day, Matt visits Riesling at the Dodge House to see how the merchants of Dodge have given in to the Texans. Bulow, from hiding, fires at Matt and misses. Matt hunts for him, deliberately turning his back to give Bulow a target. When the man emerges, Matt outguns him. "That man died about as uselessly as a man could," Matt complains to Chester. A fine demonstration of how the merchants of Dodge were not exactly supportive of their Marshal. They'd prefer to have him killed than to lose the lucrative custom of the Texan trail hands. The moral of the story is put over well, and the overall story is one of the best that the show ever made. Chester gets to give a rambling account of how to make a good pot of coffee.

GUNSMOKE

32) Dutch George
June 30th, 1956
Written by John Dunkel, Directed by Robert Stevenson
Guest Cast:Robert Middleton, Tom Pittman
 An old friend and hero of Matt's is now a horse thief. Matt is forced to try and bring him in, despite the interference of an Indian-raised man after revenge.

33) Prairie Happy
July 7th, 1956
Written by David Victor & Herbert Little, Story by John Meston, Directed by Ted Post,
Guest Cast:Robert Ellenstein, Anne Barton

 An old man disturbs Dodge with the information of an impending Indian raid. But is he telling the truth?
 This is the infamous episode, wherein Chester forgot to limp. No-one on the production or acting side noticed it, but when the episode was transmitted, numerous fans wrote in to thank them that Chester was cured!

34) Chester's Mail Order Bride
July 14th, 1956
Written by David Victor & Herbert Little, Directed by Robert Stevenson
Guest Cast:Mary Carver, Joel Ashley, Russell Thorson

 Chester, ever desperate for a girl, advertises for a mail order bride. When Girl from Philadelphia arrives, he begins to regret this decision.

35) The Guitar
July 21st, 1956
Written by Sam Peckinpah, Story by John Meston, Directed by Harry Horner
Guest Cast:Aaron Spelling, Charles Gray, Jacques Aubuchon
 Confederate soldiers meet a Union veteran in Dodge, and it looks like the Civil War might erupt anew.

36) Cara
July 28th, 1956
Written by David Victor & Herbert Little, Directed by Robert Stevenson
Guest Cast:Jorja Curtwright, Doug Odney
 An old girl-friend of Matt's is now an outlaw that he must bring to justice.

37) Mr. And Mrs. Amber
August 4th, 1956
Written by David Victor & Herbert Little, Story by John Meston, Directed by Ted Post
Guest Cast:Ainslie Pryor, Paul Richards, Gloria McGhee
 Neil and Sarah Amber try to settle down to married life, but their happiness is marred by Sarah's father,
Peak Fletcher — who is convinced he is a prophet, and that the youngsters should do as he tells them.

38) Unmarked Grave
August 18th, 1956
Written by David Victor & Herbert Little, Directed by Ted Post
Guest Cast:Ron Hagerthy, Helen Kleeb, William Hopper, Thann Wyenn, Joe Scudero
 Mrs. Randolph befriends young Rusty, an outlaw. He aims to use her faith in him to gain his own freedom.

39) Alarm At Pleasant Valley
August 25th, 1956
Written by John Dunkel, Directed by Ted Post
Guest Cast: Lew Brown, Dorothy Schuyler, Bill White, Jr, Helen Wallace
 Homesteaders attempting to move towards Dodge run into an Indian ambush.

Season Two
September 1st, 1956 through July 6th, 1957
Produced by Norman Macdonnell
Director of Photography Fleet Southcott
Art Director: Nicolai Remisoff
Property Master: Mike Gordon
Supervising Editor: Fred W. Berger, ACE
Film Editor: Sam Gold
Makeup Artist : Glen Alden
Hair Stylist: Pat Whiffing
Wardrobe: Joe E. Dowsing, Jr
Script Supervisor: Mary Chaffee
Set Decorator: G. W. Berntsen
Optical Effects: Jack Runin & Louis DeWitt
Sound: Roderick Sound, Inc.
Casting: Lynne Stalmaster

Cast
Matt Dillon: James Arness
Chester Goode: Dennis Weaver
Doc Galen Adams: Milburn Stone
Kitty Russell: Amanda Blake
Louie Pheeters: James Nusser
Barney: Charles Seel
Howie: Howard Culver
Ed O'Connor: Tom Brown
Percy Crump: John Harper
Mr. Jones: Dabbs Greer

40) Marked Man
September 1st, 1956
Guest Cast: Robert Middleton, Claude Akins, Ray Boyle, Will Wright
 After Doc witnesses a killing by the three Worth brothers,
they try to kill him to prevent his testifying against them.

41) Brush At Elkador
September 8th, 1956
Written by John Meston, Story by Les Crutchfield, Directed by Ted Post
Guest Cast: Gage Clark, Paul Lambert, Alfred Linder
 After a man is killed in Dodge, Matt and Chester go after the killer in Elkador. The man is feared by the town, and they get no cooperation at all.

GUNSMOKE

42) Custer
September 15th, 1956
Written by John Meston, Directed by Ted Post
Guest Cast: Brian Hutton, Richard Keith
Matt Dillon is forced to release a man he knows has committed murder because of the lack of evidence. The man thinks he is home free...

43) The Roundup
September 29th, 1956
Written by John Meston, Story by Sam Peckinpah, Directed by Ted Post
Guest Cast:Barney Phillips, Jacques Aubuchon, John Dierkes, Michael Hinn
Texan trailhands are heading for Dodge to whoop it up. Matt must face them alone, when none of the towns-folk — who asked his protection — will help.

44) Young Man With A Gun
October 20th, 1956
Written by John Meston, Directed by Christian Nyby
Guest Cast:Jack Diamond, Fredd Wayne, Clegg Hoyt
When a gun battle with Dillon in Dodge leaves a man dead, his younger brother plans on killing Matt in revenge.

45) Indian White
October 27th, 1956
Written by Tom Hanley, Story by David Victor & Herbert Little, Directed by Ted Post
Guest Cast:Peter Votrian, Marian Seldes
Stolen by the Cheyenne, a young boy now faces a possible return to white life — if he wants it.

46) How To Cure A Friend
November 10th, 1956
Written by John Meston, Directed by Ted Post
Guest Cast:Andrew Duggan, Simon Oakland, Joseph Mell
A Gambler who is an old friend of Matt's uses his connection with the Marshal to cheat the citizens of Dodge.

47) Legal Revenge
November 17th, 1956
Written by John Meston, Story by Sam Peckinpah, Directed by Andrew McLaglen
Guest Cast:Cloris Leachman, Philip Bourneuf

Doc Adams finds a man ill in bed, wounded by his wife — but he won't press charges, and keeps a gun under his pillow for protection. Fearing she'll kill him, he asks Matt to intervene. The man refuses Matt's protection, however.

48) The Mistake
November 24th, 1956
Written by John Meston, Directed by Andrew McLaglen
Guest Cast: Mike Connors, Cyril Delevanti
After a murder in Dodge City, Matt aims to pursue the killer. This will mean leaving the town without law for a critical period, however.

49) Greater Love
December 1st, 1956
Written by John Meston, Directed by Ted Post
Guest Cast:Claude Akins, Ray Bennett, Amzie Strickland
 When a man is wounded robbing a stage, his partner kidnaps Doc to help
him out. They cannot let Doc leave after he finishes his work, for fear that he will identify them.

50) No Indians
December 8th, 1956
Written by John Meston, Story by John Dunkel, Directed by Ted Post
Guest Cast:Dick Rich, Herbert Rudley, Mickey Simpson
 Groups of ranchers are being killed, apparently by Indians. Matt is certain that they are being framed, and
has to capture the real culprits before the Army takes reprisals against the Indians. So he and a reluctant
Chester set themselves out as bait for the killers.

51) Spring Team
December 15th, 1956
Written by John Meston, Story by Endre Bohem & Lou Vittes, Directed by Andrew McLaglen
Guest Cast:H.M. Wynant, Harry Townes, Paul Newlan, Ross Ford
 A man is killed in Dodge, and when Matt investigates the killing, he discovers that he was the intended vic-
tim.

52) Poor Pearl
December 22nd, 1956
Written by John Meston, Story by Sam Peckinpah, Directed by Andrew McLaglen
Guest Cast:Constance Ford, Denver Pyle, Michael Emmett
 Two men are in love with the same girl, and are willing to kill to eliminate their rival.

53) Cholera
December 29th, 1956
Written by John Meston, Story by Les Crutchfield, Directed by Andrew McLaglen
Guest Cast:Paul Fix, Bartlett Robinson, Peg Hillas, Stuart Whitman, Gordon Gebert
 A vicious landowner wants the land of a homesteader, and tries to evict him. When Matt prevents this, the
feud erupts, and is complicated when cholera strikes.

54) Pucket's New Year
January 5th, 1957
Written by John Meston, Story by John Dunkel, Directed by Ted Post
Guest Cast:Edgar Stehli, Grant Withers
 Two old buffalo hunters have a falling out. One leaves the other for dead, but the victim is found by Matt
and Chester.

55) The Cover-Up
January 12th, 1957
Written by John Meston, Story by William Robson, Directed by William D. Russell
Guest Cast:Tyler McVey, Vivi Janiss, Roy Engle, Marian Brash, Val Dufour, Maurice Manson
 When homesteaders outside of Dodge are killed, Matt investigates the murders.

GUNSMOKE

56) Sins Of The Father
January 19th, 1957
Written by John Meston, Story by John Dunkel, Directed by Andrew McLaglen
Guest Cast:Peter Whitney, Angie Dickinson, Gage Clarke
A hunter's Indian wife is attacked by a prejudiced man, and the hunter then goes after his own brand of revenge.

57) Kick Me
January 26th, 1957
Written by John Meston, Story by Endre Bohem & Lou Vittes, Directed by Andrew McLaglen
Guest Cast:Robert H. Harris, Frank de Kova, Julie van Zandt
Myers kills his partner for the proceeds of a robbery, then sets his wife up in Dodge as a dressmaker. The only witness to the killing was an Indian, Tobeel, who is then framed by Myers for murder.

58) The Executioner
February 2nd, 1957
Written by John Meston, Directed by Andrew McLaglen
Guest Cast:Robert Keys , Michael Hinn, Liam Sullivan
After his brother is killed by a gunman, a man goes after the killer — unarmed.

59) Gone Straight
February 9th, 1957
Written by John Meston, Story by Les Crutchfield, Directed by Ted Post
Guest Cast:Carl Betz, Marianne Stewart, Tige Andrews, John Dierkes
A former outlaw has turned over a new leaf, so when Matt and Chester arrive to arrest him, the citizens of his town refuse to allow this.

60) Bloody Hands
February 16th, 1957
Written by John Meston, Directed by Andrew McLaglen
Guest Cast: Ed Platt, Joe Perry, Bob Forrest, Lawrence Dobkin, Russell Johnson
Matt is forced to kill a man in the line of duty, and resigns, sickened by the bloodshed his task involves.

61) Skid Row
February 23rd, 1957
Written by John Meston, Directed by Ted Post
Guest Cast:Susan Morrow, Joseph Sargent, Guinn Williams
Ann Cabot arrives in Dodge to marry her fiance. Everyone attempts to cover up the fact that he's become a drunkard, and a failure. Matt sets out to reform him for her, but then she is brutally murdered...

62) Sweet And Sour
March 2nd, 1957
Written by John Meston, Directed by Andrew McLaglen
Guest Cast:Karen Sharpe, John Alderson, Walter Reed, Ken Meyer
A pretty dance hall girl flirts with men, and then provokes them into gunfights to prove their affections for her.

63) Moon
March 9th, 1957
Written by John Meston, Directed by Andrew McLaglen
Guest Cast: Mark Roberts, Harry Bartell, Paul Dubov, Dan Riss, Howard Ludwig
When a quiet rancher is challenged to a duel, it is discovered that he is actually a retired gunfighter.

64) The Bureaucrat
March 16th, 1957
Written by John Meston, Directed by Ted Post
Guest Cast: John Hoyt, Ned Glass, Bill Bryant, Al Toigo, Ken Lynch
A man from Washington DC arrives in Dodge, with the authority to become the peace officer there. The citizens, however, dislike his methods, and work on sending him home again.

65) The Last Fling
March 23rd, 1957
Written by John Meston, Directed by Andrew McLaglen
Guest Cast: Florenz Ames, Anne O'Neal , Frank de Kova, Susan Morrow
An old farmer, bored with wife and farm, runs off with a friend to Dodge City to live it up some. His furious wife chases after him. Matt tries to reconcile the pair, but in the end, she kills her husband.

66) Cain
March 30th, 1957
Written by John Meston, Directed by Ted Post,
Guest Cast: Murray Hamilton, Peggy Castle, Tom Greenway, Gage Clarke
When a drunken cowboy is killed, Chester is nearby. The cowboy had earlier threatened Chester, and the citizens of Dodge believe that Chester killed the man. Matt must prove that Chester has been framed — but Chester can't recall a thing about the killing.

67) The Photographer
April 6th, 1957
Written by John Dunkel, Directed by William D. Russell
Guest Cast: Sebastian Cabot, Dean Fredericks, Ned Glass, Charles Horvath
An photographer from the East is fascinated with the West, and sets off to capture it in pictures. Then he trespasses on sacred Indian grounds.

68) Wrong Man
April 13th, 1957
Written by John Meston, Directed by Andrew McLaglen
Guest Cast: Don Keefer, Catherine McLeod, Robert Griffin
A man kills a person whom he believes is a wanted criminal. It is discovered, however, that he has killed an innocent man. A friend of the victim then aims to get revenge.

69) Big Girl Lost
April 20th, 1957
Written by John Meston, Directed by Ted Post
Guest Cast: Michael Pate, Gloria McGhee, Judson Pratt, Gerald Melton
A Man looking for a former saloongirl can't get her whereabouts from Matt. So he hires a gunman to force Matt to talk.

GUNSMOKE

70) What The Whiskey Drummer Heard
April 27th, 1957
Written by John Meston, Directed by Andrew McLaglen
Guest Cast:Vic Perrin, Robert Karnes, Robert Burton, Bert Rumsey
Matt is being targeted by an unknown killer. A traveling salesman is the only one who might know his identity.

71) Cheap Labor
May 4th, 1957
Written by John Meston, Directed by Andrew McLaglen
Guest Cast:Andrew Duggan, Peggy Webber, Robert F. Simon
A reformed gunfighter has plans to marry, but his girlfriend causes trouble that could lead to his taking up his guns again.

72) Uncle Oliver
May 11th, 1957
Written by John Meston, Directed by William D. Russell, Assistant Director Glenn Cook
Guest Cast:Rebecca Welles, Philip Pine, Stafford Repp, Thomas Palmer, Jane Ray
A professional gambler loses to a card-wise rancher, and then kills him for the money. Matt and the dead man's gunslinging friend have to get the gambler to confess to the deed.

73) Who Lives By The Sword
May 18th, 1957
Written by John Meston, Directed by Andrew McLaglen
Guest Cast:Steve Terrell, Robert C. Ross, Harry Wood, Harold J. Stone, Sheila Noonan
A gunman avoids the law by forcing his victims to draw on him first.

74) Chester's Murder
May 25th, 1957
Written by John Meston, Directed by Andrew McLaglan
Guest Cast:Earl Hodgins, Paul Wexler, Charles Bronson
Chester is ambushed and left for dead. Matt goes after the bushwhackers with the help of two friends.

75) Daddy-O
June 1st, 1957
Written by John Meston, Directed by Andrew McLaglen
Guest Cast:John Dehner, Judson Pratt
Kitty's father arrives in Dodge City, and wants her to move , with him to New Orleans.

76) The Man Who Would Be Marshal
June 15th, 1957
Written by John Meston, Directed by William D. Russell
Guest Cast:Herbert Rudley, Alex Sharp, Clancy Cooper, Rusty Wescoatt
Matt deputizes an ex-Army officer who wants Matt's job.

77) Liar From Blackhawk
June 22nd, 1957
Written by John Meston, Story by David Victor & Herbert Little
Guest Cast:Denver Pyle, Strother Martin, John Doucette

A young man tries to impress the people in Dodge with his prowess, but the whole thing is a set-up. When a gunfighter then appears, the young liar is expected to take him on.

78) Jealousy
July 6th, 1957
Written by John Meston, Directed by Andrew McLaglen
Guest Cast:Than Wyenn, Jack Kelly, Joan Tetzel
A gambler convinces a jealous husband that his wife is spending time with Matt Dillon.

Season Three
September 14th, 1957 through July 26th, 1958
Cast
Matt Dillon: James Arness
Chester Goode: Dennis Weaver
Doc Galen Adams: Milburn Stone
Kitty Russell: Amanda Blake
Louie Pheeters: James Nusser
Barney: Charles Seel
Howie: Howard Culver
Ed O'Connor: Tom Brown
Percy Crump: John Harper
Hank: Hank Patterson
Mr. Jones: Dabbs Greer

79) Crackup
September 14th, 1957
Written by John Meston, Directed by Ted Post
Guest Cast:John Dehner, Jess Kirkpatrick, Jean Vaughn
A professional killer has just arrived in Dodge — but who has hired him, and why?

80) Gun For Chester
September 21st, 1957
Written by John Meston, Directed by Louis King
Guest Cast:Thomas Coley, George Selk, , Clayton Post
A man determined to kill Chester arrives in Dodge City. Despite his inexperience with the weapon, Chester buys a gun to defend himself.

81) Blood Money
September 28th, 1957
Written by John Meston, Directed by Louis King
Guest Cast:James Dobson, Vinton Hayworth, Lawrence Green
A man who is injured is rescued by a passing stranger, who is a wanted bank robber. The first man decides to collect the reward for the robber's capture.

GUNSMOKE

82) Kitty's Outlaw
October 5th, 1957
Written by John Meston, Story by Kathleen Hite
Guest Cast:Ainslie Pryor, Chris Alcaide
A former boyfriend of Kitty's robs the bank, and she is suspected of harboring him.

83) Potato Road
October 12th, 1957
Written by John Meston, Directed by Ted Post
Guest Cast:Tom Pittman, Robert F. Simon, Jeanette Nolan
Matt is lured out of town to investigate the murders of a boy's parents — but the murder is yet to come, and he is the target.

84) Jesse
October 19th, 1957
Written by John Meston, Direcetd by Andrew McLaglen
Guest Cast:James Maloney, George Brenlin, Edward Binns
A man arrives in Dodge City looking for the man who killed his father. He discovers that it was Matt Dillon.

85) Mavis McCloud
October 26th, 1957
Written by John Meston, Directed by Buzz Kulik
Guest Cast:Fay Spain, Casey Adams, Robert Cornthwaite, Kelly Thordsen
A young woman arrives in Dodge, and she's in a hurry to get married.

86) Born To Hang
November 2nd, 1957
Written by John Meston, Directed by Buzz Kulik
Guest Cast:Anthony Caruso, Wright King, Mort Mills
A drifter who is falsely accused and condemned to hang is saved by Matt. He won't learn his lesson, though, and tries to get his revenge on the man that was after him.

87) Romeo
November 9th, 1957
Written by John Meston, Directed by Ted Post
Guest Cast:Robert Vaughn, Barry Kelley, Barbara Eden, Robert McQueeney, Tyler McVey
It's "Romeo And Juliet" on the range, as the son and daughter of two feuding ranchers fall in love.

88) Never Pester Chester
November 16th, 1957
Written by John Meston, Directed by Richard Whorf
Guest Cast:Buddy Baer, Tom Greenway, Woodrow Chambliss
When Chester has been injured in an ambush, Matt unpins his badge in order to get his revenge without tarnishing the law.

89) Fingered
November 23rd, 1957
Written by John Meston, Directed by James Sheldon
Guest Cast:John Larch, Virginia Christine, Karl Swenson

A widower remarries, and then his second wife disappears under mysterious circumstances — as had the first.

90) How To Kill A Woman
November 30th, 1957
Written by John Meston, Story by Sam Peckinpah
Guest Cast:Robert Brubaker, Barry Atwater, Pernell Roberts, June Lockhart, Grant Withers, Peg Hillias, Ruth Storey
 Two passengers are wantonly killed during a stagecoach robbery. Matt and Chester investigate the killings, to discover the real motive.

91) Cows And Cribs
December 7th, 1957
Written by John Meston, Story by Kathleen Hite, Directed by Richard Whorf
Guest Cast:Val Avery, Kathie Browne, Judson Taylor, Anne Barton
 A homesteader accused of cattle rustling has abandoned his family on their farm

92) Doc's Reward
December 14th, 1957
Written by John Meston, Directed by Richard Whorf
Guest Cast:Jack Lord, Bruce Wendell
 Doc confesses to murder, and the man's twin brother is intent on killing him in revenge.

93) Kitty Lost
December 21st, 1957
Written by John Meston, Directed by Ted Post
Guest Cast:Warren Stevens, Gage Clarke, Brett King, Steve Ellsworth
 Kitty and a traveling companion are abandoned miles from Dodge, and must make it back through hostile territory.

94) Twelfth Night
December 28th, 1957
Written by John Meston, Directed by John Rich
Guest Cast:William Schallert, James Griffith, Rose Marie, Dick Rich
 Two feuding families are all dead except one member of each — both grimly determined to kill the other.

95) Joe Phy
January 4th, 1958
Written by John Meston, Directed by Ted Post
Guest Cast:Paul Richards, Morey Amsterdam, William Kendis
 The Marshal of a nearby town is living on a false reputation, which has now been uncovered.

96) Buffalo Man
January 11th, 1958
Written by John Meston, Story by Les Crutchfield, Directed by Ted Post
Guest Cast:Jack Klugman, John Anderson, Patricia Smith
 Matt and Chester become embroiled in a fight between Indians and white buffalo hunters.

GUNSMOKE

97) Kitty Caught
January 18th, 1958
Written by John Meston, Directed by Richard Whorf
Guest Cast:Bruce Gordon, Pat Conway, John Compton
Two bank robbers flee town with Kitty as their hostage to keep Matt at bay.

98) Claustrophobia
January 25th, 1958
Written by John Meston, Directed by Ted Post
Guest Cast:James Winslow, Will Sage, Vaughn Taylor, Joe Maross
Two claim jumpers try to evict a homesteader, but Matt gets involved.

99) Ma Tennis
February 1st, 1958
Written by John Meston, Directed by Buzz Kulik
Guest Cast:Nina Varela, Ron Hagerthy, Corey Allen
When one of her sons is wanted by Matt, Ma Tennis claims to have killed and buried him.

100) Sunday Supplement
February 8th, 1958
Written by John Meston, Directed by Richard Whorf
Guest Cast:Jack Weston, Werner Klemperer, Ed Little, David Whorf
Two newsmen from New York arrive in Dodge in search of sensational news. They discover it when they trigger a war between the Pawnees and the US Army.

101) Wild West
February 15th, 1958
Written by John Meston, Directed by Richard Whorf
Guest Cast:Paul Engel , Phyllis Coates, Philip Bourneuf, Murray Hamilton, Robert Gist
The son of an elderly man reports that his wealthy father has been kidnapped.

102) The Cabin
February 22nd, 1958
Written by John Meston, Directed by John Rich
Guest Cast:Dean Stanton, Claude Akins, Patricia Barry
Lost in a blizzard, Matt stumbles into a cabin. It's already occupied — by the two bank robbers he's after. They'd sooner see him dead than help him out.

103) Dirt
March 1st, 1958
Written by John Meston, Story by Sam Peckinpah, Directed by Ted Post
Guest Cast:June Lockhart, Wayne Morris, Gail Kobe
A young man is shot and killed as he starts his honeymoon, and the grief-stricken widow wants his killer dead.

104) Dooley Surrenders
March 8th, 1958
Written by John Meston, Directed by John Rich
Guest Cast:Strother Martin, Ken Lynch, James Maloney, Ben Wright

A hunting party goes out, and one men is killed. Dooley believes it was his fault, and flees. It's up to Matt to bring the man back.

105) Joke's On Us
March 15th, 1958
Written by John Meston, Directed by Ted Post
Guest Cast:Virginia Gregg, Bartlett Robinson, Michael Hinn, James Kevin, Herbert C. Lytton, Craig Duncan
Three ranchers lynch a man they believe is a horse thief. When their victim is proven innocent, his widow goes after revenge.

106) Tom Cassidy
March 22nd, 1958
Written by John Meston, Directed by John Rich
Guest Cast:John Dehner, Ross Martin, Peggy McKay
Tom Cassidy is the town drunk, and good for nothing. When a stranger arrives in town, Cassidy vows to kill him — but why?

107) Laughing Gas
March 29th, 1958
Written by James Fonda, Directed by Ted Post
Guest Cast:Dean Harens, June Dayton, Val Benedict, Jess Kirkpatrick
Stafford is a reformed gunfighter, now a traveling medicine showman. The Marsh brothers try and goad him to pick up his guns and face them.

108) Texas Cowboys
April 5th, 1958
Written by John Meston, Directed by John Rich
Guest Cast:Clark Gordon, Allen Lane, Ned Glass
A group of cowboys heads for Dodge and a good time. The townsfolk want them stopped, but Matt would rather talk to them.

109) Amy's Good Deed
April 12th, 1958
Written by John Meston, Story by Kathleen Hite, Directed by John Rich
Guest Cast:Jeanette Nolan, Lou Krugman
Amy Slater, an elderly lady, is convinced that Matt killed her brother. She decides that the world would be better off with Matt dead.

110) Hanging Man
April 19th, 1958
Written by John Meston, Directed by John Rich
Guest Cast:Luis van Rooten, Robert Osterloh, Zina Provendie
A businessman has apparently hung himself in his office, but Matt smells murder.

111) Innocent Broad
April 26th, 1958
Written by John Meston, Story by Kathleen Hite, Directed by John Rich
Guest Cast:Myrna Fahey, Joe Bassett, Edward Kemmer

A young lady is rudely propositioned on the stage, so her boyfriend aims to teach the ruffian a lesson.

112) The Big Con
May 3rd, 1958
Written by John Meston, Directed by John Rich
Guest Cast:Joe Kearns, Alan Dexter, Gordon Mills, Raymond Bailey
 Three men rob the bank, and then take Doc hostage as they flee Dodge City.

113) Widow's Mite
May 10th, 1958
Written by John Meston, Directed by Ted Post
Guest Cast:Marshall Thompson, Katherine Bard, Ken Mayer
 Fields marries his partner's widow, but he seems more interested in missing loot than married life.

114) Chester's Hanging
May 17th, 1958
Written by John Meston, Directed by Ted Post
Guest Cast:Charles Cooper, Sam Edwards, Walter Barnes
 After a robbery, one man is caught, but his partner remains free — and determined to get him out of jail, even at the cost of Chester's life.

115) Carmen
May 24th, 1958
Written by John Meston, Directed by Ted Post
Guest Cast:Ruta Lee , Robert Patten, Tommy Farrell, Ray Teal, Alan Gifford
 Three cavalrymen are killed during a robbery at an Army post. Major Harris intends to put Dodge under martial law if Matt can't find the killers.

116) Overland Express
May 31st, 1958
Written by John Meston, Directed by Seymour Berns
Guest Cast:Simon Oakland, Peter Mamakos, James Gavin
 Matt and Chester are traveling back to Dodge with a murderer their prisoner, but the stage is held up.

117) The Gentleman
June 7th, 1958
Written by John Meston, Directed by Ted Post
Guest Cast:Timothy Carey, Virginia Baker, Jack Cassidy
 One of the saloon girls falls for a dandy gambler, but a jealous teamster aims to kill the man and win the girl.

118) Cow Doctor
July 26th, 1958
Written by John Meston, Story by John Dunkel, Directed by Andrew McLaglen
Guest Cast:Robert H. Harris, Dorothy Adams, Tommy Kirk
 Ben Pitcher doesn't like doctors, but calls Doc Adams out to his lonely farm — to treat his cow. While Doc is gone from Dodge, a woman dies. Doc is furious with Pitcher, and is tempted when he is really hurt to leave him to his own devices.This episode was made as the final episode of the first season, but pre-empted on September 1st, 1956. It was finally shown for the first time on this date. Syndication packages restore it as episode #40.

Season Four
September 13th, 1958 through June 13th, 1959
Cast
Matt Dillon: James Arness
Chester Goode: Dennis Weaver
Doc Galen Adams: Milburn Stone
Kitty Russell: Amanda Blake
Louie Pheeters: James Nusser
Barney: Charles Seel
Howie: Howard Culver
Ed O'Connor: Tom Brown
Percy Crump: John Harper
Hank: Hank Patterson
Mr. Jones: Dabbs Greer

120) Matt For Murder
September 13th, 1958
Written by John Meston, Directed by Richard Whorf
Guest Cast:Robert Wilke, Bruce Gordon , Elisha Cook
Matt is suspended from his job, after being accused of killing the partner of a cattleman.

121) The Patsy
September 20th, 1958
Written by John Meston, Story by Les Crutchfield, Directed by Richard Whorf
Guest Cast:Peter Breck, Jan Harrison, John Alderman, Martin Landau
A young man is killed and his accused murderer taken. The boy's brother doesn't want to wait for justice, however, and plans to kill the captive himself.

122) Gunsmuggler
September 27th, 1958
Written by John Meston, Story by Les Crutchfield, Directed by Richard Whorf
Guest Cast:Paul Langton, Frank de Kova
A family has been massacred by Indians, and both Major Evans and Matt Dillon want to discover who has been giving them rifles.
Note: Toheel had appeared in the previous season's "Kick Me"

123) Monopoly
October 4th, 1957
Written by John Meston, Story by Les Crutchfield, Directed by Seymour Berns
Guest Cast:Harry Townes, Robert Gist, Pat O'Malley
A newcomer to Dodge City buys up all the freighting lines, but the owner of the last one refuses to sell.

124) Letter Of The Law
October 11th, 1958
Written by John Meston, Story by Les Crutchfield, Directed by Richard Whorf
Guest Cast:Clifton James, Mary Carver, Harold J. Stone
When Matt is ordered to evict a former gunslinger and his wife, he prefers to help the man. But can he do it and still uphold the law?

GUNSMOKE

125) Thoroughbreds
October 18th, 1958
Written by John Meston, Directed by Richard Whorf
Guest Cast:Ron Randell, Walter Barnes, Dan Blocker
Jack Portis has hardly arrived in Dodge City before he gets himself into a gunfight.

126) Stage Holdup
October 25th, 1958
Written by John Meston, Story by Les Crutchfield, Directed by Ted Post
Guest Cast:Bob Morgan, John Anderson, Charles Aidman
A stage that Matt and Chester are in is robbed. Later, Matt hears a man he thinks was one of the robbers asking Doc's help for an injured friend.

127) The Lost Rifle
November 1st, 1958
Written by John Meston, Directed by Richard Whorf
Guest Cast:Charles Bronson, Paul Engel, Lew Gallo, Tom Greenway
One of Matt's friends is accused of murder when his rifle is found near the body. Matt has to prove the man's claim that he lost the rifle before the murder.

128) Land Deal
November 8th, 1958
Written by John Meston, Story by Les Crutchfield, Directed by Ted Post
Guest Cast:Dennis Patrick, Nita Talbot, Murray Hamilton, Ross Martin
A land agent's extravagant promises arouse Matt's suspicions that he is a con man.

129) Lynching Man
November 15th, 1958
Written by John Meston, Directed by Richard Whorf
Guest Cast:George Macready, Bing Russell, Charles Gray, O.Z. Whitehead
Two transients kill a homesteader, and the townspeople want to lynch them.

130) How To Kill A Friend
November 22nd, 1958
Written by John Meston, Directed by Richard Whorf
Guest Cast:James Westerfield, Philip Abbott, Pat Conway
Two gamblers try to bribe Matt to be allowed to stay in Dodge. When he refuses, they hire a gunman to kill him.

131) Grass
November 29th, 1958
Written by John Meston, Directed by Richard Whorf
Guest Cast:Philip Coolidge, Charles Fredericks, Chris Alcaide
With marauding Indians nearby, Matt recommends a farmer buy a rifle for protection. The farmer then accidentally shoots a cowboy with the gun.

132) The Guest Cast:December 6th, 1958
Written by John Meston, Directed by Jesse Hibbs
Guest Cast:Robert F. Simon

A woman who swallowed a nail dies despite Doc's efforts. The husband then vows to kill Doc in return.

133) Robber And Bridegroom
December 13th, 1958
Written by John Meston, Directed by Richard Whorf
Guest Cast:Burt Douglas, Jan Harrison, Donald Randolph, Frank Maxwell
A girl is traveling to Dodge City to get married. Her stage is held up, and she is taken off. She later turns up in town, and will not testify against the men who held her. Matt suspects that her fiance was one of the men.

134) Snakebite
December 20th, 1958
Written by John Meston, Directed by Ted Post
Guest Cast:Andy Clyde, Charles Maxwell, Warren Oates
Two drifters kill an old man's dog out of spite. The following day, one of the men is found murdered, and the old man is suspected.

135) The Gypsum Hills Feud
December 27th, 1958
Written by John Meston, Story by Les Crutchfield, Directed by Richard Whorf
Guest Cast:Anne Barton, William Schallert, Albert Linville, Hope Summers, Sam Edwards
Two families are feuding in the hills, and while they are out hunting Matt and Chester run into the center of the problem.

136) Young Love
January 3rd, 1959
Written by John Meston, Directed by Seymour Berns
Guest Cast:Joan Taylor, Jon Lormer, Wesley Lau, Charles Cooper, Stephen Chase
When a rancher is murdered, the prime suspect is the man who is in love with his wife.

137) Marshal Proudfoot
January 10th, 1959
Written by Tom Hanley, Story by John Meston, Directed by Jesse Hibbs
Guest Cast: Charles Fredericks, Earle Parker, Robert Brubaker
Chester's Uncle Wesley comes to town, thinking that Chester is the marshal, and Matt the deputy.
Note: In the radio series, Chester's surname was Proudfoot; for the tv, it was changed to Goode.

138) Passive Resistance
January 17th, 1959
Written by John Meston, Directed by Ted Post
Guest Cast:Carl Benton Reid, Alfred Ryder, Read Morgan
Seek is a pacifist for religious reasons, and refuses to fight or to take action even when his home is burned and sheep killed during a range war.

139) Love Of A Good Woman
January 24th, 1959
Written by John Meston, Story by Les Crutchfield, Directed by Arthur Hiller
Guest Cast:Kevin Hagen, Jacqueline Scott
A paroled convict wants revenge on Matt, but a local woman thinks she can tame his wild nature.

GUNSMOKE

140) Jayhawkers
January 31st, 1959
Written by John Meston, Directed by Andrew McLaglen
Guest Cast:Jack Elam, Ken Curtis, Chuck Hayward, Lane Bradford, Earl Parker
 A Texan herd is passing Dodge, and the trail boss asks Matt for help, fearing raids by a rival.
Note: Ken Curtis later played regular Festus; he made a number of guest appearances before then, however, and this was the first.

141) Kitty's Rebellion
February 7th, 1959
Written by John Meston, Story by Marian Clark, Directed by Jesse Hibbs
Guest Cast:Barry McGuire, Addison Powell, Robert Brubaker, Ben Wright
 Kitty's younger brother arrives in Dodge City, and is appalled to find his sister working as a saloon girl.

142) Sky
February 14th, 1959
Written by Les Crutchfield, Story by John Meston, Directed by Ted Post
Guest Cast:Allen Case, Charles Thompson, Linda Watkins, Olive Blakeney, Patricia Huston
 A saloon girl from the Long Branch is killed, and Matt tracks down the killer.

143) Doc Quits
February 21st, 1959
Written by John Meston, Directed by Edward Ludlum
Guest Cast:Fiona Hale, Bartlett Robinson, Wendell Holmes, Jack Grinnage, Jack Younger, Bert Rumsey
 A new doctor in town starts to put Doc out of business, and when Doc warns the townsfolks that the man is a quack, they accuse him of simple jealousy.

144) Mike Blocker
February 28th, 1959
Written by John Meston, Directed by Jesse Hibbs
Guest Cast:Denver Pyle, Grant Williams, Norma Crane
 A former saloon girl is about to marry a rancher, but her old boyfriend is determined to win her back any way he can.

145) The Coward
March 7th, 1959
Written by John Meston, Directed by Jesse Hibbs
Guest Cast:Barry Atwater, Jim Beck, House Peters, Jr
 A killer aims to slay Matt to cover his tracks, but he accidentally kills a rancher who resembles the marshal.

146) Al Clovis
March 14th, 1956
Written by John Meston, Directed by Andrew McLaglen
Guest Cast:Bert Freed, Joe Flynn, Fay Roope
 Al Clovis gets into a deadly quarrel with another man; after killing him, he tries to flee Dodge.

147) Wind
March 21st, 1959
Written by John Meston, Directed by Arthur Hiller

Guest Cast:Whitney Blake, Mark Miller, Roy Engel
 Matt suspects that a saloon girl is helping a gambler to win his games, and orders the man out of Dodge.

148) Fawn
April 4th, 1959
Written by John Meston, Directed by Andrew McLaglen
Guest Cast:Peggy Stewart, Robert Rockwell, Robert Karnes, Wendy Stewart
 When two Indian women are rescued from slavery by Matt, he discovers that one of them is a white woman, and the other her half-breed daughter.

149) Renegade White
April 11th, 1959
Written by Les Crutchfield, Story by John Meston, Directed by Andrew McLaglen
Guest Cast:Barney Phillips, Michael Pate, Bob Brubaker
 A man accused of murder is set free — and is shortly afterwards discovered selling guns to the Indians.

150) Murder Warrant
April 18th, 1959
Written by John Meston, Directed by Andrew McLaglen
Guest Cast:Ed Nelson, Onslow Stevens, Mort Mills
 A deputy hunting a wanted man kills him — but from ambush.

151) Change Of Heart
April 25th, 1959
Written by John Meston, Directed by Andrew McLaglen
Guest Cast:James Drury, Ken Curtis, Lucy Marlowe
 A man plans on marrying a saloon girl, but his brother's objections stop the wedding.

152) Buffalo Hunter
May 2nd, 1959
Written by John Meston, Directed by Ted Post
Guest Cast:Harold J. Stone, Garry Walberg, Lou Krugman, Sam Buffington, Scott Stevens
 Two buffalo hunters are murdered, and Matt suspects that their boss knows more about the crime than he is telling.

153) The Choice
May 9th, 1959
Written by John Meston, Directed by Ted Post
Guest Cast:Darryl Hickman, Bob Brubaker, Charles Maxwell
 Andy Hill arrives in Dodge and gets a job with the stage line. Matt discovers he has a wanted poster on the man, however.

154) There Never Was A Horse
May 16th, 1959
Written by John Meston, Directed by Andrew McLaglen
Guest Cast:Jack Lambert, Bill Wellman, Jr, Joseph Sargent
 A gunman kills a drunk in self-defense, but prefers to draw on Matt than be locked up.

155) Print Asper
May 23rd, 1959
Written by John Meston, Directed by Ted Post
Guest Cast:Pat O'Malley, Ted Knight, Lew Brown, Robert Ivers
A Lawyer is supposed to deed over a ranch to the old man's sons; instead, he takes over the title himself.

156) The Constable
May 30th, 1959
Written by John Meston, Directed by Arthur Hiller
Guest Cast:John Larch, Pitt Herbert, Strother Martin
To stop a group of cowboys from causing trouble, Matt insists that they check their guns on entering Dodge. Their boss threatens to boycott Dodge if this continues, and the merchants attempt to pressure Matt into giving up the check.

157) Blue Horse
June 6th, 1959
Written by John Meston, Story by Marian Clark, Directed by Andrew McLaglen
Guest Cast:Gene Nelson, Michael Pate, Bill Murphy, Monte Hale
Matt and Chester are taking an Indian to jail in Dodge when they are stopped by an Army patrol searching for reservation jumpers.

158) Cheyennes
June 13th, 1959
Written by John Meston, Directed by Ted Post
Guest Cast:Walter Brooke, Chuck Robertson, Ralph Moody, Little Sky, Tim Brown
A band of settlers has been killed by some Cheyenne. Captain Nichols wants to ride into the local village and kill them all. Matt hopes instead to convince the chief to hand over the guilty braves for trail, and thus avert an Indian war.

Season Five
September 5th, 1959 through June 18th, 1960
Cast
Matt Dillon: James Arness
Chester Goode: Dennis Weaver
Doc Galen Adams: Milburn Stone
Kitty Russell: Amanda Blake
Louie Pheeters: James Nusser
Barney: Charles Seel
Howie: Howard Culver
Ed O'Connor: Tom Brown
Percy Crump: John Harper
Hank: Hank Patterson
Mr. Jones: Dabbs Greer

159) Target
September 5th, 1959
Written by John Meston, Story by Les Crutchfield, Directed by Andrew McLaglen
Guest Cast:Darryl Hickman, John Carradine, Susan Lloyd, Frank de Kova
A young man wants to marry a gypsy girl, but both families are violently opposed to the wedding.

160) Kitty's Injury
September 19th, 1959
Written by John Meston, Story by Marian Clark, Directed by Buzz Kulik
Guest Cast:Don Dubbins, Anne Seymour, Karl Swenson
Out riding with Matt, Kitty is thrown from her horse. Matt tries to get help
from the Judsons, who live close by, but they refuse to help.

161) Horse Deal
September 26th, 1959
Written by John Meston, Directed by Andrew McLaglen
Guest Cast:Bartlett Robinson, Harry Carey, Jr, Trevor Bardette, Michael Hinn, Fred Grossinger
Matt discovers that several ranchers about Dodge City have been unwittingly buying stolen horses.

162) Johnny Red
October 3rd, 1959
Written by John Meston, Story by Les Crutchfield, Directed by Buzz Kulik
Guest Cast:James Drury, Josephine Hutchinson, Abel Fernandez, Dennis McMullan
Matt recognizes Johnny Red as a habitual criminal, but he can't order the man out of Dodge without evidence.

163) Tail To The Wind
October 10th, 1959
Written by John Meston, Directed by Andrew McLaglen
Guest Cast:Peter Whitney, John Crawford, Richard Rust
A crazy old man and his sons try to beat up a cowboy, but he is saved by Matt and Chester. Furious, the
three men aim to kidnap Chester and take it out on him.

164) Annie Oakley
October 17th, 1959
Written by John Meston, Story by Les Crutchfield, Directed by Christian Nyby
Guest Cast:Harry Townes, Alice Backes, Harry Swoger, Alan Reed, Jr
The Reeses want to buy the Neller farm, but Pezzy and Cora won't sell. The Reeses then aim to run the
Nellers off and take the farm by force.

165) Kangaroo
October 24th, 1959
Written by John Meston, Directed by Jesse Hibbs
Guest Cast:Florence MacMichael, George Mitchell, John Anderson
Kate Kinsman wants more attention from her husband, so she attempts to make him jealous by flirting with
a neighbor. Tempers flare, and later Kinsman is found murdered.

166) Saludos
October 31st, 1959
Written by John Meston, Story by Les Crutchfield, Directed by Andrew McLaglen
Guest Cast:Connie Buck, Gene Nelson, Jack Elam, Robert J. Wilke
Sochi, a half-breed Indian girl, arrives in Dodge City, shot by a man. Matt and Chester go looking for the
bushwhacker, and find that there are three suspects.

69

GUNSMOKE

167) Brother Whelp
November 7th, 1959
Written by John Meston, Story by Les Crutchfield, Directed by R.G. "Bud" Springsteen
Guest Cast:Lew Gallo, Ellen Clark, John Clarke
A man returns to Dodge City to discover that his fiance has married his brother while he was awaiting trial.

168) The Boots
November 14th, 1959
Written by John Meston, Directed by Jesse Hibbs
Guest Cast:John Larch, Richard Eyer, Wynn Pearce
A townsman takes in a young boy, and they become friends. Then a stranger arrives in town, and problems arise.

169) Odd Man Out
November 21st, 1959
Written by John Meston, Story by Les Crutchfield, Directed by Andrew McLaglen
Guest Cast:Elisha Cook, Elizabeth York, William Phipps
A townsman claims that his wife has left him, but Matt becomes suspicious, since she hasn't been seen for a while.

170) Miguel's Daughter
November 28th, 1959
Written by John Meston, Story by Marian Clark, Directed by Andrew McLaglen
Guest Cast:Finton Meyer, Simon Oakland, Wesley Lau, Ed Nelson
Miss Kitty stops two trail hands from pestering a pretty young girl, and takes her home to her grateful father.

171) Box o' Rocks
December 5th, 1959
Written by Les Crutchfield, Directed by R.G. "Bud" Springsteen
Guest Cast:Vaughn Taylor, Larry Blake, William Fawcett, Gertrude Flynn, Howard McNear
Matt Dillon finds that a coffin supposedly containing the body of miner Packy Rountree actually is filled with gold ore.

172) False Witness
December 12th, 1959
Written by John Meston, Story by Marian Clark, Directed by Ted Post
Guest Cast:Wright King, Wayne Rogers, Robert Griffin
A Dodge City man, desiring a little fame, claims to be the only witness to a murder. Naturally, he is the next target of the killer.

173) Tag, You're It
December 19th, 1959
Written by Les Crutchfield, Directed by Jesse Hibbs
Guest Cast:Paul Langton, Madlyn Rhue, Gregg Stewart
Gunman Karl Killion arrives in Dodge, scaring the townsfolk. Matt can't do anything, however, unless he breaks the law.

70

174) Thick'n'Thin
December 26th, 1959
Written by John Meston, Story by Les Crutchfield, Directed by Stuart Heisler
Guest Cast:Robert Emhardt, Percy Helton, Tina Menard
 Two old men have been ranching together for years, but have finally fallen out. Each wants Matt to evict the other from their ranch.

175) Groat's Grudge
January 2nd, 1960
Written by John Meston, Story by Marian Clark, Directed by Andrew McLaglen
Guest Cast:Ross Elliott, Thomas Coley, Ben Wright
 The Civil War is over, but Confederate soldier Lee Grayson can't forget it. He is after Tom Haskett, whom he accuses of killing his wife during Sherman's march through Georgia.

176) Big Tom
January 9th, 1960
Written by John Mestion, Story by Marian Clark, Directed by Andrew McLaglen
Guest Cast:Harry Lauter, Don Megowan, Robert J. Wilke
 An unscrupulous boxing promoter knows that an opponent has heart trouble. He aims to take advantage of this by staging a fight with him.

177) Till Death Do Us
January 16th, 1960
Written by Les Crutchfield, Directed by Stanley Yarbrough
Guest Cast:Milton Selzer, Mary Field, Rayford Barnes
 An assassin tries to kill the Cobbs, and Matt discovers that it was one of the Long Branch girls who hired the man.

178) The Tragedian
January 23rd, 1960
Written by John Meston, Story by Les Crutchfield, Directed by Arthur Hiller
Guest Cast:John Abbott, Stanley Clements, Harry Woods, Howard McNear
 An unemployed actor is discovered cheating in the Long Branch at cards. Matt takes pity on the man, and finds him a job.

179) Hinka Do
January 30th, 1960
Written by Les Crutchfield, Directed by Andrew McLaglen
Guest Cast:Mamie Nino Varela, Walter Burke, Mike Green, Richard Reeves, Ric Roman, Bob Hopkins
 The Lady Gay Saloon — rival of the Long Branch — acquires a new owner, Mamie. She's quite used to using a gun to enforce her rules, too.

180) Doc Judge
February 6th, 1960
Written by John Meston, Directed by Arthur Hiller
Guest Cast:Barry Atwater, Dennis Cross, George Selk
 When Doc is threatened by a gunman, he discovers that Matt is out of town, and his only protection is Chester — which may be worse than nothing!

GUNSMOKE

181) Moo Moo Raid
February 13th, 1960
Written by John Meston, Story by Les Crutchfield, Directed by Andrew McLaglen
Guest Cast:Raymond Hatton, Lane Bradford, Robert Karnes, Tyler McVey, Richard Evans, Ron Hayes, John Close, Clem Fuller
 Two herds of cattle are being driven towards Dodge, with a large wager on who will reach there first. A swollen river bars the way as the race heats up.
Note: When this was broadcasted, this episode was the highest-rated episode of any tv show to this point, an example of how popular "Gunsmoke" had become.

182) Kitty's Killing
February 20th, 1960
Written by John Meston, Story by Marian Clark, Directed by Arthur Hiller
Guest Cast:Abraham Sofaer, John Pickard
 Kitty risks her own life to stop an insane killer from shooting a harmless old man.

183) Jailbait Janet
February 27th, 1960
Written by Les Crutchfield, Directed by Jesee Hibbs
Guest Cast:John Larch, Nan Peterson, Steve Terrell
 Two teenage children help their mother rob a train, but in the process, they kill a man.

184) Unwanted Deputy
March 5th, 1960
Written by John Meston, Story by Marian Clark, Directed by Andrew McLaglen
Guest Cast:Charles Aidman, Mary Carver, Marlowe Jenson, Dick Rich
 When Matt arrests a man for murder, the man's brother attempts to get Matt fired as marshal.

185) Where'd They Go?
March 12th, 1960
Written by John Meston, Story by Les Crutchfield, Directed by Jesse Hibbs
Guest Cast:Jack Elam, Betty Hartford
 Jonas's store has been robbed, and Jonas accuses farmer Clint Dodie of the deed. Matt can't believe it, but has to go and arrest the man.

186) Crowbait Bob
March 26th, 1960
Written by Les Crutchfield, Directed by Andrew McLaglen
Guest Cast: Ned Glass, Shirley O'Hara, John Apone
 As Crowbait Bob lies dying, his greedy relatives come to stake their claims. He wills all his possessions to Kitty instead.

187) Colleen So Green
April 2nd, 1960
Written by Les Crutchfield, Directed by Stanley Yarbrough
Guest Cast:Joanna Moore, Harry Swoger, Robert Brubaker, Percy Ivins, Clem Fuller, Harold Goodwin
 Colleen is a Southern belle, and she soon has all of the young men in town running about after her favors.

188) The Ex-Urbanites
April 9th, 1960
Written by John Meston, Directed by Andrew McLaglen
Guest Cast:Ken Curtis, Lew Brown, Robert J. Wilke
Doc is shot, and Chester is left to both look after him and guard them both against the would-be killers.

189) I Thee Wed
April 16th, 1960
Written by John Meston, Story by Les Crutchfield, Directed by Jesse Hibbs
Guest Cast:Allyn Joslyn, Alice Frost
Sam Lackett is continually getting thrown in jail for beating his wife — yet Hester constantly bails him out again.

190) The Lady Killer
April 23rd, 1960
Written by John Meston, Directed by Andrew McLaglen
Guest Cast:Jan Harrison, Harry Lauter, Ross Elliott, George Selk, Clem Fuller, Charles Starrett
Mae is a new hostess at the Long Branch, with a temper. She kills a cowboy, then aims to kill Matt.

191) Gentleman's Disagreement
April 30th, 1960
Written by Les Crutchfield, Directed by Jesse Hibbs
Guest Cast:Adam Kennedy, Finton Meyler, Val Dufour
Beaudry arrives in Dodge furious to discover his girlfriend has married blacksmith Wells. Determined to revenge this, he challenges Wells to a fight the blacksmith can't win.

192) Speak Me Fair
May 7th, 1960
Written by Les Crutchfield, Directed by Andrew McLaglen
Guest Cast:Douglas Kennedy , Ken Curtis, Chuck Robertson, Perry Cook
Matt, Doc and Chester go hunting, and they find a young Indian, badly beaten. They attempt to track down his attackers.

193) Belle's Back
May 14th, 1960
Written by Les Crutchfield, Directed by Jesse Hibbs
Guest Cast:Nita Talbot, Nancy Rennick, Gage Clarke, Daniel White
Belle left Dodge with a wanted criminal three years ago. Now she returns, but no-one wants her back again.

194) The Bobsy Twins
May 21st, 1960
Written by John Meston, Directed by Jesse Hibbs
Guest Cast:Ralph Moody, Morris Ankrum, Jean Howell, Buck Young, Charles MacArthur
Two brothers decide that they will rid the area of Indians by killing them all off.

195) Old Flame
May 28th, 1960
Written by John Meston, Story by Marian Clark, Directed by Jesse Hibbs

Guest Cast:Marilyn Maxwell, Lee van Cleef, Peggy Stewart, Hal Smith, Clem Fuller
An old girl-friend of Matt's arrives in town. She claims her husband is trying to kill her, and asks Matt to help.

196) The Deserter
June 6th, 1960
Written by John Meston, Story by Marian Clark, Directed by Arthur Hiller
Guest Cast:Rudy Solari, Joe Perry, Harry Bartell, Jean Inness, Henry Brandon, Charles Fredericks
Lurie James and a civilian, Radin, aim to rob the Army payroll and escape.

197) Slim O'Dell
June 11th, 1960
Written by Les Crutchfield, Directed by Andrew McLaglen
Guest Cast:Joanna Moore, Arthur Franz, Douglas Kennedy
A stage holdup leaves O'Dell dead, but Matt is interested in catching the man's escaped partner.

198) Cherry Red
June 18th, 1960
Guest Cast:Florenz Ames, Frank de Kova, Susan Morrow, Annie O'Neal
A couple of old farmers come to Dodge for a last fling. One of them annoys Kitty with his constant attentions. Later, the man is shot at, and he accuses Kitty of the deed.

Season Six

September 3rd, 1960 through June 17th, 1961
Produced by Norman MacDonnell
Associate Producer: James Arness
Production Supervisor : Dewey Starkey
Assistant to Producer: Frank Paris
Director of Photography: Fleet Southcott
Art Director : Walter E. Keller
Film Editor: Otto Meyer, Al Joseph, ACE
Set Decorator : Herman N. Schoenbrun
Sound Effects Editor : Gene Eliot, MPSE
Music Editor : Gene Feldman
Script Supervisor: Adele Cannon
Production Sound Mixer: Vernon W. Kramer
Recording: Joel Moss
Casting: Stalmaster-Lister Co
Property Master : Clem R. Widrig
Costumes: Alexander Velcoff, Thelma Hilborn, Ruth Stella
Makeup: Glen Alden
Hairstylist : Pat Whiffing, CHS
Titles & Opticals: Pacific Title

Cast

Matt Dillon: James Arness
Chester Goode: Dennis Weaver
Doc Galen Adams: Milburn Stone
Kitty Russell: Amanda Blake
Louie Pheeters: James Nusser
Barney: Charles Seel
Howie: Howard Culver
Ed O'Connor: Tom Brown
Percy Crump: John Harper
Hank: Hank Patterson

199) Friend's Pay-Off
September 3rd, 1960
Written by John Meston Story by Marian Clark Directed by Jesse Hibbs
Guest Cast: Mike Road, Tom Reese, Jay Hector, George Selk, Clem Fuller
A friend of Matt Dillon is accused of robbery, but is found dying.

200) The Blacksmith
September 17th, 1960
Written by John Meston Story by Norman MacDonnell Directed by Andrew McLaglen
Guest Cast: Anna-Lisa, George Kennedy, Bob Anderson
The blacksmith has sent for a mail-order bride, but one of the local ranchers tries to win her away from him.

201) Small Water
September 24th, 1960
Written by John Meston Directed by Andrew McLaglen
Guest Cast: Trevor Bardette, Warren Oates, Rex Holman
Matt is forced to kill one of the Pickett boys when he won't surrender. Finn Pickett then plans his revenge for the killing.

202) Say Uncle
October 1st, 1960
Written by John Meston Directed by Andrew McLaglen
Guest Cast: Richard Rust, Gene Nelson, Harry Lauter, Dorothy Green, Roy Barcroft
When a man dies in what is claimed as an accident, his son believes that a drifter killed him.

203) Shooting Stopover
October 8th, 1960
Written by John Meston Story by Marian Clark Directed by Andrew McLaglen
Guest Cast: Anthony Caruso, Patricia Barry, Paul Guilfoyle, Robert Brubaker
Matt and Chester are transporting a killer to Wichita on a stage that also carries a gold shipment.

204) The Peace Officer
October 15th, 1960
Written by John Meston Story by Norman MacDonnell Directed by Jesse Hibbs
Cast Clegg Rawlins Lane Bradford Stella Susan Cummings Ponce John Zaccaro, John Close
A nearby sheriff decides to take over control of his town. The citizens send a messenger to Matt asking him for help.

GUNSMOKE

205) Don Matteo
October 22nd, 1960
Written by John Meston Directed by Marian Clark
Guest Cast: Lawrence Dobkin, Bing Russell, Ben Wright
A gunman is hunting a man that Matt has thrown out of Dodge City.

206) The Worm
October 29th, 1960
Written by John Meston Directed by Arthur Hiller
Guest Cast: Kenneth Tobey, Stewart Bradley, Ned Glass, H.M. Wynant, Gage Clarke
Spadden is a bully used to getting his own way, but his latest victim finally turns on him.

207) The Wake
November 5th, 1960
Written by John Meston Directed by Gerald H. Mayer
Guest Cast: Denver Pyle , Anne Seymour, George Selk, Joel Ashley, Gregg Schilling, Michael Hinn, Clem Fuller
Gus Mather arrives in Dodge with the body of Boggs. Claiming to be the man's friend, he inaugurates a grand wake, even though Mrs. Boggs disbelieves his claims.

208) The Badge
November 12th, 1960
Written by John Meston Story by Marian Clark Directed by Andrew McLaglen
Guest Cast: John Dehner, Conlan Carter, Allan Lane, Harry Swoger, Mike Mikler
Matt is tracking down two killers, but is wounded and taken captive by the men.

209) Distant Drummer
November 19th, 1960
Written by John Meston Story by Marian Clark Directed by Arthur Hiller
Guest Cast: Jack Grinnage, George Mitchell, Bruce Gordon, George Selk, William Newell, Phil Chambers
A man who was a drummer boy in the Civil War runs afoul of two cruel muleskinners.

210) Ben Tolliver's Stud
November 26th, 1960
Written by John Meston Story by Norman MacDonnell Directed by Andrew McLaglen
Guest Cast: John Lupton, Roy Barcroft, Jean Ingram
Ben Tolliver is fired by rancher Jake Creed, because he is courting Jake's daughter. When Ben leaves, he takes along a horse he's broken, and Jake accuses him of horse theft.

211) No Chop
December 3rd, 1960
Written by John Meston Directed by Stanley Yarbrough
Guest Cast: John Hoyt, Rex Holman, Leo Gordon, Mark Allen, Guy Stockwell
When cattle stray from the Dolan herd onto Mossman land, the Mossmans drive them off. The Dolans are furious with this, and begin a range war.

212) The Cook
December 17th, 1960
Written by John Meston Directed by Ted Post Assistant Director Robert Beche

Guest Cast: Guy Stockwell, Sue Randall, John Pickard, Ken Mayer, Tom Greenway, Harry Swoger, John Milford, Gene Benton, Brad Trumbull, Craig Duncan, Sam Woody

A drifter, Sandy, is hired on as a cook in Delmonico's, but an irate customer complains. Sany accidentally kills the man, then runs. Matt and Chester set out after him, but when they arrest him, the move isn't too popular in town. Sandy is the only good cook that the town has known, and Texans want him freed - or they'll tree the town.

213) Old Fool
December 24th, 1960
Written by John Meston Directed by Ted Post Assistant Director Robert Beche
Guest Cast: Buddy Ebsen, Hope Summers, Linda Watkins, Hampton Fancher
Hannibal Bass is flattered by the attentions of attractive widow Elsie - but his wife, Della, is not so pleased. She knows the woman is after her husband, and aims to keep her old fool. When she fires off a rifle at her rival, Elsie swears out a warrant for her arrest.

214) Brother Love
December 31st, 1960
Written by John Meston
Guest Cast: Lurene Tuttle, Kevin Hagen, Gene Lyons, Jack Grinnage, Jan Harrison
A storekeeper is shot, and as he dies, he names his killer as Cumbers - but which of the brothers did he mean?

215) Bad Sheriff
January 7th, 1961
Written by John Meston Directed by Andrew McLaglen
Guest Cast: Russell Arms, Harry Carey, Jr, Ken Lynch, Don Keefer
A stagecoach robber flees as Matt and Chester track him - and he runs into an ambush by two other robbers. When Matt arrives, the man claims that these men robbed the stage, and that he is a sheriff who was tracking them...

216) Unloaded Gun
January 14th, 1961
Written by John Meston Story by Marian Clark Directed by Jesse Hibbs
Guest Cast: William Redfield, Lew Brown, Greg Dunn, James Malcolm, Rik Nervik

217) The Trapper
January 21st, 1961
Written by John Meston Story by Marian Clark Directed by Harry Harris, Jr
Guest Cast: Tom Reese, Strother Martin, Jan Shepard, George Selk
A man and his wife spend the night in a trapper's camp, and in the morning the wife is found dead.

218) Love Thy Neighbor
January 28th, 1961
Written by John Meston Directed by Dennis Weaver
Guest Cast: Jeanette Nolan, Jack Elam, Ken Lynch, Warren Oates, David Kent
A young boy steals a sack of potatoes from his neighbor, but is caught on a barbed wire fence while running away.
Note: This was the first story that series' regular Dennis Weaver directed.

GUNSMOKE

219) Bad Seed
February 4th, 1961
Written by John Meston Story by Norman MacDonnell Directed by Harry Harris, Jr
Guest Cast: Ann Helm, Roy Barcroft, Burt Douglas
A young girl wants to escape from her father, who beats her when he gets drunk. She asks Matt to intervene.

220) Kitty Shot
February 11th, 1961
Written by John Meston Directed by Andrew McLaglen
Guest Cast: George Kennedy, Christopher Gray, Rayford Barnes, Joseph Mell
Two miners in the Long Branch get a little too drunk and start a gunfight. Kitty is caught by one of the stray bullets.

221) About Chester
February 25th, 1961
Written by John Meston Story by Frank Paris Directed by Alan Crosland, Jr Assistant Director Robert Beche
Guest Cast: Charles Aidman, House Peters, Jr, Mary Munday, Harry Shannon, George Eldredge
Doc Adams has been missing for several days, so Matt and Chester start searching for him. They split up, and when Chester's horse goes lame, he stops at a remote farm for help. Instead, he's captured by horse thief Dack and his woman, Lilymae. Dack aims to kill Chester, but Lilymae helps him to escape.

222) Harriet
March 4th, 1961
Written by John Meston Directed by W.P. Fowler
Guest Cast: Suzanne Lloyd, Joseph Hamilton, Tom Reese, Ron Hayes
On their way to Colorado, a schoolteacher and his daughter are attacked by gunmen. James Horne is killed, but Harriet escapes to Dodge City.

223) Hot Shot
March 11th, 1961
Written by John Meston Directed by Harry Harris, Jr
Guest Cast: Karl Swenson, Gage Clarke, Joseph Mell, Dallas Mitchell
Two bank robbers are fleeing towards Dodge, so the sheriff of the town they hit wires Matt to intercept them. Before he can, however, someone ambushes and critically wounds Chester.

224) Old Faces
March 18th, 1961
Written by John Meston Directed by Harry Harris, Jr
Guest Cast: James Drury, Jan Shepard, George Keymas, Ron Hayes
The Cooks are newlyweds, aiming to settle in Dodge. Some of the people there recognize Mrs. Cook from her days as a saloon hostess and gambler.

225) Big Man
March 25th, 1961
Written by John Meston Directed by Gerald H. Meyer
Guest Cast: John McLiam, Sandy Kenyon, Rayford Barnes, George Kennedy, Jack Chaplain, Ricky Sorenson, Robert G. Anderson, Barney Phillips, Steve Warren, Mathew McCue, Jim Nusser
Pat Swarner tries to force his attentions on Kitty, so Matt throws him out of town. When Swarner is found dead just outside of town, a witness claims to have seen Matt kill him.

226) Little Girl
April 1st, 1961
Written by John Meston Story by Kathleen Hite Directed by Dennis Weaver
Guest Cast: Susan Gordon, Billy McLean, Wright King, Ann Morrison, Doc Lucas, Ricky Weaver, Bobby Weaver, Rusty Weaver, Megan King, Michael King, Rip King
When his house burns down, Hi Stevens is killed in the fire. Matt and Chester come across his young daughter, who leads them to the rest of the orphaned family.

227) Stolen Horses
April 8th, 1961
Written by John Meston Story by Norman MacDonnell Directed by Andrew McLaglen
Guest Cast: Jack Lambert, Guy Raymond, Shirley O'Hara, Henry Brandon
Horse thieves kill a man for his horses. The only witness is the man's friend, who has very poor eyesight, which hinders identifying the killers.

228) Minnie
April 15th, 1961
Written by John Meston Directed by Harry Harris, Jr
Guest Cast: Virginia Gregg, Alan Hale, Jr, George Selk, Mathew McCue, Barry Cahill, Robert Human
Minnie has been a tomboy all of her life, but when she comes to Doc with a bullet wound, she vows to settle down and behave herself.

229) Bless Me Till I Die
April 22nd, 1961
Written by John Meston Story by Ray Kemper Directed by Ted Post
Guest Cast: Ronald Foster, Phyllis Love, Vic Perrin, Dabbs Greer
Nate Bush tries to stop the Treadwells coming into Dodge City, so Matt is forced to jail the man. He won't explain his actions, but intends to stop the couple somehow.

230) Long Hours, Short Pay
April 29th, 1961
Written by John Meston Directed by Andrew McLaglen
Guest Cast: John Larch, Lalo Rios, Frank Sentry, Dawn Little Sky, Allan Lane, Steve Warren, Fred McDougall
Matt catches a man selling guns to the Indians. He arrests him, but can he make it back to Dodge with his captive?

231) Hard Virtue
May 6th, 1961
Written by John Meston Directed by Dennis Weaver
Guest Cast: Lea Waggner, Lew Brown, Robert Karnes, George Selk, James Maloney
When a man starts paying too much attention to his boss's wife, the boss then starts packing a gun and looking for an excuse to use it.

232) The Imposter
May 13th, 1961
Written by John Meston Story by Kathleen Hite Directed by Vaughn Paul
Guest Cast: Jim Davis , Virginia Gregg, Paul Langton, Garry Walberg

GUNSMOKE

A man who says he is a Texas sheriff arrives in Dodge City, but Matt has been informed that the sheriff is dead.

233) Chester's Dilemma
May 20th, 1961
Written by John Meston Script by Vic Perrin Directed by Ted Post
Guest Cast: Patricia Smith, John Van Dreelen, Dabbs Greer
Chester's luck with women is running true to form - Edna Walstrom seems taken with him, but is very interested in the mail he delivers to Matt. Chester begins to suspect that she is up to something.

234) The Love Of Money
May 27th, 1961
Written by John Meston Directed by Ted Post
Guest Cast: Cloris Leachman, Warren Kemmerling, Tod Andrews
An ex-lawman friend of Matt's passes through Dodge, heading for California. When he stops in at the Long Branch, though, he takes a shine to Boni, one of the hostesses there.

235) Melinda Miles
June 3rd, 1961
Written by John Meston Directed by William D. Faralla
Guest Cast: Diana Millay, Burt Douglas, Walter Sande, Christopher Gray, Glenn Strange , Rand Brooks
Harry Miles doesn't want his daughter romancing one of the hands; he'd rather she marry his foreman.

236) Colorado Sheriff
June 17th, 1961
Written by John Meston Directed by Jesse Hibbs
Guest Cast: Wright King, Robert Karnes, Wayne West, Kelton Garwood
Two men from Colorado arrive in Dodge City. One is a sheriff, the other his escaped prisoner. Both are wounded, and which is which?

Season Seven

September 30th, 1961 through May 26th, 1962
Now an hour-long show
Produced by: Norman MacDonnell
Associate Producer: Frank Paris
Director of Photography: Fleet Southcott
Art Director: Albert Herschong
Film Editor: Al Joseph, ACE
Set Decorator: Herman N. Schoenbrun
Sound Effects Editor: Gene Eliot, MPSC
Music Editor: Gene Feldman
Script Supervisor: Edla Bakke
Production Sound Mixer: Vernon W. Kramer
Recording: Joel Moss
Casting: Stalmaster-Lister Co.
Property Master: Clem R. Widrig
Costumers: Alexander Velcoff, Thelma Wilborn
Makeup Artist : Glen Alden

Hairdresser: Pat Whiffing, CHS
Titles & Optical: Pacific Title

Cast

Matt Dillon: James Arness
Chester Goode: Dennis Weaver
Doc Galen Adams: Milburn Stone
Kitty Russell: Amanda Blak
Louie Pheeters: James Nusser
Barney: Charles Seel
Howie: Howard Culver
Ed O'Connor: Tom Brown
Percy Crump: John Harper
Hank: Hank Patterson
Sam: Glenn Strange

237) Perce
September 30th, 1961
Written by John Meston Directed by Harry Harris
Guest Cast: Ed Nelson, Chuck Bail, Chuck Hayward, Alex Sharp, Norma Crane, Ken Lynch
Three outlaws attack Matt on his way back to Dodge, but Matt gets unexpected help from Perce McCall.

238) Old Yellow Boots
October 7th, 1961
Written by John Meston Directed by Ted Post
Guest Cast: Warren Stevens, Joanna Linville, Dean Stanton, Steve Brodie, Bing Russell, Dabbs Greer
A cowboy starts romancing Beulah Parker, in the hopes of marrying her for the Parker Ranch. To his frustration, he discovers that it actually belongs to her brother.

239) Miss Kitty
October 14th, 1961
Written by Kathleen Hite Directed by Harry Harris
Guest Cast: Roger Mobley, Harold J. Stone, Linda Watkins, John Lasell, Frank Sutton
All of Dodge is speculating about why Kitty met a stagecoach and took off a young boy. She refuses to talk about it.

240) Harper's Blood
October 21st, 1961
Written by John Meston Directed by Andrew McLaglen
Guest Cast: Peter Whitney, Dan Stafford, Conlan Carter, Evan Evans, Warren Kemmerling, William Yip, Moira Turner
Gip Cooley treats his sons very harshly, intending that the "bad blood" they inherited from their outlaw grandfather will never come through.

241) All That
October 28th, 1961
Written by John Meston Directed by Harry Harris
Guest Cast: John Larch, Buddy Ebsen, Frances Helm, Guy Raymond, Gage Clarke
Cliff and Clara Shanks are evicted from their home after they fail to pay off his mortgage.

GUNSMOKE

242) Long, Long Trail
November 4th, 1961
Written by Kathleen Hite Directed by Andrew McLaglen
Guest Cast: Barbara Lord, Alan Baxter, Peggy Stewart, Mabel Albertson, Robert Dix
Sarah Drew wants to join her husband at Forth Wallace, but there is no transportation available in Dodge.

243) The Squaw
November 11th, 1961
Written by John Dunkel Directed by Gerald H. Mayer
Cast , John Dehner, Vitina Marcus, Paul Carr, Bob Hastings, Jeb McDonald, Jack Orrison, Bill Erwin
Hardy Tate's stern, unloving wife dies, and Hardy wants an Indian as his next bride - much to his son Cully's intense dislike.

244) Chesterland
November 18th, 1961
Written by Kathleen Hite Directed by Ted Post Assistant Director Wes McAfee
Cast , Sondra Kerr, Earl Hodgins, Sarah Selby, Harold Innocent, Arthur Peterson
Chester has taken a strong shine to Miss Daisy Fair, and is worried that he asked her to marry him after she fell asleep. He collects advice on the subject, but then proposes again when she's awake. Daisy agrees, but on the stipulation that they wait and get to know one another better. She came out West to marry, but wants a home and comforts above all. Chester is worried, knowing he can't manage that on his salary. He promptly buys a homestead up for grabs, but it's very thin soil, and the shack on the ground ready to fall over. Chester tries his best to farm the land, without any success. He's working so hard at that and being deputy that he falls asleep all the time. Matt tells him that two jobs are too much for him, and Chester reluctantly quits as deputy. Matt promises him the job again whenever he wants it.
 Back at the shack, Chester's attempts at improving the place are the butt of criticism from Tubby, one of the neighbors. Annoyed, Chester tries too hard, and the whole place collapses. He throws Tubby out, then starts to rebuild. Doc visits him with food that he manages to convince Chester he needs help in eating. Afterwards, Chester decides that the perfect thing for the place is a dug-out. He works hard, and makes a respectable finished product. When Daisy sees it, however, she's furious. There is no way she'll live in a hole in the ground. Demoralized, Chester spends the night, only to waken with the place awash. He thinks that it rained, but the prairie is as dry as dust - he's hit a well. Inspiration strikes, and Chester starts a pump for the farmers thereabouts, which saves them going into Dodge for their water. Chester makes a small fortune, which Daisy collects and banks. When Chester tries to draw out some money, though, he is told that Daisy drew it all out the previous day. Doc saw her leave town on the night stage... When Matt arrives at the jail the next day, he finds Chester back at work again, trying hard to forget his latest disappointment.
 A typical Chester romance - when he thinks he's finally won, the girl runs off with his money, caring nothing for him. Chester tried hard all the time to get a girl, but always without any luck whatsoever. The humor in this tale is also very strong, with Chester's efforts at farming and building.

245) Milly
November 25th, 1961
Written by John Meston Story by Hal Moffett Directed by Richard Whorf
Guest Cast: Jena Engstrom, Billy Hughes, Malcolm Atterbury, James Griffith, Harry Swoger, Don Dubbins, Sue Randall
Bart Glover is incapable of taking care of his daughter, Milly, and her brother, so Milly grabs the first chance she can to marry and leave with her brother.

246) Indian Ford
December 2nd, 1961
Written by John Dunkel Directed by Andrew McLaglen
Guest Cast: R.G. Armstrong, Pippa Scott, Robert Dix, John Newton
A Dodge girl has been seen meeting with Arapahoe Indians. Captain Benter,
wanting a chance to kill Indians, conducts his own investigation.

247) Apprentice Doc
December 9th, 1961
Written by Kathleen Hite Directed by Harry Harris
Guest Cast: Ben Cooper, Crahan Denton, Robert Sorrells
Doc is kidnapped to look after a wounded desperado. Pitt is supposed to kill Doc afterwards, but turns him
loose instead. Then, later, Pitt turns up in Dodge - asking to become Doc's apprentice.

248) Nina's Revenge
December 16th, 1961
Written by John Meston Directed by Tay Garnett
Guest Cast: Lois Nettleton, William Windom, Ron Foster, Johnny Seven
Lee Sharky is getting very fed up with his wealthy father-in- law, who refuses to help him and his wife out.

249) Marry Me
December 23rd, 1961
Written by Kathleen Hite Directed by Dennis Weaver Assistant Director Wes McAfee
Guest Cast: Don Dubbins, Warren Oates, Taylor McPeters
 Three mountain men, Pa Cathcart, Orkey and the younger son, Sweet Billy, have been living outside of
Dodge City for some months. Sweet Billy has been courting, and wants to marry, but Cathcarts always marry in line. While Orkey is tending the Widow Akin, Billy asks Pa to talk to Orkey. Pa does when his son returns, suggesting that Orkey think on wifin'. Orkey agrees, and heads into Dodge to pick himself a wife. He
sees Kitty in the Long Branch, and decides that she'll do. She's puzzled by his attentions, and Sam gets annoyed and tosses him out. When Chester hears about it, he rushes off to fetch Matt, bubbling over with a terrible story about a mountain man trying to haul off Miss Kitty. When Matt arrives, everything is quite peaceful. Kitty thinks it's all over - but the Cathcarts don't. Unable to understand why Kitty didn't come, Orkey
says: "I chose; she didn't choose back." Sweet Billy points out that things are different here from their home.
Pa finally decides that Kitty is just plain shy, and she needs a good man to draw her out - or to cuff her, if
need be.
 That evening, Matt and Doc talk. Rob Cotter is sick, and Doc is afraid that it's the cholera. Matt asks is he
has heard about the mountain man. "I heard it twice," Doc answers. "Chester's version and the truth." Meanwhile, the Cathcarts kidnap Miss Kitty unobserved, and take her out to their shack. Kitty is furious, and
starts throwing things at them. They're polite and cheerful, but firm. Pa thinks she just needs a little drawing
out. Orkey tries to talk to her, but she's in no mood to listen. By morning, Kitty is missed in town, and Matt
starts a search. It seems obvious that the mountain man took her, but no-one knows where he might be. At
the shack, Pa returns from visiting Widow Akin, feeling rather poorly. Orkey takes his turn with the old
woman. In the night, Kitty seizes her chance and sneaks out of the house - only to fall into one of the pits
that the Cathcarts have dug. Pa and Sweet Billy haul her out, and cover the pit over again.
 In the morning, Matt and Chester find Doc at Cotter's farm. Rob Cotter has died of the cholera. His next call
is on the widow Akin, who saw Cotter last week. At the shack, Orkey returns to the family. Widow Akin is
over the worst of it now, but Pa is badly sick. The widow gives Doc the lead to the shack, and he heads out
with Matt and Chester. Matt has Chester circle around, and then the limping deputy just vanishes. He's fallen
in one of the pits... Sweet Billy investigates, and Matt gets the drop on him. Matt calls for Kitty, and she and

GUNSMOKE

Orkey emerge from the shack. Pa has died of the cholera, and Orkey and Sweet Billy agree that they had best take him home. Orkey asks Kitty to release him from marryin' - he just doesn't have the time to teach her the business now. Kitty agrees, realizing that Orkey is a good soul at heart. She heads back to Dodge with her friends.

This was one of the all-time best episodes, with a fine mixture of humor and drama. The Cathcarts are excellently drawn and played. They're not villains, and they try to do what they believe is right - only it isn't what everyone else things is right. They do tend the Widow Akin while she's sick, and they are, in their own weird way, kind to Kitty. Fine acting from the three guests make them completely believable. Chester gets a terrific, if minor part, in this tale, especially when he falls down the pit.

250) A Man A Day
December 20th, 1961
Written by John Meston Directed by Harry Harris
Cast , Val Dufour, Fay Spain, Leonard Nimoy, Garry Walberg, Roy Wright, Ann Morrell, Arthur Peterson, Jr
To stop Matt from interfering with a robbery they have planned, a gang threatens to shoot a man a day unless Matt leaves Dodge.

251) The Do-Badder
January 6th, 1962
Written by John Meston Directed by Andrew McLaglen
Guest Cast: Abraham Sofaer, Strother Martin, Warren Oates, Mercedes Shirley, H.M. Wynant, James Anderson, Adam Williams
Harvey Easter is a prospector who has finally struck it rich. On his way back to Dodge, he is ambushed and robbed.

252) Lacey
January 13th, 1962
Written by Kathleen Hite Directed by Harry Harris
Guest Cast: Sherry Jackson, Jeremy Slate, Dorothy Green, Oliver McGowan, Sarah Selby, Nora Hayden
Lacey Parcher wants to marry Jess Ayley, but her stubborn father refuses to allow her. When Parcher is murdered, the marriage can go ahead - but did Ayley kill Parcher?

253) Cody's Code
January 20th, 1962
Written by John Meston Directed by Andrew McLaglen
Guest Cast: Anthony Caruso, Gloria Talbott, Robert Knapp, Wayne Rogers, Ken Becker
Cody Denham wants only to marry Rose Loring and settle in Dodge, but Sam Dukes has very violent objections to the plan.

254) Old Dan
January 27th, 1962
Written by Kathleen Hite Directed by Andrew McLaglen
Cast , Edgar Buchanan, Philip Coolidge, William Campbell, Dorothy Neumann, Sharon Wiley, Sharon Joslyn, Joe Hayworth
Doc decides that he is going to reform drunkard Dan Witter. He tries to get him a job, and makes the saloons refuse to serve him. Dan manages to get drunk anyhow, and get fired, so Doc gets him a job on Lem Petch's farm. The two men get along fine until Luke, Petch's shiftless son, returns, and starts taunting the old drunk with whisky.

255) Catawomper
February 10th, 1962
Written by John Meston Story by Gil Favor Directed by Harry Harris
Guest Cast: Sue Ann Langdon, Dick Sargent, Roy Wright, Frank Sutton,
Warren Vanders, Harold Innocent
Kate Tassel decides that her boyfriend, Bud Bones, is taking her too much for granted. She flattens him in a blazing row, and announces that she'll be taking new admirers any time. Naturally, Chester is among them. Bud decides that he'll run off anyone who tries to romance his girl.

256) Half Straight
February 17th, 1962
Written by John Meston Directed by Ted Post
Guest Cast: John Kerr, Elizabeth MacRae, William Bramley, J. Edward McKinley
Lute Willis, a gun for hire, is given his next target - Matt Dillon.

257) He Learned About Women
February 24th, 1962
Written by John Meston Story by John Rosser Directed by Tay Garnett
Guest Cast: Barbara Luna, Robert J. Wilke, Claude Akins, Ted de Corsia, Miriam Colon
A band of Comacheros kills Chavela's family and takes her captive. Garvey, their leader, aims to marry her, but his first wife, Kisla, objects. Matt is out hunting them when Kitty and Chester run afoul of the Comancheros. Chester holds them off so Kitty can get away, but is captured himself. The Comancheros stake him out to die in the sun, but Kisla frees him so he can take Chavela away. Solis kills Garvey and sets out to hunt them down. Chester is apparently betrayed by Chavela, and left to die in the desert.

258) The Gallows
March 3rd, 1962
Written by John Meston Directed by Andrew McLaglen
Guest Cast: Jeremy Slate, Robert J. Stevenson, William Challee, Joseph Ruskin
A strange bargain has been struck between Pruit Dover and Ax Parsons, in which Parsons must forfeit his life if he fails to deliver.

259) Reprisal
March 10th, 1962
Written by John Meston Directed by Harry Harris
Guest Cast: Diane Foster, Jason Evers, Tom Reese , George Lambert, Joe di Reda, Brad Trumball, Grace Lee Whitney
Oren Conrad leaves his wife at home on Saturday nights, spending his time with saloon girl Pearl. One Saturday, he arrives late, and Pearl has another "guest" for the evening.

260) Coventy
March 17th, 1962
Written by John Meston Directed by Christian Nyby
Guest Cast: Joe Maross, Paul Birch, Mary Field, Don Keefer, Walter Burke, Helen Wallace, John Harmon
Jessie Ott is heading into Dodge City with his pregnant wife, Clara, when their horse goes lame and they are stranded.

GUNSMOKE

261) The Widow
March 24th, 1962
Written by John Dunkel Directed by Ted Post
Guest Cast: Joan Hackett, Alan Reed, Jr, J. Edward McKinley, Alexander Lockwood
Drunken Emil Peck dunks Kitty in a horse-trough, but she gets no sympathy from widowed Mady Arthur.

262) Durham Bull
March 31st, 1962
Written by John Meston Story by Jack Shuttleworth
Guest Cast: Andy Clyde, Ricky Kelman, John Kellogg, Gilbert Green, George Keymas, Ted Jordan
An outlaw gang decides that Dodge City should provide them with riches. They hear an old man and his young grandson planning to bring a valuable Durham Bull to Dodge for breeding, and decide to steal it. After all, how much trouble can an old man and a boy be? They soon discover their mistake...

263) Wagon Girls
April 7th, 1962
Written by John Meston Directed by Andrew McLaglen
Guest Cast: Arch Johnson, Kevin Hagen, Ellen McRae (Ellen Burstyn), Constance Ford, Joan Marshall, Rayford Barnes
On the prairie, Matt meets Polly, who is trying to escape from wagon master Karl Feester. Matt is intrigued and investigates her story, which is loudly disputed by Feester himself.

264) The Dealer
April 14th, 1962
Written by John Dunkel Directed by Harry Harris
Guest Cast: Judi Meredith, Gary Clarke, George Mathews, Roy Roberts, Jess Kirkpatrick
Johnny Cole is fond of Lily Baskin, who is not interested in him. Her father attacks Johnny, who is forced to kill the old man in self-defence...

265) The Summons
April 21st, 1962
Written by Kathleen Hite Story by Marian Clark Directed by Andrew McLaglen
Guest Cast: Bethel Leslie, John Crawford, Cal Bolder, Robert J. Stevenson, Myron Healey, Shug Fisher, Percy Helton, Tom Hennesey, Joyce Jameson
Loy Bishop kills his partner in a robbery, then is amazed to learn that he is not a wanted man. He had hoped to collect the bounty on the man, but instead he faces charges of murder.

266) The Dreamers
April 28th, 1962
Written by John Meston Directed by Andrew McLaglen
Guest Cast: Liam Redmond, J. Pat O'Malley, Valerie Allen, CeCe Whitney, Gage Clarke, Dabbs Greer, Shug Fisher
Two miners have made a big strike, and head into Dodge to celebrate. One of the old men falls head over heels in love with Miss Kitty, and is determined to get her to marry him.

267) Cale
May 5th, 1962
Written by Kathleen Hite Directed by Harry Harris
Guest Cast: Carl Reindal, Robert Karnes, Joseph Hamilton, Peter Ashley

Cale is shot and wounded when he is taken to be the friend of a wanted horse-thief.

268) Chester's Indian
May 12th, 1962
Written by Kathleen Hite Directed by Dick Sargent
Guest Cast: Jena Engstrom, Eddie Little Sky, Karl Swenson, Lew Brown, Michael Barrier, Peggy Rea, Shug Fisher, Gene Benton
Chester is looking forward to a nice fishing trip when he stops at a small ranch to ask directions. He gets involved with a young woman's attempts to help an Indian escape from the local reservation. Callie, kept on a tight rein by her father, is convinced she loves the Indian, and Chester tries to talk sense into her - only to discover that he has to nurse the man back to health!

269) The Prisoner
May 19th, 1962
Written by Tommy Thompson Directed by Andrew McLaglen
Guest Cast: Andrew Prine, Nancy Gates, Conrad Nagel, Ed Nelson, William Phipps
A prisoner escapes from the military stockade in Fort Dodge, and heads into town.

270) The Boys
May 26th, 1962
Written by John Meston Directed by Harry Harris
Guest Cast: Malcolm Atterbury, George Kennedy, Dean Stanton, Michael Parks, May Heatherton
Professor Eliot arrives in Dodge City with his snake-oil elixir, determined to get rich in the quickest possible way.

Season Eight
September 15th, 1962 through June 1st, 1963
Produced by Norman MacDonnell
Assistant Producer: Frank Paris
Director Of Photography: Fleet Southcott
Art Director: Albert Herschong
Film Editor: Al Joseph, ACE
Set Decorator: Herman N. Schoenbrun
Sound Effects Editor: Gene Eliot, MPSE
Music Editor: Gene Feldman
Script Supervisor: Edla Bakke
Production Sound Mixer: Vernon W. Kramer
Recording: Joel Moss
Casting: Stalmaster-Lister Co
Property Master: Clem R. Widrig
Costumes: Alexander Velcoff, Thelma Hilborn
Makeup Artist: Glen Alden
Hairstylist: Pat Whiffing, CHS

GUNSMOKE

Cast
Matt Dillon: James Arness
Chester Goode: Dennis Weaver
Doc Galen Adams: Milburn Stone
Kitty Russell: Amanda Blak
Louie Pheeters: James Nusser
Barney: Charles Seel
Howie: Howard Culver
Ed O'Connor: Tom Brown
Percy Crump: John Harper
Hank: Hank Patterson
Quint Asper: Burt Reynolds
Sam: Glenn Strange

271) The Search
September 15th, 1962
Written by Kathleen Hite Directed by Harry Harris
Guest Cast: Carl Reindal, Ford Rainey, Virginia Gregg, Raymond Griffith, Leonard Nimoy
Cale takes off on a horse belonging to his employer, Tate Gifford, for no apparent reason. Gifford brands him a thief, but Matt isn't so certain. He goes looking for the man, and both are stranded on the prairie without a horse.
This was a sequel to "Cale" (5.5.62).

272) Call Me Dodie
September 22nd, 1962
Written by Kathleen Hite Directed by Harry Harris
Guest Cast: Kathy Nolan, Jack Searl, Mary Patton , Diane Mountford, Carol Seffinger, Dallas McKennon
Addie and Floyd Bagge run their orphanage like a slave camp. Dodie manages to escape and seeks help for the other children imprisoned by the evil brother and sister.

273) Quint Asper Comes Home
September 29th, 1962
Written by John Meston Directed by Andrew McLaglen
Guest Cast: Angela Clarke, Bill Zuckert, Earl Hodgins, Myron Healey, Harry Carey, Jr, James Doohan
Quint Asper is a half-breed Comanche who returns home when two Indian-haters shoot his father. He decides that he will leave white society and avenge his father's killing. Matt, taking a liking to Quint, manages to persuade him that justice is better than revenge. Quint then settles in Dodge as the new blacksmith.
Note: This was the first episode to feature semi-regular Quint Asper.

274) Root Down
October 6th, 1962
Written by Kathleen Hite Directed by Sobey Martin Assistant Director Wes McAfee
Guest Cast:John Dehner, Sherry Jackson, Robert Doyle, Howard McNear, George Selk, Michael Carr, Ollie O'Toole
Luke Dutton and his children, Aggie and Grudie, have settled for a moment outside of Dodge, on their drifting way to join Uncle Solon in Colorado. Luke is a dreamer, and likes to idle the time away. Aggie, on the other hand, wants to see Dodge and meet a nice fella and settle down. Luke has Grudie take her into town, and she's enchanted. Grudie goes for a drink, and she looks in Jonas's store. She sees Chester, and is smit-

ten, asking Doc if he's Chester's father. "He's not my son!" Doc snaps. "I'm too young to have a boy that old - and a little too particular!" In the meantime, Grudie has gotten into a fight in the Long Branch, and used a set of brass knuckles. Matt tells him to leave town.

Back at the cabin, Aggie waxes lyrical about Dodge, but Luke isn't listening. He's aiming to drift on again, and she's frustrated. She wants to root down, and that night, she thinks up a brilliant plan. She gets up early, and rides to Dodge, where she asks Chester to come fishing with her. Naturally he agrees. The two male Dutton's realize Aggie is gone, and when she returns, she brings Chester. She then claims that she spent the night with Chester, which floors everyone - especially Chester. He is even more embarrassed when she says that Chester's come to do the right thing and marry her. When he tries to explain it, Grudie knocks him down with his knuckledusters. Aggie then gets to tend him, and tries to convince him of her story. Luke won't believe his side of the story, and sets him to working, watched by the mean-spirited Grudie.

Aggie tries to get Chester to understand how badly she just wants to settle down, and he begins to sympathize a little with her. In town, Matt thinks that Chester's simply off having fun with a pretty girl, until he realizes that the horse she rode was the one that Grudie also rode - and that Chester might be in trouble. Luke has a letter at last from Solon, telling them to come on out, so they strike camp and start up. Solon is a preacher, so they aim to have him marry Aggie and Chester. Matt arrives and stops them, refusing to accept for a moment the preposterous story about Chester having slept with Aggie. Aggie realizes she has to tell the truth to prevent further trouble. Chester, predictably, then stands up for her, telling her father that she just wants to root down somewhere. Luke promises she will. He finds Grudie's brass knuckles, and throws them away, determined to start over with his children. Chester won't press charges. "I don't think they meant any harm," he explains. "They're just kinda peculiar." He and Matt watch them leave for Colorado - and a new home?

Another of Kathleen Hite's excellent odd families, and again brilliantly played. Poor old Chester really gets it this time, stalked by a predatory female...

275) Jenny
October 13th, 1962
Written by John Meston Directed by Andrew McLaglen
Guest Cast: Ruta Lee, Ron Hayes, John Duke, Monte Montana, Jr, Ken Hudginsx

Meyers is a bank-robber who has fled to Dodge with his girl-friend, Jenny. She finds work in the Long Branch, but he gambles away the money he stole, and looks for another way to make it back fast.

276) Collie's Free
October 20th, 1962
Written by Kathleen Hite Directed by Harry Harris
Guest Cast: Jason Evers, Jacqueline Scott, James Halferty, William Bramley
After eight years in prisoner, Collie Patten is free. He's spent the whole time thinking of a way to get even with Matt, who captured him, and now begins to put that plan into action.

277) The Ditch
October 27th, 1962
Written by Les Crutchfield Directed by Harry Harris
Guest Cast: Joanne Linville, Jay Lanin, Christopher Dark, Hardie Albright, Dehi Bertt
Homesteaders have intruded in an area that Susan believed was hers. She is egged on by a gunman to divert the water that they need to survive. As a result, a water ditch is begun, and a pitched battle between the two sides begins...

GUNSMOKE

278) The Trappers
November 3rd, 1962
Written by John Dunkel Directed by Andrew McLaglen
Guest Cast: Strother Martin, Richard Shannon, Doris Singleton
Tug Marsh and Billy Logan have worked together for years, but when Indians capture Tug, Billy runs for his life.

279) Phoebe Strunk
November 10th, 1962
Written by John Meston Directed by Andrew McLaglen
Guest Cast: Joan Freeman , Virginia Gregg, Don Megowan, Dick Peabody, Gregg Palmer, Harry Raybould
Phoebe Strunck manages to look after her four sons - by making them into an efficient band of robbers under her direction.

280) The Hunger
November 17th, 1962
Written by Jack Curtis Directed by Harry Harris
Guest Cast: Ellen Willard, Robert Middleton, Hampton Fancher, Linda Watkins
When making a call on the Dorf family, Doc is appalled to discover that Dorf "disciplines" his willful daughter by locking her away in a small hut, with no food. He and Matt get the girl taken away from the family, and Doc starts to treat her nicely. Althea then falls in love with Doc, who simply cannot cope with the prospect.

281) Abe Blocker
November 24th, 1962
Written by John Meston Directed by Andrew McLaglen
Guest Cast: Chill Wills, Wright King, Miranda Jones, Harry Carey, Jr
Abe Blocker is a mountain man, who hates the intrusion of modern ranchers on what he regards as his land. When his efforts to scare them off don't work, he turns to murder. Matt, an old friend of his, is appalled, but has no choice. He has to hunt down and kill his old friend before Blocker kills again.

282) The Way It Is
December 1st, 1962
Written by Kathleen Hite Story by Frank Paris Directed by Harry Harris
Guest Cast:Claude Akins, Garry Walberg, Virginia Lewis, Duane Grey
Kitty is furious with Matt for standing her up again because of his job. She rides out to cool off, and finds an injured man on the trail. After nursing him back to health, she finds him kind and considerate. She is falling in love with him when she discovers that he is also violent and possessive, and determined to slay his "rival" for her affections when Matt returns to town.

283) Us Haggens
December 8th, 1962
Written by Les Crutchfield Directed by Andrew McLaglen
Guest Cast: Ken Curtis, Denver Pyle, Elizabeth MacRae
Black Jack Haggen is a wanted killer that Matt is trailing. He is joined by the man's nephew, Festus, who has his own reasons for wanting revenge on his slippery uncle.
Note: This was the first appearance of Festus. He would return the following year as a regular character. In the meantime, Ken Curtis played two other guest-spots in different roles.

284) Uncle Sunday
December 15th, 1962
Written by John Meston Directed by Joseph Sargent Assistant Director Robert
L. Rosen Incidental Music Tommy Morgan Conducted by Lud Gluskin
Guest Cast: Henry Beckman, Joyce Bulifant, Ed Nelson, Dabbs Greer, Gage
Clarke, Wallace Rooney, Nora Marlowe

When Chester gets a letter from his Uncle Sunday Meechum, he panics, and starts looking for extra work. Doc and Matt are puzzled until Chester explains that Sunday has to leave Waxahachie, Texas, due to trouble with the law. He wants to go on to California, but can only afford to reach Dodge. Chester is hoping to raise the money to get rid of him again - preferably as far as China! Chester views his uncle as probably the biggest crook in Texas. Sadly, Chester's efforts don't pay off. When he tries to work for Quint, he manages to start a fire; when he works in Jonas's store, he insults one of the customers accidentally; at Dan's pool hall, he looses the job when two drunken cowboys rip one of the felts. Nothing is going right.

A drifter called Burt Curry then approaches Chester with an offer. If Chester supplies him with bank and stage shipment times, he'll give Chester a share of the robbery loot. Chester is furious, and Curry claims it was only a joke. Chester doesn't believe that for a second. The next day, Uncle Sunday arrives, and charms Matt with his cheerful humor and manners. He also has a cousin along, Ellie, that Chester has never heard of. She's pretty, though, and Chester jumps at the chance to show her around - even if Uncle Sunday accompanies them. Sunday makes a favorable impression all around, mostly because everyone in town likes Chester, and assumes any of his relatives are equally pleasant. Curry sees Ellie, and likes the look of her. She in her turn admires his good looks, and makes an appointment to see him that night. By accident, Chester mistakenly makes the same appointment.

Doc is worried that Chester is trying to date a relative of his, but again Chester proves smarter - he knows Ellie isn't really Sunday's niece. That night, Chester tries to romance Ellie, but she gets rid of him so she can meet Curry. Chester observes this, and listens in. Curry and Ellie have sized each other up: he knows she's Meechum's kept woman, and she knows he's a crook. She tells him that Mr. Botkin will be working late at the bank the next night. Sunday, as Chester's uncle, can get in without arousing suspicion, and they can rob them. Ellie wants a younger, more handsome man, though, and will leave the bank first with the money. If Curry can have two horses ready...

Chester visits his Uncle in the morning, with the news - and a plan. Sunday admits a weakness for pretty women, and a need for money to keep them entertained. That night, Sunday and Ellie visit the bank, and Botkin lets them in. He is held up, and Ellie takes the money in her bag. While Sunday is tying up the banker, she slips out and meets Curry. He takes the bag and jumps on his horse, leaving her behind. As she screams curses after him, Chester arrests her. This was all his idea, and down the road, Matt grabs the fleeing Curry. With the two villains out of the way, Sunday is something of a hero - an appropriate time to leave town...

Chester's relatives are always trouble (a pattern followed by Festus's relatives in the future). They are also humorous, not really villainous, like Sunday. Inevitably, they decide that Dodge isn't the place for them, and move along. Poor old Chester suffered the double embarrassment this time of meeting another relative and losing a girl in a single episode. Nothing ever goes right for him, it seems.

285) False Front
December 22nd, 1962
Written by John Meston Story by Hal Moffett Directed by Andrew McLaglen
Guest Cast: Andrew Prine, William Windom, Art Lund , Charles Fredericks
Journalist Paul Hill believes that gunslingers out West are just reputations, and bets a friend that he can make anyone into a feared man with the right publicity. He picks youthful Clay Tatum, and goes to Dodge City. After spreading word about the "legendary" Clay Tatum, Hill brings the youth into town. Tatum is indeed feared. The notoriety goes to his head and he starts believing in the tales himself.

GUNSMOKE

286) Old Comrade
December 29th, 1962
Written by John Dunkel Directed by Harry Harris
Guest Cast:J. Pat O'Malley, Frank Sutton, Ralph Moody
Colonel Wislon arrives in Dodge looking for the son of his commanding general, who is dying. He discovers that Billy is the town fool.

287) Pheeters
January 5th, 1963
Written by John Meston Directed by Harry Harris
Guest Cast: Larry Ward, John Larkin, Gloria McGhee
Bart Felder is jealous of his wife, and kills a man she claims is pestering her. She was lying to cover her real lover, and now they try and fix the blame on the town drunk, Louie Pheeters.
Note: This was the first story to feature Louie Pheeters, who made many further appearances over the years.

288) The Renegades
January 12th, 1963
Written by John Meston Directed by Andrew McLaglen
Guest Cast: Audrey Dalton, Ben Wright, Jack Lambert, Donald Barry
A colonel's daughter hates all Indians, and Quint Asper is included in that field. When an Indian attack involves the Army, she refuses to believe Quint's claims that the Indians are being framed by white raiders.

289) Cotter's Girl
January 19th, 1963
Written by Kathleen Hite Directed by Harry Harris
Guest Cast: Mariette Hartley, Roy Barcroft, John Clark, Jesselyn Fax
Old man Cotter dies in Dodge, and asks Matt to take his daughter a letter. Matt agrees, but the daughter is nowhere near as sweet as the old man claims she is.

290) The Bad One
January 26th, 1963
Written by Gwen Bagni Guilguid Directed by Sobey Martin
Guest Cast: Chris Robinson, Dolores Sutton, Booth Coleman , Ken Kenosha
Jenny Parker rather likes the handsome young robber who holds up their stage, and is convinced that he isn't as bad as Matt claims. She refuses to help Matt track down and capture the escaped man.

291) The Cousin
February 2nd, 1963
Written by Kathleen Hite Story by Marian Clark Directed by Harry Harris
Guest Cast: Michael Forest, John Anderson, Joseph Perry, Gloria Talbott
Chance Hopper was raised by the same foster parents as Matt, but he turned bad and was jailed. Now he is free again, he arrives in Dodge to meet his old foster brother. Matt, however, is convinced that Chance is after something else as well.

292) Shona
February 9th, 1963
Written by John Meston Directed by Ted Post
Guest Cast: Miriam Colon, Robert Bray, John Crawford , Robert Palmer, Bart Burns, Steve Stevens
Gib, a friend of Quint's, brings his Indian wife to town for treatment. The folks of Dodge don't like this,

since they are rather prejudiced against Indians.

293) Ash
February 16th, 1963
Written by John Meston Directed by Harry Harris
Guest Cast: John Dehner, Anthony Caruso, Dee Hartford, Adam West, Sheldon Allman
Ben Galt is struck on the head, and this induces wild mood swings in him that turn him from a gentle person into a raging maniac.

294) Blind Man's Bluff
February 23rd, 1963
Written by John Meston Directed by Ted Post
Guest Cast: Will Hutchins, Crahan Denton, John Alderson, Herbert Lytton
Matt is blinded when he is attacked on the trail by the gang of the killer he is tracking.

295) Quint's Indian
March 1st, 1963
Written by John Meston Story by Marian Clark Directed by Fred H. Jackman
Guest Cast: Will Corey, James Brown, Patrick McVey, James Griffith
When a horse is stolen by someone versed in Comanche ways, the townsfolk assume that Quint was to blame, and attack him.

296) Anybody Can Kill A Marshal
March 8th, 1963
Written by Kathleen Hite Directed by Harry Harris
Guest Cast: Warren Stevens, James Westerfield, Milton Selzer, Brenda Scott
Two outlaws bungle the job of killing Matt, so they hire a professional to do the job for them.

297) Two Of A Kind
March 16th, 1963
Written by Merwin Gerard Directed by Andrew McLaglen
Cast , Richard Jaekel, Michael Higgins, Kent Smith, Garry Walberg, Ben Wright, John Mitchum
Two Irishmen work together in a mine, but fall out over a woman and start feuding. Clay Bealton sees this as the perfect opportunity to get his hands on their gold.

298) I Call Him Wonder
March 23rd, 1963
Written by Kathleen Hite Directed by Harry Harris
Guest Cast: Ron Hayes, Edmund Vargas, Sandy Kenyon, Leonard Nimoy, Duane Gray
Jud Sorrell is an amiable drifter who finds an Indian boy on the trail. Reluctantly, he takes care of the tyke, and as a result he falls foul of prejudice and abuse. Somehow, though, he comes to actually care for the boy.

299) With A Smile
March 30th, 1963
Written by John Meston Directed by Andrew McLaglen
Guest Cast: R.G. Armstrong, James Best, Sharon Farrell, Linden Chiles, Dick Foran, Dan Stafford
Major Creed is the richest rancher in the area. His son, Dal, believes he can have whatever he wants - but Lottie Foy makes it quite clear to him that this does not include her in any way, shape or form.

93

GUNSMOKE

300) The Far Places
April 6th, 1963
Written by John Dunkel Directed by Harry Harris
Guest Cast: Angela Clarke, Rees Vaughn, Bennye Gatteys, Orville Sherman , Dennis Cross
Carrie Newcomb is annoyed with her son's choice of who he wants to marry. She then plans on selling out her ranch and moving East to separate the couple.

301) Panacea Sikes
April 13th, 1963
Written by Kathleen Hite Directed by William Conrad
Guest Cast: Nellie Burt, Dan Tobin, Charles Watts, Lindsay Workman
Panacea arrives in Dodge City, claiming that she is Kitty's mother - and presuming upon this supposed relationship. Kitty isn't fooled, but the old lady wins her larcenous way into Kitty's heart.

302) Tell Chester
April 20th, 1963
Written by Frank Paris Directed by Joseph Sargent
Guest Cast: Lonny Chapman, Mitzi Hoag, Jo Halton, Sara Taft
Polly Donahue is Chester's latest lady - at least in his mind. She, on the other hand, has her eyes set on Wade Stringer. The fact that he's already married seems never to have been mentioned to her.

303) Quint-Cident
April 27th, 1963
Written by Kathleen Hite Directed by Andrew McLaglen
Guest Cast:Mary la Roche, Ben Johnson, Don Keefer
Widow Willa Devlin sets her sights on Quint; he, in his turn, sets his eyes on the horizon, uninterested in her.

304) Old York
May 4th, 1963
Written by John Meston Directed by Harry Harris
Guest Cast: Edgar Buchanan, H.M. Wynant, Robert Knapp, Ed Madden, Alex Sharp, Michael Constantine, Rudy Dolan
Years ago, Matt almost turned outlaw, and joined a gang. When he wants out, their leader plans on killing Matt. Dan York saved Matt's life. Now, Dan turns up in Dodge, and plays on Matt's gratitude to plan a crime spree in the town.

305) Daddy Went Away
May 11th, 1963
Written by Kathleen Hite Story by John Rosser Directed by Joseph Sargent
Guest Cast: Mary Carver, Suzanne Cupito, William Schallert
Lucy Damon and her daughter, Jessica, arrive in Dodge. She sets up a dressmaker's shop, and Chester is smitten. When Jessica tells Chester that "Daddy went away," he assumes her to mean that her mother is a widow. In fact, he simply literally went away - fishing - to avoid his responsibilities.

306) The Odyssey Of Jubal Tanner
May 18th, 1963
Written by Paul Savage Directed by Andrew McLaglen
Guest Cast: Beverly Garland, Peter Breck, Gregg Palmer, Denver Pyle

Colie Fletcher comes across Jubal Tanner on the trail and shoots him, to steal his horse. He has already killed Leah Brunson's fiance. Tanner and Leah join forces to get the criminal captured.

307) Jeb
May 25th, 1963
Written by Paul Savage Directed by Harry Harris
Guest Cast: Jim Hampton, Roy Thinnes, Emile Genest, William Hunt, Buck Young
A farm boy is accused of stealing a horse. When he denies the accusation, the man guns him down in cold blood.

308) The Quest For Asa Janin
June 1st, 1963
Written by Paul Savage Directed by Andrew McLaglen
Guest Cast: Anthony Caruso, Richard Devon, Gene Darfier, George Keymas, Joseph Sirola, Harry Carey, Jr, Jack Lambert
When a friend of Matt's is condemned to hang, he asks Matt to track down the real killer before the deed is done.

Ninth Season
September 28th, 1963 through June 11th, 1964
Produced by Norman Macdonnell
Associate Producer: Frank Paris
Director of Photography: Frank Phillips, ASC
Production Manager : Robert M. Beche
Art Director: James D. Vance
Set Decorator: Herman N. Schoenbrun
Script Supervisor: Edla Bakke
Film Editor: Otto Meyer, ACE
Sound Effects Editor : Gene Eliot, MPSE
Music Editor: Gene Feldman Production
Sound Mixer: Vernon W. Kramer
Casting: Stalmaster-Lister Co
Property Master: Clem R. Widrig
Costumes: Alexander Velcoff, Thelma Hildborn
Makeup Artist: Glen Alden
Hair Stylist: Patt Whiffing, CHS

GUNSMOKE

Cast

Matt Dillon: James Arness
Chester Goode: Dennis Weaver
Doc Galen Adams: Milburn Stone
Kitty Russell: Amanda Blak
Louie Pheeters: James Nusser
Barney: Charles Seel
Howie: Howard Culver
Ed O'Connor: Tom Brown
Percy Crump: John Harper
Hank: Hank Patterson
Sam: Glenn Strange
Nathan Burke: Ted Jordan

309) Kate Heller
September 28th, 1963
Written by John Meston Directed by Andrew McLaglen
Guest Cast: Mabel Albertson, Tom Lowell, Robert Knapp, Betsy Jones-Moreland, Harry Bartell, Ted Jordan, Duane Eddy
Matt is ambushed and shot down by a killer and a thief.

310) Lover Boy
October 5th, 1963
Written by John Meston Directed by Andrew McLaglen
Guest Cast: Sheree North, Richard Coogan, Alan Baxter, Ken Curtis, Dorothy Konrad
Kyle Kelly has just jilted one girl, and is now paying court to a second.

311) Legends Don't Sleep
October 12th, 1963
Written by Kathleen Hite Directed by Harry Harris
Guest Cast: Hope Summers , William Talman, Scott Marlowe, Robert Bice, Alan Bestor, Ken Kenoka , Don Haggerty
A famous gunslinger on release from prison finds that he has a young admirer who wants to be just like him.

312) Tobe
October 19th, 1963
Written by Paul Savage Directed by John W. English
Guest Cast: Mary la Roche, Harry Townes, Philip Abbott, L.Q. Jones, Sarah Selby
When her boyfriend becomes a gambler, Mae Young throws him over, and becomes a hostess in the Long Branch. There she meets up with Tobe, and the two become more than friends.

313) Easy Come
October 26th, 1963
Written by John Meston Directed by Andrew McLaglen
Guest Cast: Andrew Prine, Carl Reindal, George Wallace, Charles Briggs
Everyone thinks that Elmo Sippy is the most even-tempered, easy-going man. This is just a front, however, for his cold and murderous nature.

314) My Sister's Keeper
November 2nd, 1963
Written by Kathleen Hite Directed by Harry Harris
Guest Cast: Nancy Wickwire, James Broderick Jennifer Billingsley
Two unmarried sisters hire on a widower to help with their ranch. Both then
start becoming attracted to him.

315) Quint's Trail
November 9th, 1963
Written by Kathleen Hite Directed by Harry Harris
Guest Cast: Everett Sloane, Don Haggerty, Sharon Farrell, Shirley O'Hara
The Neff family are passing through Dodge on their way to Oregon. Their guide leaves them, taking all of
their money with him. The family (and especially Belle) prevail upon Quint to help them out.

316) Carter Caper
November 16th, 1963
Written by John Meston Directed by Jerry Hopper
Guest Cast: Jeremy Slate, William Phipps, Rayford Barnes, Anjanette Comer, Michael Fox, I. Stanford Jolley
Joe Stark wants revenge from Billy Hargis. Stark had tried to steal Billy's horse, but Billy beat him up. Now
in Dodge, Stark has a chance to get even.

317) Ex-Con
November 30th, 1963
Written by John Meston Directed by Thomas Carr
Guest Cast: John Kellogg , Jean Cooper, Richard Devon, Roy Roberts, Raymond Guth, Harry Lauter
Leo Pitts is out of jail, and heads straight for Dodge City with two intentions: first, to marry Lily; second, to
kill Matt Dillon. He manages the first, but is killed in trying the second. His brother then takes up the quest
for vengeance.

318) Extradition (Part One)
December 7th, 1963
Written by Anthony Ellis Directed by John W. English
Guest Cast: Gilbert Roland, Gene Evans, Andy Albin, Alex Montoya, Anna Novarro, Walter Burke, Miguel
Landa, Pepe Hern, Rico Alani
Charlie Hacker flees to Mexico after killing a man. Matt is hot on his trail, but is stopped by Chavez at the
border. Chavez agrees to act in an official capacity to help Matt find Chavez, but seems to spend most of his
time swindling Dillon. When Matt finally reaches his quarry, both he and Hacker are thrown into a Mexican
jail.

319) Extradition (Part Two)
December 14th, 1963
Written by Anthony Ellis Directed by John W. English
Guest Cast: Gilbert Roland, Gene Evans, Andy Albin, Alex Montoya, Anna Novarro, Walter Burke, Miguel
Landa, Pepe Hern, Rico Alani
Matt manages to get out of the jail, and heads back towards to border with Hacker - plus Mexican bandits on
his trail.

GUNSMOKE

320) The Magician
December 21st, 1963
Written by John Kneubuhl Directed by Harry Harris
Guest Cast: Lloyd Corrigan, Brooke Bundy, Crahan Denton, Tom Simcox, William Zuckert, Ken Tiliesas, Sheldon Allman
A traveling salesman of dubious medicines arrives in Dodge. In a game of cards, he is accused of cheating.

321) Pa Hack's Brood
December 28th, 1963
Written by Paul Savage Directed by Jerry Hopper
Guest Cast: Lynn Loring, James Hampton, Milton Selzer, Charles Kuenstle, Marianne Hill, George Lindsey
Pa Hack is worried about impending old age, so he decides that his best bet is to marry off his daughter to a nearby wealthy rancher.

322) The Glory And The Mud
January 4th, 1964
Written by Gwen Bagni Gielgud Directed by Jerry Hopper
Guest Cast: Kent Smith, James Best, Marsha Hunt, Robert Sorrells
Sam Beal wants to become Matt's deputy, thinking he can gain glory that way. Matt realizes the youth only wants a reputation, and refuses to hire him on. Then famed western sideshow owner Jack Dakota comes to town, to wed his long-time girl, Sarah Carr. Beal figures that killing Dakota will make his name. The only problem for Dakota is that he is going blind, and doesn't want anyone to know this - he can't afford to fight, but neither can he back down.

323) Dry Well
January 11th, 1964
Written by John Meston Directed by Harry Harris
Guest Cast: Bill Henry, Ned Glass, Karen Sharpe, Tom Simcox, John Hanek
Yuma Linz may be just married, but she's still taking every chance to see her old boy-friend.

324) Prairie Wolfer
January 18th, 1964
Written by John Dunkel Directed by Andrew McLaglen
Guest Cast: Noah Beery , Don Dubbins, Frank Coby, Holly McIntire
Festus Haggen returns to Dodge City, now a wolfer. He is trapping wolves for the Cattleman's Association. Nate Guthrie is blaming wolves for deeds he is doing, to steal hides and sell them to Rolly Wendt. Sarah, Nate's daughter, takes a shine to Festus, despite her father's objections. Festus discovers the truth, and is then framed by Nate for Wendt's murder.
Note: Festus's first episode as a regular. At the end, he's still a wolfer, not the deputy as yet.

325) Once A Hangman
January 25th, 1963
Written by Kathleen Hite Directed by Harry Harris
Guest Cast: Tom Reese, Ben Wright, Jan Shepard, Ralph Moody, Butch Patrick, George Keymas
An old friend of Matt's has died a suspicious death. Matt goes to investigate this, despite the fact that no-one wants him to. He discovers that his friend is not dead - just hiding out.

326) Friend
February 1st, 1964
Written by Les Crutchfield Directed by Andrew McLaglen
Guest Cast: Slim Pickens, Elizabeth MacRae, Roy Barcroft, Ken Tobey, John Hudson, William Bryant
Festus and his friend Bucko lose rather a lot of money in a poker game. Later, the winner is found murdered, and accusations begin to fly.

327) No Hands
February 8th, 1964
Written by John Meston Directed by Andrew McLaglen
Guest Cast: Strother Martin, Denver Pyle, Kevin Hagen, Rayford Barnes, Wright King
Doc is busy with a patient when the Ginnis's arrive. They refuse to wait, and start to mistreat the man Doc is dealing with.

328) May Blossoms
February 15th, 1964
Written by Kathleen Hite Directed by Andrew McLaglen
Guest Cast: Laurie Peters , Richard X. Slattery, Charles Gray, Roger Torrey, Sarah Selby, Mary Munday
Festus's cousin, Mayblossom, arrives in Dodge City - to marry him. She claims that their fathers arranged this years ago, when they were children. Despite the fact that she's a very attractive girl, Festus doesn't like the idea of settling down at all.

329) The Bassops
February 22nd, 1963
Written by Tom Hanley Directed by Andrew McLaglen
Guest Cast: Robert Wilke, Warren Oates, Eunice Pollis, Mickey Sholdar
The Bassop family find Matt and Kelby stranded near their farm. Both men are handcuffed together, and both claim to be the Marshal. The young couple don't know what they should do.

330) The Kite
February 29th, 1963
Written by John Meston Directed by Andrew McLaglen
Guest Cast: Lyle Bettger, Michael Higgins, Betsy Hale, Allyson Ames
Mrs. Cassidy has been killed, and her daughter, Letty, saw the deed. Until the man responsible can be brought to trail, Matt has to protect the girl.

331) Comanches Is Safe
March 7th, 1964
Written by Kathleen Hite Directed by Harry Harris
Guest Cast: Kathy Nolan, Don Megowan, Ted Jordan , Robert Gravage, Dean Stanton, Rex Holman
 Quint and Festus have a time of it in Wichita, but later back in Dodge, they regret this. Liz turns up, a saloon girl they met, and claims that they invited her out.

332) Father Love
March 14th, 1964
Written by John Meston Directed by Harry Harris
Guest Cast: Ed Nelson, Shary Marshall, Robert F. Simon, Anthony Caruso
Cora is just married. She discovers that her husband's uncle seems to have some romantic interests in her.

GUNSMOKE

333) Now That April's There
March 21st, 1964
Written by Les Crutchfield Directed by Andrew McLaglen
Guest Cast: Elizabeth MacRae, Royal Dano, Hal Baylor
April has a reputation for telling tall stories, but her latest is unfortunately true: she witnessed a murder. The only people that believe her are the killers themselves.

334) Homecoming
March 28th, 1964
Written by Paul Savage Directed by Harry Harris
Guest Cast: Dabbs Greer, John Dehner, Lane Bradford , Dorothy Green
Caleb Marr has had enough of farming, and decides he'll sample the life in Dodge City instead.

335) Owney Tupper Had A Daughter
April 4th, 1964
Written by Paul Savage Directed by Jerry Hopper
Cast , Jay C. Flippen, Andrea Darvi, Noreen Corcoran, James Seay, Howard Wendell, Orville Sherman, Dolores Quinton, Vernon Rich, Berkeley Harris, Steve Gaynor
Owney Tupper is a widower, and he finds that he can't make ends meet, despite all his efforts. He is forced by the busy-body old ladies of Dodge to give his daughter away until he can support her.

336) Bently
April 11th, 1964
Written by John Kneubuhl Directed by Harry Harris
Guest Cast: Jan Clayton, Charles MacGraw, Gene Lyons, June Dayton, Bill Erwin
Ned Wright was found innocent of murder by a jury, but when he is dying, he sends for Chester to make a strange confession.
This was the final episode to feature Chester.

337) Kitty Cornered
April 18th, 1964
Written by Kathleen Hite Directed by John Brahm
Guest Cast: Jacqueline Scott, Shug Fisher, Joseph Sirola, Viki Raaf
Stella Damon wants to buy out Kitty and take over the Long Branch. When Kitty won't sell, Stella starts to play dirty.

338) The Promoter
April 25th, 1964
Written by John Meston Directed by Andrew McLaglen
Guest Cast: Vic Perrin, Allen Case, Don Collier, Robert Fortier, Larry Blake, Wilheim von Homburg
Henry Huckaby is tired of farming, so he decides to become a demon of the boxing ring instead.

339) Trip West
May 2nd, 1964
Written by John Dunkel Directed by Harry Harris
Guest Cast: Herbert Anderson, Sharon Farrell, H.M. Wynant
Elwood Hardacre is a shy bank clerk, but when a fortune teller predicts he will die in the near future, he decides to take chances, and his entire personality changes.

340) Scot-Free
May 9th, 1964
Written by Kathleen Hite Directed by Harry Harris
Guest Cast: Patricia Owens, Anne Barton, Jay Lanin, Julie Sommers, Harry Bartel, Robert Bice
Rob Scott leaves his wife, Anne, and their children to move in with Nora Brand. First, he has to dispose of Nora's husband, though.

341) Cool Dawn
May 16th, 1964
Written by Les Crutchfield Directed by Andrew McLaglen
Guest Cast: Julie Parrish, George Kennedy, Anthony Caruso, Christopher Connelly
Cool Dawn is sold by her father, Bull Foot, to Stark. She hates the man, and runs away, taking refuge with Festus.

342) Orville Bass
May 23rd, 1964
Written by John Meston Story by Shimon Wincelberg Directed by Harry Harris
Guest Cast: Harold J. Stone, Phyllis Coates, Jack Elam , Tom Lowell, Emile Geneste
Orville Bass arrives in Dodge City, claiming to be the legitimate husband of Edna Lowell, and that the Lowell property really belongs to him.

343) The Other Half
May 30th, 1964
Written by John Dunkel Directed by Andrew McLaglen
Guest Cast: Lee Kinsolving, Donna J. Anderson, Paul Fix, Larry Fix
Nancy Otis is loved by two twin brothers, but cannot decide which of them she prefers.

344) Journey For Three
June 4th, 1964
Written by Frank Paris Directed by Harry Harris
Guest Cast: William Arvin Michael Pollard, Mark Goddard
Boyd Lambert falls in with the Gifford brothers, who are off to California. It soon becomes apparent that Lambert is rotten through and through, and aims on dragging the brothers down with him.

345) Cornelia Conrad
June 11th, 1964
Guest Cast: Diane Foster, Jason Evers, Tom Reese, George Lambert, Joe di Reda, Gene Benton, Joe Devlin, Harold Innocent, Gage Clarke
No other information.

Season Ten

September 26th, 1964 through May 29th, 1965
Produced by Philip Leacock
Script Consultant: John Mantley
Director of Photography: Harry Stradling, Jr
Production Manager: Robert M. Beche
Assistant to Producer: Herbert DuFine
Art Director: Albert Herschong, Malcolm, C. Bert

GUNSMOKE

Set Decorator: Herman N. Schoenbrun
Script Supervisor: Edle Bakke
Film Editor: Al Joseph, Otto Meyer
Sound Effects Editor: Gene Eliot, MPSE
Music Editor: Gene Feldman
Production Sound Mixer: Vernon W. Kramer
Casting: James Lister
Property Master: Clem R. Widrig
Costumes: Alexander Velcoff
Makeup Artist: Glen Alden

Cast:

Matt: James Arness
Doc: Milburn Stone
Kitty: Amanda Blake
Festus: Ken Curtis
Sam: Glenn Strange
Quint: Burt Reynolds
Louie Pheeters: James Nusser
Barney: Charles Seel
Howie: Howard Culver
Ed O'Connor: Tom Brown
Percy Crump: John Harper
Hank: Hank Patterson
Nathan Burke Ted Jordan

346) Blue Heaven
September 26th, 1964
Written by Les Crutchfield, Directed by Michael O'Herlihy
Guest Cast: Tim O'Connor, Kurt Russell, Diane Ladd, Karl Swenson, Jan Merlin
A man on the run from the law teams up with a young scamp.

347) Crooked Mile
October 3rd, 1964
Written by Les Crutchfield, Directed by Andrew McLaglen
Guest Cast: Katharine Ross, Royal Dano, George Kennedy
Cyrus Degler doesn't like Quint paying attention to his daughter, so he uses a bullwhip to teach Quint to stay away.

348) Old Man
October 10th, 1964
Written by John Meston, Directed by Harry Harris
Guest Cast: Ed Peck, Ned Glass, Rayford Barnes, Robert Hogan, Howard Wendell
When Joe Silva is murdered, the wrong man is arrested for the killing.

349) The Violators
October 17th, 1964
Written by John Dunkel, Directed by Harry Harris
Guest Cast: Denver Pyle, James Anderson, Arthur Batanides, Michael Pate, Amzie Strickland, Garry Wal-

berg, Martin Blaine
When a peaceable young man is killed and scalped by renegade Indians, hatred runs rife in Dodge City.

350) Doctor's Wife
October 24th, 1964
Written by George Eckstein, Directed by Harry Harris
Guest Cast: James Broderick, Phyllis Love, Harold Gould, Anne Barton, Helen Kleeb, Robert Brubaker
Dr. May moves to Dodge City, and to ensure that her husband is a success, Jennifer May starts to spread malicious rumors about Doc Adams.

351) Take Her, She's Cheap
October 31st, 1964
Written by Kathleen Hite, Directed by Harry Harris
Guest Cast: Laurie Peters, Willard Sage, Linda Watkins, Mort Mills
When Matt helps the Carp family out of difficulties on the trail, he is offered their daughter as a wife as a way of saying thanks.

352) Help Me, Kitty
November 7th, 1964
Written by Kathleen Hite, Directed by Harry Harris
Guest Cast: Betty Conner, Jack Elam, James Frawley, Burt Douglas, Peggy Stewart, Hal Shaw, Joe Conley, Larry Blake
The daughter of one of Kitty's friends comes to her for advice. She's unmarried and pregnant, and doesn't know what to do.

353) Hung High
November 14th, 1964
Written by John Meston, Directed by Mark Rydell
Guest Cast: Robert Culp, Scott Marlowe, Harold J. Stone, Ed Asner, Elisha Cook, George Lindsay, Steven Marlo, Michael Conrad, Robert Anderson, Buck Young, Clegg Hoyt, Karl Lukas
A friend of Matt's has retired from being a lawman. He is then killed by a young man who hates all lawmen.

354) Jonah Hutchinson
November 21st, 1964
Written by Calvin Clements, Direcetd by Harry Harris
Guest Cast: Robert F. Simon, Richard Anderson, June Dayton, Tommy Alexander, Claude Johnson, David Macklin
Jonah Hutchinson returns home after thirteen years of prison, determined to make a new life for himself and his family.

355) Big Man, Big Target
November 28th, 1964
Written by John Mantley, Directed by Michael O'Herlihy
Guest Cast: Mariette Hartley, J.D. Cannon, Mike Road, Harry Lauter, John McLiam , Frank Ferguson
Pike Beechum likes the looks of Ellie Merchant, so he frames her husband Joe for horse stealing to get a free field at her.

356) Chicken
December 5th, 1964
Written by John Meston, Directed by Andrew McLaglen
Guest Cast: Glenn Corbett, Gigi Perreau, John Lupton, L.Q. Jones, Lane Chandler, Chubby Johnson, Dave Willock, Lane Bradford
Dan Collins is reputed to have killed four outlaws, and this makes him a big man about town. The truth is that he didn't do the deed, and is in fact a coward.

357) Innocence
December 12th, 1964
Written by John Meston, Directed by Harry Harris
Guest Cast: Bethel Leslie, Michael Forest, Claude Akins, Jason Evers, Jacqie Shelton, Lee Krieger, Ric Roman
Elsa Poe is the latest hostess in the Long Branch, and becomes unintentionally the spark that sets two feuding cowboys at one another.

358) Aunt Thede
December 19th, 1964
Written by Kathleen Hite, Directed by Sutton Roley
Guest Cast: Jeanette Nolan, Dyan Cannon, James Stacy, Frank Cady, Howard McNear, Jennie Lee Aurness
Festus's Aunt Thede arrives in town, looking for a fine man to marry. At the same time, Ivy Norton is looking for one also, to escape her brutal father.

359) Hammerhead
December 26th, 1964
Written by Anthony Ellis, Directed by Christian Nyby
Guest Cast: Arch Johnson, Linda Foster, Chubby Johnson, John Fiedler
Race fever hits Dodge when a gambler comes there to buy horses, and everyone wants to sell. When the claims of all are disputed, a race is the outcome.

360) Double Entry
January 2nd, 1965
Written by Les Crutchfield, Directed by Joseph Sargent
Guest Cast: Forrest Tucker, Cyril Delevanti, Mel Gallagher, Lew Brown, Nora Marlowe
Brad McClain is an old friend of Matt's, and plans to take advantage of the friendship to make his fortune.

361) Run, Sheep, Run
January 9th, 1965
Written by John Meston, Directed by Harry Harris
Guest Cast: Burt Brinkerhoff, Davey Davison, Peter Whitney, Arthur Malet
Tom and Mary Stocker have sold their ranch, but the man who is buying it won't pay them the money right away.

362) Deputy Festus
January 16th, 1965
Written by Calvin Clements, Directed by Harry Harris
Guest Cast: Denver Pyle, Royal Dano, Carl Reindel, Shug Fisher, Don Beddoe, Bill Zuckert
When three drunken fur trappers are thrown into jail, Festus is only slightly surprised to discover that they are more of his disreputable kin.

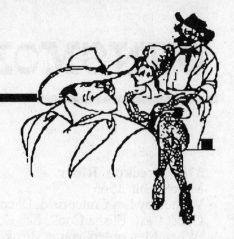

363) One Killer On Ice
January 23rd, 1965
Written by Richard Carr
Guest Cast: John Drew Barrymore, Anne Helm, Philip Coolidge, Dennis
Hopper, Richard Carlyle
 Two bounty hunters have captured a wanted man, but are afraid that his gang will try and ambush them.
They ask for Matt's help to bring the man in.

364) Chief Joseph
January 30th, 1965
Written by Clyde Ware, Story by Thomas Warner, Directed by Mark Rydell
Guest Cast: Victor Jory, Robert Loggia, Joe Maross, Michael Keep, Leonard Stone
 Chief Joseph is passing through Dodge, but is refused lodging at the Dodge House because he is an Indian.
Lt. Tripp is worried that this might stir up hostile reprisals that Joseph is supposed to be resolving.

365) Circus Trick
February 6th, 1965
Written by Les Crutchfield, Directed by William F. Claxton
Guest Cast: Elizabeth MacRae, Walter Burke, Warren Oates, Ken Scott
 April, Festus's girl-friend, gets a sideshow job in a circus that has stopped in Dodge.
 Elizabeth MacRae was a semi-regular for a while as Festus's girl-friend.

366) Song For Dying
February 13th, 1965
Written by Harry Kronman, Directed by Allen Reisner
Guest Cast: Theodore Bikel, Robert F. Simon, Ford Rainey, Sheldon Allman, Lee Majors, Russell Thorson
 The Lukens follow a minstrel to Dodge City, aiming to kill him.

367) Winner Take All
February 20th, 1965
Written by Les Crutchfield, Directed by Vincent McEveety
Guest Cast: Tom Simcox, Margaret Bly, John Milford, H.M. Wynant, Red Rowe
 When cattle are sold, the Renner brothers disagree on the shares of the money due to each of them.

368) Eliab's Aim
February 27th, 1965
Written by Will Corry, Directed by Richard Sarafian
Guest Cast: James Hampton, Dee J. Thompson, Donald O'Kelly, Gregg Palmer
 Eliab, one of Festus's nephews, comes to Dodge City, aiming to enforce the code of the Haggens.

369) Thurdsay's Child
March 6th, 1965
Written by Robert Lewin, Directed by Joseph H. Lewis, Assistant Director Paul Nichols, Incidental Music
Richard Shores, Supervised and Conducted by Herschel Burke Gilbert
Guest Cast: Jean Arthur, Scott Marlowe, Joe Raciti, Suzanne Benoit, Roy Barcroft, Fred Coby
Julie Blane comes to Dodge to visit her daughter and son-in-law. Kitty is an old friend of hers, and very up-
set when Julie disappears by night.

GUNSMOKE

370) Breckon Rider
March 13th, 1965
Written by Les Crutchfield, Directed by Vincent McEveety
Guest Cast: Elisha Cook, Ben Cooper, Robert Sorrells, John Warburton
When Matt orders young Breck Taylor out of town, a lawyer from the East stands up for the young man's rights, and insists that he be allowed to stay.

371) Bank Baby
March 20th, 1965
Written by John Meston, Direcetd by Andrew McLaglen
Guest Cast: Jacques Aubuchon, Virginia Christine, Harry Carey, Hampton Fancher, Gail Kobe
The Clum's are a deeply religious family, and on their way to their new home, they stop outside of Dodge. There they are robbed, and are unable to go on.

372) The Lady
March 27th, 1965
Written by John Mantley, Directed by Mark Rydell
Guest Cast: Katharine Ross, Eileen Heckart, R.G. Armstrong, Michael Forest, Clifton James
Hattie Silks is a lady from New Orleans now down on her luck. To her distaste, the only job she can get is as a hostess in the Long Branch.

373) Dry Road To Nowhere
April 3rd, 1965
Written by Harry Kronman, Directed by Vincent McEveety
Guest Cast: James Whitmore, Julie Sommars, John Saxon, L.Q. Jones, Reed Morgan, Carol Brewster, Steven McEveety
A temperance crusader arrives in Dodge City to preach the virtues of abstinence. Hard on his heels is Tebbetts, a gunfighter who has sworn to kill him.

374) Twenty Miles From Dodge
April 10th, 1965
Written by Clyde Ware, Directed by Mark Rydell
Guest Cast: Darren McGavin, Everett Sloane, Aneta Corsault, Gerald S. O'Loughlin, Tony Haig, Pat Cardi, Val Avery, Stafford Repp, William Fawcett, Noam Pitlik, Paul Barselow, Jennifer Lea, Danny Fowler
A stage is held up, and the passengers are all kidnapped. One of them is Kitty.

375) The Pariah
April 17th, 1965
Written by Calvin Clements, Directed by Harry Harris
Guest Cast: John Dehner, Steve Ihnat, Tom Reese, Ika Windish, Donald Loseby
A farmer kills an outlaw, but is then ostracized by the citizens of Dodge City for the deed.

376) Bad Lady From Brookline
April 24th, 1965
Written by Kathleen Hite, Directed by Harry Harris
Guest Cast: Jan Clayton, Andrew Duggan, Peter Brooks
Doc discovers that his friend Sully and his mother have scurvy.

377) Guilt Built
May 1st, 1965
Written by Gustave Field, Directed by Michael O'Herlihy, Assistant Director
Robert L. Rosen, Incidental Music Richard Shores
Guest Cast: Betty Hutton, Claude Akins, Billy Bowles, John Hubbard, Jonathan Kidd, Ollie O'Toole, Jan Peters, Eddie Hice, Tom McCauley
 Molly McConnell and her young son arrive in Dodge City, only to learn that McConnell has been killed in a gun fight.

378) Two Tall Men
May 8th, 1965
Written by Frank Q. Dobbs & Robert C. Stewart, Directed by Vincent McEveety
Guest Cast: Ben Cooper, Harry Townes, George Lindsey, Jay Ripley
 Doc Adams has been attacked and left unconscious. He is found by an old buffalo hunter, and nursed back to health.

379) Honey Pot
May 15th, 1965
Written by Clyde Ware, Directed by Vincent McEveety
Guest Cast: Rory Calhoun, Joanna Moore, John Crawford, Dick Wessel, Charles Maxwell, Mort Mills
 Ben Stack, a friend of Matt's, arrives in Dodge. He likes the look of one of the saloon girls, but she's not interested in him at all.

380) The New Society
May 22nd, 1965
Written by John Meston, Directed by Harry Harris
Guest Cast: , Jeremy Slate, James Gregory, Elizabeth Perry, Richard X. Slattery, Sandy Kenyon, Jack Weston, Ian Wolfe, Linda James, Dennis Cross
 Matt visits a new town to investigate a murder case, but the townspeople there look after their own.

381) He Who Steals
May 29th, 1965
Written by John Meston, Directed by Harry Harris
Guest Cast: Russ Tamblyn, Harold J. Stone, Len Wayland, Stanley Adams, Larry Ward, Roger Torrey
 A young cowboy, Billy Waters, idolizes Jim Donner, an old mountain man. When Donner steals a calf, though, Billy has to decide whether to report the theft.

Season Eleven
September 18th, 1965 through May 7th, 1966
Produced by Philip Leacock
Associate Producer: John Mantley
Director of Photography: Harry Stradling, Jr
Production Manager: Robert M. Besche
Assistant to Producer: Herbert DuFine
Art Director: Raymond Beal
Set Decorator: Herman N. Schoenbrun
Script Supervisor: Edla Bakke
Film Editor: Otto Meyer, ACE

GUNSMOKE

Sound Effects Editor: Jack A. Finlay
Music Editor: Gene Feldman
Production Sound Mixer: Vernon W. Kramer
Casting: James Lister
Property Master: Clem R. Widrig
Costumer: Alexander Velcoff
Makeup Artist: Glen Alden
Hair Stylist: Pat Whiffing, CHS

Cast:

Matt: James Arness
Doc: Milburn Stone
Kitty: Amanda Blake
Festus: Ken Curtis
Sam: Glenn Strange
Quint: Burt Reynolds
Louie Pheeters: James Nusser
Barney: Charles Seel
Howie: Howard Culver
Ed O'Connor: Tom Brown
Percy Crump: John Harper
Hank: Hank Patterson
Nathan Burke Ted Jordan
Clayton Thaddeus "Thad" Greenwood: Roger Ewing
Mr. Bodking: Roy Roberts

382) Seven Hours To Dawn
September 18th, 1965
Written by Clyde Ware, Directed by Vincent McEveety
Guest Cast: John Drew Barrymore, Johnny Seven, Anthony Lettier, Jerry Douglas, Michael Vandever, Bernadette Hale, Gary Paggett, Joseph Perry, Rusty Lane, Allen Jaffe, Morgan Woodward
An outlaw gang takes over Dodge City, and holds the town hostage, preventing Matt from interfering.

383) The Storm
September 25th, 1965
Written by Paul Savage, Directed by Joseph Sargent
Guest Cast: Forrest Tucker, Tim McIntire, Ruth Warwick, Richard Evans, Willard Sage, Kelly Thordsen, Mary Lou Tyler, Victor Izay, Steven Darrell
The Benteen brothers are two of Matt's friends, but they are willing to let an innocent buffalo hunter hang for the murder that they committed.

384) Clayton Thaddeus Greenwood
October 2nd, 1965
Written by Calvin Clements, Directed by Joseph Sargent
Guest Cast: Robert Sorrells, Sherwood Price, Jack Elam, Allen Jaffe, Paul Fix
When four men cause his father's death, Thad Greenwood arrives in Dodge to settle the scores.
This was the first episode with Thad, who became a semi-regular for a while.

385) Ten Little Indians
October 9th, 1965
Written by George Eckstein, Directed by Mark Rydell
Guest Cast: Nehemiah Persoff, Warren Oates, Bruce Dern, Zalman King,
Nina Roman, John Marley, Rafael Campos, Stanja Lowe
 On his way back to Dodge, Matt is attacked by a gunman. Matt kills the man, only to find that there are others waiting for him back in Dodge.

386) Taps For Old Jeb
October 16th, 1965
Written by Les Crutchfield, Directed by James Sheldon, Assistant Director Christopher Seiter, Incidental
Music Leon Klatzkin
Guest Cast: Ed Begley, Wayne Rogers, Morgan Woodward, Arthur Batanides, Don Keefer, Rudy Sooter
 An old prospector finds gold, but he doesn't trust banks. Instead, he hires a bodyguard.

387) Kioga
October 23rd, 1965
Written by Robert Lewin, Directed by Harry Harris
Guest Cast: Neville Brand, Teno Pollick, Nina Roman, John Hubbard
 Kioga wants revenge on the fur trapper that killed his father and tried to rape his sister.

388) The Bounty Hunter
October 30th, 1965
Written by Paul Savage, Directed by Harry Harris
Guest Cast: Robert Lansing, Wright King, Lisabeth Hush, Amber Flower, Bert Freed, Gregg Palmer, Victor
Izay, John Kowal, Jason Johnson
 When his son is killed, Chris Thornton hires bounty hunter Luke Frazer to bring in the man who did it.

389) The Reward
November 6th, 1965
Written by Scott Hunt & Beth Keele, Story by Gil Ralston, Directed by Marc Daniels
Guest Cast: James Whitmore, David Ladd, Fred J. Scollay, Julio Medina, Gil Rankin, Peter Whitney,
Berkeley Harris, Normann Burton

Jim Forbes was sent to jail for gold mine swindles, but on his release, his victims want their money from
him.

390) Malachi
November 13th, 1965
Written by Paul Savage, Directed by Gene Nelson
Guest Cast: Harry Townes, Edward Andrews, Jack Elam, Robert Sorrells, Woodrow Chambliss
 Matt is out hunting down a killer, and Malachi Harper takes over as the marshal in order to impress his
brother.

391) The Pretender
November 20th, 1965
Written by Calvin Clements, Directed by Vincent McEveety
Guest Cast: Nehemiah Persoff, Tom Simcox, Tom Skerritt, Harry Davis, Gregg Palmer, Julie Sommars,
Athena Lorde, Sam Edwards

GUNSMOKE

Frank Dano is captured rustling cattle, and his father refuses to forgive him — especially since Frank was teaching his own ways to his younger brother Edmund also.

392) South Wind
November 27th, 1965
Written by Juanita Bartlett, Directed by Allen Reisner
Guest Cast: Pat Cardi, Bruce Dern, Bob Random, Michael Davis, Gregg Palmer, Michael Whitney
 Homer Bonney and his father meet up with Judd Print on the trail. They join forces, but Print kills Bonney, and then goes after Homer.

393) The Hostage December 4th, 1965
Written by Clyde Ware, Story by JoAnne Johnson, Directed by Vincent McEveety
Guest Cast: Darren McGavin, Simon Oakland, Tom Reese, I. Stanford Jolley, Willis Bouchey, Vito Scotti
 Four convicts escape, and while they are making their way to the Mexican border, they take Matt as a hostage.

394) Outlaw's Woman
December 11th, 1965
Written by Clyde Ware, Directed by Mark Rydell
Guest Cast: Lane Bradbury, Vincent Beck, Lonny Chapman, Peggy Rae, Lou Antonio, Gene Tyburn
 Matt is surprised when the outlaw he wounds during a raid on a train turns out to be a woman.

395) Judge Calvin Strom
December 18th, 1965
Written by Don Mullally, Directed by Vincent McEveety
Guest Cast: John Saxon, James Gregory, Les Brown, William Campbell, Tom Reese, X Brands, Olan Soule
 Kitty and Festus are captured by Judge Strom and his two sons. They are accused of murdering one of the family, and put on a mock trial for their lives.

396) Gold Mine
December 25th, 1965
Written by Scott Hunt & Beth Keele, Directed by Abner Biberman
Guest Cast: Tom Nardini, John Anderson, Paul Carr, Argentina Brunetti, Michael Vandever
 Kitty has been left a gold mine, and on her way to look it over, she meets and befriends a mute young boy.

397) Death Watch
January 8th, 1966
Written by Calvin Clements, Directed by Mark Rydell
Guest Cast: Albert Salmi, Frank Silvera, Alfred Ryder, Willard Sage, Richard Evans, Arlene Quinn, Charles Wagenheim, Steve Gravers
 John Drago is worth thirty thousand dollars in Mexico. Two bounty hunters capture and wound him. They aim to take him in for the reward dead or alive.

398) Sweet Billy, Singer Of Songs
January 15th, 1966
Written by Gustave Field, Directed by Alvin Ganzer
Guest Cast: Bob Random, Royal Dano, Brooke Bundy, Slim Pickins, Shug Fisher, Judy Carne
 Festus is asked to help out in getting a bride for his nephew, Sweet Billy.

399) The Raid (Part One)
January 22nd, 1966
Written by Clyde Ware, Directed by Vincent McEveety
Guest Cast: Gary Lockwood, Richard Jaekel, Jeremy Slate, Michael Conrad, John Anderson, John Kellogg, Jim Davis, Preston Pierce

Jim Stark and his gang have robbed the bank of Sedalia, and aim to make Dodge's bank their second.

400) The Raid (Part Two)
January 29th, 1966
Written by Clyde Ware, Directed by Vincent McEveety
Guest Cast: Gary Lockwood, Richard Jaekel, Jeremy Slate, Michael Conrad, John Anderson, John Kellogg, Jim Davis, Preston Pierce
To cover their getaway, the Stark gang kidnaps Doc and starts a fire in the town.

401) Killer At Large
February 5th, 1966
Written by Calvin Clements, Directed by Marc Daniels
Guest Cast: Geraldine Brooks, Stewart Erwin, John Pickard, Cyril Delevanti, Tim O'Kelly, Craig Hundley, Gilman Rankin, James Beggs
Doc Brown is a medicine show man, claiming to be a fast gun. Festus mocks him, and is issued a challenge to prove his own worth.

402) My Father's Guitar
February 12th, 1966
Written by Hal Sitowitz, Directed by Robert Totten
Guest Cast: Beau Bridges, Charles Dierkop, Steve Ihnat, Dub Taylor
Jason's most precious possession is the guitar that his father gave him. When this is the subject of rough-housing, Jason kills the man who started it.

403) Wishbone
February 19th, 1966
Written by Paul Savage, Directed by Marc Daniels
Guest Cast: Lew Gallo , Victor French, Lyle Waggoner, Billy Beck
When three outlaws gun down the driver and guard of a stage, Matt sets off after them.

404) Sanctuary
February 26th, 1966
Written by Calvin Clements, Directed by Harry Harris
Guest Cast: Richard Bradford, Sean Garrison, Virginia Gregg, Joan Blackman, Larry Ward, Charles Wagenheim
A wounded outlaw takes refuge in a church, taking the minister and two women hostage to hold off Matt.

405) Honor Before Justice
March 5th, 1966
Written by Frank Q. Dobbs & Robert C. Stewart, Directed by Harry Harris
Guest Cast: France Nuyen, Michael Ansara, George Keymas, Noah Beery, Harry Bartell, Ralph Moody, Barton MacLane, James Almanzar, Richard Gilden, Ken Renard
When her father is sentenced to hang for a murder he did not commit, his daughter Sarah asks Thad to help her out.

GUNSMOKE

406) The Brothers
March 12th, 1966
Written by Tom Hanley, Directed by Tay Garnett
Guest Cast: Scott Marlowe, Tom Reese, Joseph Hoover, Bobby Crawford, Warren Vanders
When Matt imprisons a man, his older brother attempts to break him out of jail.

407) Witch Doctor
March 19th, 1966
Written by Les Crutchfield, Directed by Peter Graves
Guest Cast: R.G. Armstrong, Shelley Morrison, Claire Wilcox, Elizabeth Fraser, Gregg Palmer, George Lindsey
Doc and Festus are enjoying their fishing trip, until they are kidnapped by buffalo hunters.
Peter Graves, the star of Mission Impossible, is the brother of James Arness.

408) Harvest
March 26th, 1966
Written by Les Crutchfield, Directed by Harry Harris
Guest Cast: James MacArthur, Lesley Ann Warren, George Kennedy, Karl Swenson, Alma Platt, Fred Colby
Ben Payson is furious with homesteaders who have settled on what he thinks is his land. He gets even more annoyed when his daughter falls in love with one of them.

409) Byline
April 9th, 1966
Written by Les Crutchfield, Directed by Allen Reisner
Guest Cast: Chips Rafferty, Dabbs Greer, Denver Pyle, Ted de Corsia, Stefan Arngrim, Maudie Prickett, Gertrude Flynn
Even though Festus is unable to read or write, he somehow lands a job on the local newspaper.

410) Treasure Of John Walking Fox
April 16th, 1966
Written by Clyde Ware, Story by Gwen Bagby, Directed by Marc Daniels
Guest Cast: Leonard Nimoy, Richard Webb, `Lloyd Gough, Jim Davis , Ted Gehring, Tom McCauley
Aaron Tigue and John Walking Fox are friends and buffalo hunters, but because John is an Indian, the people in Dodge give both men a hard time.

411) My Father, My Son
April 23rd, 1966
Written by Hal Sitowitz, Directed by Robert Totten
Guest Cast: Jack Elam, Lee van Cleef, Zalman King, Teno Pollick, Charles Kuenstle, Del Monroe , James Gammon, John McLiam, Billy Halop, Scott Hale
A brash young gunfighter, David Barrett, challenges Ike Jeffords to a fight. Jeffords kills the young man, but his family want revenge.

412) Parson Comes To Town
April 30th, 1966
Written by Verne Jay, Directed by Marc Daniels
Guest Cast: Sam Wanamaker, Lonny Chapman, John McLiam, Charles Wagenheim, Woodrow Chambliss, John Granville, Kevin Burchette

On his way to Dodge City, a clergyman is killed. Later, in town, a man turns up wearing his clothes on a strange mission.

413) Prime Of Life
May 7th, 1966
Written by Dan Ullman, Directed by Robert Totten
Guest Cast: Douglas Kennedy, Joe Don Baker, Martin West, Jonathan Lippe, Victor French
 Kyle Stoner discovers that his girl-friend has been seeing another man, so he starts planning to kill his rival.

GUNSMOKE

Season Twelve

September 17th 1966 through April 15th, 1967
Now filmed in color

Produced by John Mantley
Executive Producer: Philip Leacock
Story Consultant: Paul Savage
Music Supervision: Morton Stevens
Director of Photography: Harry Stradling, Jr
Art Director: John B. Goodman
Film Editor: Al Joseph, ACE
Production Manager: Robert M. Beche
Assistant to Producer: Herbert DuFine
Casting: Pam Polifroni
Music Editor: Gene Feldman
Sound Effects Editor: Jack A. Finlay
Production Sound Mixer: Vernon W. Kramer
Script Supervisor: Edla Bakke
Set Decorator: Herman N. Schoenbrun
Property Master: Clem R. Widrig
Costumer: Alexander Velcoff
Makeup Artist: Glen Alden
Hairstylist: Pat Whiffing, CHS
Musical theme "Gunsmoke" also known as "Old Trails": Glenn Spencer and Rex Kouty

Cast:

Marshall Matt Dillon: James Arness
Doc Galen Adams: Milburn Stone
Kitty Russell: Amanda Blake
Festus Haggen: Ken Curtis
Sam, the bartender: Glenn Strange
Clayton Thaddeus "Thad" Greenwood: Roger Ewing
Louie Pheeters: James Nusser
Barney: Charles Seel
Howie: Howard Culver
Ed O'Connor: Tom Brown
Percy Crump: John Harper
Hank: Hank Patterson
Ma Smalley: Sarah Selby
Nathan Burke: Ted Jordan
Mr. Bodkin: Roy Roberts
Mr. Lathrop: Woodrow Chambliss
Halligan Charles Wagenheim

414) Snap Decision

September 17th, 1966

Written by Richard Carr, Directed by Mark Rydell

Guest Cast: Claude Akins, Michael Strong, Michael Cole, Sam Gilman, Orville Sherman

Matt kills a horse thief, a man who was once his friend. Discouraged, he turns in his badge. The problem is that he simply cannot stand back and let another man do his job.

415) The Goldtakers

September 24th, 1966

Written by Clyde Ware, Directed by Vincent McEveety

Guest Cast: Martin Landau, Roy Jenson, Brad Weston, William Bramley, Denver Pyle, John Boyer, Charles Francisco

Matt has gone fishing, and while Dodge is undefended, a group of thieves that have stolen a giant piece of gold and commandeer the blacksmith shop in order to divide the loot.

416) The Jailer

October 1st, 1966

Written by Hal Sitowitz, Directed by Vincent McEveety

Guest Cast: Bette Davis , Bruce Dern, Robert Sorrells, Julie Sommars, Tom Skerritt, Zalman King

Her husband was hung six years ago, and her three sons sent to jail. Now widow Etta Stone is getting her revenge. She has captured Matt and condemned him to hang in the morning.

417) The Mission

October 8th, 1966

Written by Richard Carr, Directed by Mark Rydell

Guest Cast: Bob Random, Robert F. Simon, Warren Oates, Steve Ihnat, Jim Davis, Arch Johnson, Robert Tafur, Rafael Campos, Reuben Moreno, Bert Madrid, Mike Abelar
Matt is in Mexico to claim a prisoner, when he is bushwacked by three thieves.

GUNSMOKE

418) The Good People

October 15th, 1966

Written by Paul Landis, Directed by Robert Totten

Guest Cast: Tom Simcox, Morgan Woodward, Allen Case, Shug Fisher, Ted Jordan, Frederic Downs, James O'Hara, Clyde Howdy, Steve Gravers

A Man is hanged unjustly for cattle rustling. He is then cut down and left unburied.

419) Gunfighter, RIP

October 22nd, 1966

Written by Hal Sitowitz, Story by Michael Fisher, Directed by Mark Rydell

Guest Cast: Darren McGavin, France Nuyen, Michael Conrad, Stefan Gierasch, Don Hanmer, Allen Emerson

Joe Bascome is hired by the Douglas brothers to kill Matt. Bascome is seriously wounded before he can take on Matt, however, and must be nursed back to health by Ching Lee.

420) The Wrong Man

October 29th, 1966

Written by Clyde Ware, Directed by Robert Totten

Guest Cast: Carroll O'Connor, Clifton James, James Anderson, Kevin O'Neal, Gilman Rankin, Charles Kuenstle, Mel Gaines, Victor Izay, James Almanzer v

Hootie Kyle is desperate for money to save his farm. He borrows from Matt, then enters a poker game. After he loses, the man he played against is found murdered and robbed.

421) The Whispering Tree

November 12th, 1966

Written by Calvin Clements, Directed by Vincent McEveety

Guest Cast: John Saxon, Jacqueline Scott, Ed Asner, Morgan Woodward, Donald Losby, Christopher Pate, Rex Holman, Allen Jaffe, Kathleen O'Malley, Stephen McEveety

Virgil Stanley is released after eight years in jail and returns to his farm. The money from his robbery was never recovered, so Redmond, the lawman, is still after him. It's hidden on the farm, and Stanley is afraid that Redmond will discover it.

422) The Well

November 19th, 1966

Written by Francis Cockrell, Directed by Marc Daniels

Guest Cast: Guy Raymond, Joan Payne, Ted Jordan, Ted Gehring, Karl Lukas, Elizabeth Rogers, Lawrence Casey, Pete Kellett, Robert Ballew

Dodge City is experiencing a terrible drought. Then a rainmaker is hired — but will he settle the problem or increase it?

423) Stage Stop

November 26th, 1966

Written by Hal Sitowitz, Directed by Irving Moore

Guest Cast: John Ireland, Anne Whitfield, Jack Ging, Steve Raines, Joseph Ruskin, Michael Vandever, Sid Haig, Andy Albin

Doc is on a stage coach with a blind man and an expectant woman. Doc Adams takes up arms to protect the stage first when robbers make an attack on the stage which fails. and then when the stage stops later at a way station, and they make a second attack.

424) The Newcomers

December 3rd, 1966

Written by Calvin Clements, Directed by Robert Totten

Guest Cast: Karl Swenson, John Voight, Robert Sorrells, John Pickard, Charles Kierkop , James Murdock, Ben Wright, Lawrence Aten, Daniel Ades

A young Swedish immigrant is heading west with his father when he accidentally kills a cowboy. The only witness is a man called Handley, who offers to keep quiet — for a price.

GUNSMOKE

425) Quaker Girl

December 10th, 1966

Written by Preston Wood, Directed by Bernard Kowalski

Guest Cast: William Shatner, Ariane Quinn, Liam Sullivan, Ben Johnson, Warren Vanders, Tom Reese , William Bryant, Timothy Carey, Joseph Breen

Thad is in trouble with a gang, and their misapprehension as to just who his prisoner is. His only helper is a Quaker girl.

426) The Moonstone

December 17th, 1966

Written by Paul Savage, Directed by Richard Colla

Guest Cast: Mike Kellin, Warren Kemmerling, Tom Skerritt, Gail Kobe, Jeff Palmer, Ted Jordan, Fred Colby

Orv Simpson is not at all fond of his brother Chad's girl-friend, but has no idea what information she has on Chad or his own past. It all may be revealed if she gets mad enough.

427) Champion Of The World

December 24th, 1966

Written by Les Crutchfield, Directed by Marc Daniels

Guest Cast: Alan Hale, Jr, Dan Tobin, Ralph Ross, Jane Dulo, Arthur Pederson, Gail Robbins, Don Keefer, Ted Jordan

Bull Bannock is a retired fighter — heavyweight champion of the world! — who is conned into trying to buy the Long Branch as the front man for a trickster.

428) The Hanging

December 31st, 1966

Written by Calvin Clements, Directed by Bernard Kowalski

Guest Cast: Tom Stern, Kit Smythe, Robert Knapp, Henry Darrow, Anna Navaro, Edmund Hashim, Larry Ward, Richard Bakalyan

When a convicted murderer is sentenced to hang, the man's gang gets ready to try and rescue him.

429) Saturday Night

January 7th, 1967

Written by Clyde Ware, Directed by Robert Totten

Guest Cast: Leif Erickson, Dub Taylor, Victor French, William C. Watson, Lawrence D. Mann, James Almanzar, Link Harget, Rudy Sooter, Frederick Downs

Matt and a prisoner are saved from death by a group of cowboys. That Saturday night, after whooping it up, one of them frees the prisoner for a lark. The man then aims to kill Matt for locking him up.

430) Mad Dog

January 14th, 1967

Written by Jay Simms, Directed by Charles Rondeau

Guest Cast: George Lindsey, Denver Pyle, Hoke Howell, George Murdock, Iggie Wolfington, Sammy Reese, Iggie Wolfington, Butch Patrick, Dub Taylor

Festus accepts a saddle from a dying man, unaware that the man was a famous mad dog killer. The saddle is beautiful — and distinctive. When Festus reaches the next town, he is taken for the mad dog killer on the loose and offered $300 to fight the three sons of a man his cousin is accused of killing.

431) Muley

January 21st, 1967

Written by Les Crutchfield, Directed by Allen Resiner

Guest Cast: Zalman King, Lane Bradbury, Ross Hagen, Marc Cavell, Anthony Call, Ted Jordan

Muley plans to kill Matt and rob the bank, but is sidetracked when he falls for the attractive saloon hostess, Lucky.

GUNSMOKE

CLIPPING FILE: MATT DILLON

Matt was orphaned at any early age, as many people in the early West had been. He was raised by foster parents, along with Chance Hopper. In his late teens, Matt drifted off. He had become pretty good with a gun, and uncertain of his future.

He threw his lot in with a gang, but had serious reservations about the correctness of what he was doing. Dan York then saved his life, and Matt went straight.

After a fair number of jobs, from ranching to scouting, Matt became a lawman, and finally the Marshal of Dodge City. His experiences had toughened him, and his abilities as a lawman were related to his previous jobs. Matt has a firm sense of right and wrong, and is willing to bend the letter of the law in order to preserve its spirit. He will from time to time allow someone to be freed, if he thinks that they have had enough of a lesson. At other times he is inclined to lock them up to prevent them from wrong-doing. He applies his own beliefs to his tasks, a kind of benevolent dictator.

Matt is not the fastest shot, but he is willing to take that extra fraction of a second to aim before he fires, so that he very rarely misses. His choice of weapon is a Colt Navy revolver, with a slightly elongated barrel, adding to its accuracy.

Matt does not make friends easily, mostly because of his job. He has a continuing relationship with Kitty Russell, but is more committed to his job than he is to her. He will probably never marry her, but enjoys her company. He has from time to time shown interest in other women, but, again, always subservient to his duties as a lawman.

With Chester, Matt is a firm boss, often privately amused at Chester's antics. He is not above teasing Chester, but he clearly feels responsible for him. Festus, on the other hand, is more independent. Matt has a more professional and less fatherly attitude towards his newer deputy.

Doc provides Matt with a rare chance to sit and enjoy good conversation. Matt and Doc enjoy sitting and talking on a peaceful, warm evening, outside of the jail.

432) Mail Drop

January 28th, 1967

Written by Calvin Clements, Directed by Robert Totten

Guest Cast: Eddie Hodges, John Anderson, Bing Russell, Steve Raines, Ted French, Pete Kellett

The only man who can help Matt track down an outlaw is the man's reluctant son.

433) Old Friend

February 4th, 1967

Written by Clyde Ware, Directed by Allen Resiner

Guest Cast: Fritz Weaver, Delphi Lawrence, Valentin de Vargas, Carlos Rivas, David Renard, Lew Brown, William Benedict

Marshal Burl Masters arrives in Dodge, hunting down a gang of outlaws — at any cost, either to himself or to his friends. They had destroyed his town and taken away his wife.

434) Fandango

February 11th, 1967

Written by Don Ingalls, Directed by Paul Landis

Guest Cast: Marie Alcaide, Torin Thatcher, Diana Muldaur, Paul Fix, Shug Fisher, Joe Higgins, Walter Baldwin

Matt has caught the man who killed a rancher and three hands. The brother of the dead rancher wants his revenge without waiting for the law, and Matt is in the terrible position of having to arm his prisoner in order to bring him in — most likely to hang.

435) The Returning

February 18th, 1967

Written by Paul Landis, Directed by Marc Daniels

Guest Cast: Michael Ansara, Lois Nettleton, Ted Jordan, Steve Sanders, Jonathan Lippe, Johnnie Whitaker, Roy Barcroft, Billy Halop, Richard Webb, Kenneth Mars

Tired of years of struggling as a dirt farmer, Luke Todd decides to return to his life of crime. His wife doesn't want any part of this — until he leaves a stolen $20,000 with her when she is in desperate need of money.

GUNSMOKE

436) The Lure

February 25th, 1967

Written by Clyde Ware, Directed by Marc Daniels

Guest Cast: Stephen McNally, Kim Darby, Warren Vanders, John Pickard, Paul Picerni, Fred Coby, Len Wayland, Martin Brooks, Val Avery, Troy Melton

Private detectives use Kitty and the daughter of an outlaw as lures to trap the girl's fugitive father.

437) Noose Of Gold

March 4th, 1967

Written by Clyde Ware, Directed by Irving Moore

Guest Cast: Vincent Gardenia, Barton MacLane, Steve Ihnat, Sam Gilman, Jan Shepard, Michael Preece, Jack Bailey, Harry Basch

An old friend of Matt's is now a wanted man, with a price on his head. This friendship may be the noose that captures the man, and Matt is reluctant to use it. An assistant attorney general with political aspirations has no such compunctions.

438) The Favor

March 11th, 1967

Written by Don Ingalls, Directed by Marc Daniels, Assistant Director Al Kraus

Guest Cast: James Daley, William Bramley, Diane Ladd, Troy Melton, Shirley Wilson, Fred J. Scolay, Lew Gallo, Bill Hart, Robert Miles, Jr.

Kitty is on a stage that breaks down. She is saved from Indian attackers by her fellow passenger, John Crowley. Later, in Dodge, she discovers that Matt is after Crowley, and the relationship between her and Matt becomes very strained.

439) Mistaken Identity

March 18th, 1967

Written by Les Crutchfield & Paul Savage, Directed by Robert Totten

Guest Cast: Albert Salmi, Hal Lynch, Ken Mayer, Sam Melville, Ted Jordan

Ed Carstairs is posing as Mel Gates to hide out from the law. When Matt discovers the real Gates injured in the brush, Carstairs' deception becomes known.

122

440) Ladies From St. Louis

March 25th, 1967

Written by Clyde Ware, Directed by Irving Moore

Guest Cast: Claude Akins, Josephine Hutchinson, Aneta Corsault, Kelly Jean Peters, Henry Darrow, Venita Wolf, Lois Roberts, Vic Tayback, Ralph Roberts, John Carter, Lew Brown, Ted Jordan

A group of traveling nuns is attacked. Their savior is the unlikely person of Sweeney, a fugitive from justice. He is wounded helping them, and they feel duty bound to hide him from Matt.

441) Nitro! [or Tiger By The Tail] (Part One)

April 8th, 1967

Written by Preston Wood, Directed by Robert Totten

Guest Cast: David Canary, Bonnie Beecher, Dub Taylor, Tom Reese, Eddie Firestone, Robert Rothwell, Rudy Sooter

A gang of bank robbers need nitroglycerine in their latest attack. They persuade McClaney to boil it off of dynamite, because he needs money to court the saloon girl he loves.

442) Nitro! [or Tiger By The Tail] (Part Two)

April 15th, 1967

Written by Preston Wood, Directed by Robert Totten

Guest Cast: David Canary, Bonnie Beecher, Dub Taylor, Tom Reese, Eddie Firestone, Robert Rothwell, Rudy Sooter

After the raid on the bank, the gang flees. Matt goes after the men, but they still have some of the dangerous nitro left — to stop his pursuit.

GUNSMOKE

Season Thirteen
September 11th, 1967 through March 4th, 1968

Produced by John Mantley
Associate Producer: Joseph Dackow
Story Consultant: Paul Savage
Director Of Photography: Monroe Askins, ASC
Art Director: Joseph R. Jennings
Film Editor: Bill Mosher, ACE
Production Manager: Robert M. Beche
Assistant to Producer: Herbert DuFine
Casting: Pam Polifroni
Music Editor: Gene Feldman
Sound Effects Editor: Jack A. Finlay
Production Sound Mixer: Vernon W. Kramer
Script Supervisor: Edla Bakke
Musical theme "Gunsmoke" also known as "Old Trails": Glenn Spencer and Rex Kouty

Cast:

Marshall Matt Dillon: James Arness
Doc Galen Adams: Milburn Stone
Kitty Russell: Amanda Blake
Festus Haggen: Ken Curtis
Newly O'Brien: Buck Taylor
Sam, the bartender: Glenn Strange
Louie Pheeters: James Nusser
Barney: Charles Seel
Howie: Howard Culver
Ed O'Connor: Tom Brown
Percy Crump: John Harper
Hank: Hank Patterson
Ma Smalley: Sarah Selby
Nathan Burke: Ted Jordan
Mr. Bodkin: Roy Roberts
Mr. Lathrop: Woodrow Chambliss
Halligan Charles Wagenheim

443) The Wreckers

September 11th, 1967

Written by Hal Sitowitz, Directed by Robert Totten

Guest Cast: Warren Oates, Rex Holman, Trevor Bardette, Warren Vanders, Charles Kuenstle, Edmund Hashim, James Almanzar, Gene Rutherford

Matt and Kitty are traveling to Dodge City with a prisoner when their stage is wrecked by outlaws. To save Matt's life, Kitty puts his badge on the prisoner.

444) Cattle Barons

September 18th, 1967

Written by Clyde Ware, Directed by Gunnar Helstrom

Guest Cast: Forrest Tucker, John Milford, Robert Wilke, Robert Sampson, Lew Brown, Fred Colby, Brad Johnson

A cattle drive approaching Dodge spells even more trouble than usual — two different men claim that they own it.

445) The Prodigal

September 25th, 1967

Written by Calvin Clements, Directed by Bernard McEveety

Guest Cast: Lew Ayres, Lamont Johnson, Richard Evans, Charles Robinson, Lee Krieger, Ted Gehring, Kelly Thordsen

A reporter after a story and a dead man's son want to reopen a case that Matt settled twelve years ago. This story was filmed for season twelve, but aired the following season.

446) Vengeance (Part One)

October 2nd, 1967

Written by Calvin Clements, Directed by Richard Sarafian

Guest Cast: John Ireland, Kim Darby, James Anderson, Victor French, James Stacy, Morgan Woodward, Buck Taylor, Paul Fix, Royal Dano, Sandy Kevin

Parker runs his town with an iron fist, and his men do as they please. When they kill Bob Johnson's friends, however, Johnson swears to get his revenge. Parker is later found dead, and Matt is forced to arrest

Johnson for the deed. Angel, a saloon hostess, testifies that he was with her when the killing took place.

447) Vengeance (Part Two)

October 9th, 1967

Written by Calvin Clements, Directed by Richard Sarafian

Guest Cast: John Ireland, Kim Darby, James Anderson, Victor French, James Stacy, Morgan Woodward, Buck Taylor, Paul Fix, Royal Dano, Sandy Kevin

448) A Hat

October 16th, 1967

Written by Ron Bishop, Directed by Robert Totten

Guest Cast: Chill Wills, Gene Evans, Tom Simcox, H.M. Wynant, Robert Sorrells

When a mountain man's hat is ruined by a bullet, he sees the act as an affront to his dignity. He takes a very terrible revenge for the deed, and matters begin to escalate.

449) Hard Luck Henry

October 23rd, 1967

Written by Warren Douglas, Directed by John Rich

Guest Cast: John Astin, Royal Dano, John Shank, Ken Drake, Anthony James, Mayf Nutter, Charles Kuenstle, Bo Hopkins, Michael Fox , Mary Lou Taylor

Festus visits his folks back home, but they're too busy squabbling about a chestful of Confederate gold that Hard Luck Henry has found to pay him any attention.

450) Major Glory

October 30th, 1967

Written by Richard Carr, Story by Richard Carr & Clyde Ware, Directed by Robert Totten

Guest Cast: Carroll O'Connor, Victor French, Robert F. Lyons, Link Wyler, Lawrence Mann, Don G. Ross, Cal Naylor, Chris Stephens, Russ Sier

Major Vanscoy refuses to allow Matt to pursue two Army deserters, despite the fact that Festus is their captive. They are being tracked by Sgt. Spear, and the Major insists that this is purely a military matter.

451) The Pillagers

November 6th, 1967

Written by Calvin Clements, Directed by Bernard McEveety

Guest Cast: John Saxon, Vito Scotti, Paul Picerni, Joseph Schneider, William Bramley, Harry Harvey, Sr., Allen Jaffe

Kitty and Newly O'Brien are kidnapped by a gang, which believes that Newly is a doctor and can operate on one of their wounded members.
This was the first episode in which Newly O'Brien appeared.

452) Prairie Wolfers

November 13th, 1967

Written by Calvin Clements, Directed by Robert Butler

Guest Cast: Charles McGraw, Jon Voigt, Lou Antonio, Kelly Jean Peters, I. Stanford Jolley, Matt Emery

Cory and Rich are two rambunctious wolfers, in town to sell their pelts. When the trader refuses to buy them, they rob him of $20,000. With Matt out of town, it's up to Festus to track them down and bring them back.

453) Stranger In Town

November 20th, 1967

Written by John Dunkel, Story by John Dunkel & Emily Mosher, Directed by E. Darrell Hallenbeck

Guest Cast: Pernell Roberts, Jacqueline Scott, Henry Jones, R.G. Armstrong, Billy Halop, Pete Kellett, John Kowal, Eric Shea, Barry MacLane

Gunman Dave Reeves arrives in Dodge with the assignment to kill a local businessman. Then he sees his estranged wife, who is now living in Dodge — with the son he has never met and courting the man he has come to kill.

454) Death Train

November 27th, 1967

Written by Ken Trevey, Directed by Gunnar Hellstrom

Guest Cast: Dana Wynter, Morgan Woodward, Mort Mills, Ed Bakey, Norman Alden, Trevor Bardette, Zalman King, Sam Melville

A private railroad car pulls into Dodge, and the people insides are all sick. Doc thinks it's Rocky Mountain spotted fever, and a local preacher incites the town, fearing the plague will spread.

455) Rope Fever

December 4th, 1967

Written by Chris Rellas, Directed by David Alexander

Guest Cast: Ralph Bellamy, Anna Lee, George Murdock, Ted Gehring, Ken Mayer, Sam Gilman, Dennis Cross, Hal Baylor

Festus is arrested for murder and bank robbery after befriending a wounded bank robber. The sheriff insists that he show them where the stolen money is hidden.

456) Wonder

December 18th, 1967

Written by William Blinn, Story by William Blinn & Mary Worrell, Directed by Irving Moore

Guest Cast: Tony Davis, Warren Berlinger, Richard Mulligan, Ken Swofford, Norman Alden, Jackie Russell, Fay Spain,

Wonder (from "I Call Him Wonder") returns to Dodge to get help for his friend, who is being tracked down by a group of cowboys that want to kill him.

457) Baker's Dozen

December 25th, 1967

Written by Charles Joseph Stone, Directed by Irving Moore

Guest Cast: Denver Pyle, Peggy Rea, Harry Lauter, Harry Carey, Mitzi Hoag, Sam Greene, Phyllis Coghlan, Ed McReady

When a mother dies bearing triplets, Doc decides that the three orphans should be adopted together. The Ronigers offer this, but they already have ten children of their own.

CLIPPING FILE:
KITTY RUSSELL

Kitty lost her mother mother at an early age. Her father, John, was an itinerant gambler. Accordingly, he left her with foster parents to bring her up, and would only now and then show up in her life.

Kitty grew up with a wild streak, and eventually drifted into being a saloon hostess. When she moved to Dodge, she proved to be a fine attraction in the Long Branch, and soon began to accumulate funds. She also met Matt, and fell in love.

Though she longs for Matt to marry her and settle down, she realizes that he never really intends to do so. From time to time, she would take up with other men, mostly to assure herself of her own attractiveness. She could never, however, stray far from Matt, and other relationships always fell apart.

After several years, Kitty bought a part-ownership in the Long Branch, and then worked hard to prove how well she could run the place. She eventually bought out her silent partner, and came into full ownership of the place. Under her guidance, the saloon turned a fine profit. She hired on Sam as her bartender, and her choice proved excellent; he was efficient both at serving the customers and evicting drunks and breaking up fights.

Kitty has an adventurous spirit and a zest for life. Settling down quietly has no appeal at all to her. She prefers to be on the go, and travels a lot. She is also inclined to get involved in the affairs of others, simply out of her caring heart. She is fairly easy with her money, and will loan it out to individuals she feels will benefit from her help.

GUNSMOKE

458) The Victim

January 1st, 1968

Written by Hal Sitowitz, Directed by Vincent McEveety

Guest Cast: Beverly Garland, James Gregory, Kevin Hagen, Cliff Osmond, Edmund Hashim, John Kellogg, Warren Vanders, Roy Jenson, Willis Bouchey, Greg Palmer, Tim O'Kelly

In Martin's Bend, the townsfolk want to lynch a man who accidentally killed a popular cowboy. Matt helps the sheriff to keep the man safe until the circuit judge arrives.

459) Dead Man's Law

January 8th, 1968

Written by Calvin Clements, Jr, Directed by John Rich, Assistant Director Paul Nichols, Incidental Music Leon Klatzkin

Guest Cast: John Dehner, Gunnar Hellstrom, Eddie Little Sky, Craig Curtis, Ralph Manza, Gregg Palmer, Robert Brubaker, Steve Raines, Baynes Barron, Alex Sharp, Ted Jordan, Jonathan Harper

Matt goes missing, and Festus wants to go and search for him. The problem is that Matt left him in charge of Dodge, and Sam Wall is taking advantage of Matt's absence to organize a troop of vigilantes that will give him power in the town. If Festus leaves, he will be virtually handing control over to Wall.

460) Nowhere To Run

January 16th, 1968

Written by Ron Honthaner, Story by Robert Totten, Directed by Vincent McEveety

Guest Cast: Slim Pickens, J. Robert Porter, Bob Random, Ilka Windish, Mark Lenard, Dan Ferrone, Michael Burns

Mark Stonecipher was a member of the gang that robbed Dodge, and has returned to his home ranch. There, he has fallen into the well, and his only hope of rescue is that Matt and Festus track him down.

461) Blood Money

January 22nd, 1968

Written by Hal Sitowitz, Directed by Robert Totten

Guest Cast: Nehemiah Persoff, Anthony Zerbe, James Anderson, Donna Baccala, Hank Brandt, Lee de Broux, Mills Watson

Nick Skouras is becoming a gunfighter, to his father's disgust. Alex then deliberately maims his son's gunhand to stop his "career" short. Then three men arrive with a score to settle, and Nick is unable to stand up to them.

462) Hill Girl

January 29th, 1968

Written by Calvin Clements, Directed by Robert Totten

Guest Cast: Lane Bradbury, Victor French, Anthony James, Dabbs Greer, Ted Jordan, Burt Mustin

Hillbilly girl Merry Florene is the butt of her half-brothers' jokes. Newly takes pity on her and helps her escape to Dodge City. The brothers then follow her to Dodge and start trouble there.

463) The Gunrunners [or Buffalo Man]

February 5th, 1968

Written by Hal Sitowitz, Directed by Irving Moore

Guest Cast: Michael Constantine, Dan Ferrone, Jim Davis, John McLiam, James Griffith, Dick Peabody, X Brands, Lane Bradford

An old trapper whose adopted Indian son is beated and left to die by five Army deserters sets out to track down the assailants.

464) The Jackals

February 12th, 1968

Written by Calvin Clements, Directed by Alvin Ganzer

Guest Cast: Paul Richards, Ward Wood, Felice Orlandi, Michael Vandever, Joe de Santis, Tige Andrews

When his friend Sheriff Hardin is gunned to death, Matt tracks the killers into Mexico.

465) The First People

February 19th, 1968

Written by Calvin Clements, Directed by Robert Totten

Guest Cast: Gene Evans, Todd Armstrong, Jack Elam, Richard Hale, James Alamanza, Felix Locher, James Lydon

GUNSMOKE

When the Indian Agent places unduly strern restrictions on the Elm Fork Reservation and trouble ensues, Matt is implicated in a murder. The agent begins the process for a Federal investigation to strip Matt of his badge.

466) Mister Sam'l

February 26th, 1968

Written by Harry Kronman, Directed by Gunnar Hellstrom

Guest Cast: Ed Begley, Mark Richman, Larry Pennell, Sandra Smith, Duke Hobbie

Mr. Sam'l is a rainmaker, hired to help out drought-stricken Dodge City. Ben Akins is trying to make him fail, so he can then buy up the land very cheaply to sell at a profit when it finally does rain.

467) A Noose For Dobie Price

March 4th, 1968

Written by Anthony Ellis, Directed by Richard Sarafian

Guest Cast: Chill Wills, Robert Donner, Sheldon Allman, Shug Fisher, E. J. Andre, Rose Hobart, Owen Bush, Michael Greene

Former outlaw Eliah Gorman is Matt's only hope in his hunt for escaped killer Dobie Price — but can he trust the man?

Season Fourteen

September 23rd, 1968 through March 24th, 1969

Produced by Joseph Dackow
Executive Producer: John Mantley
Executive Story Consultant: Paul Savage
Director of Photography: Monroe Askins, ACE
Art Director: Joseph R. Jennings
Film Editor: Donald W. Ernst
Production Manager: Robert M. Beche
Assistant Story Consultant: Jim Byrnes
Assistant to Producer: Ron Honthaner
Casting: Pam Polifroni
Music Editor: Gene Feldman
Sound Effects Editor: Jack A. Finlay
Production Sound Mixer: Vernon W. Kramer
Script Supervisor: Erika Werner
Set Decorator: Herman N. Schoenbrun
Property Master: Clem R. Widrig
Costumer: Alexander Velcoff
Makeup Artists: Glen Alden, Newton Jones
Hair Stylist: Gertrude Wheeler
Musical theme "Gunsmoke" also known as "Old Trails": Glenn Spencer and Rex Kouty

Cast:

Marshall Matt Dillon: James Arness
Doc Galen Adams: Milburn Stone
Kitty Russell: Amanda Blake
Festus Haggen: Ken Curtis
Sam, the bartender: Glenn Strange
Louie Pheeters: James Nusser
Barney: Charles Seel
Howie: Howard Culver
Ed O'Connor: Tom Brown
Percy Crump: John Harper
Hank: Hank Patterson
Ma Smalley:Sarah Selby
Nathan Burke: Ted Jordan
Mr. Bodkin: Roy Roberts
Mr. Lathrop: Woodrow Chambliss
Halligan Charles Wagenheim

GUNSMOKE

468) Lyle's Kid

September 23rd, 1968

Written by Calvin Clements, Directed by Bernard McEveety

Guest Cast: Morgan Woodward, Robert Pine, Joe de Santis, Charlotte Considine, Jonathan Harper

Grant Lyle was once a lawman, forced to retire after he was crippled. His twisted mind now plans his vengeance, using his son as his instrument of retribution.

469) The Hide Cutters

September 30th, 1968

Written by Jack Turley, Directed by Bernard McEveety

Guest Cast: Joseph Campanella, Michael Burns, Conlan Carter, Ken Swofford, Cliff Osmond, Eddie Firestone, Gregg Palmer

Matt joins in with a cattle drive in order to trap two renegade hide hunters.

470) Zavala

October 7th, 1968

Written by Paul Savage, Directed by Bernard McEveety

Guest Cast: Manuel Padilla, Jr, Miriam Colon, Jim Davis, Jose Chavez, Ricardo Alaniz, Rex Holman, Jonathan Lippe, Robert Sorrells, Larry D. Mann, Warren Vanders, Nacho Galindo, Elizabeth Germaine, Bobby E. Clark

On the hunt for bandits, Matt stops in a small Mexican town. He makes friends with young Paco, who promptly sees in him a fine new husband for his widowed mother.

471) Uncle Finney

October 14th, 1968

Written by Calvin Clements, Directed by Bernard McEveety

Guest Cast: Burt Mustin, Victor French, Anthony James, Lane Bradbury, Pete Kellett, John Dolan, Steve Raines, Monte Hale

Roland and Elbert bring in their father to collect an outstanding warrant for his arrest. The warrant is almost sixty years old and the man is 103 now. Their actions are simply part of a plan to rob the incoming freight

shipment which is thwarted by Festus who is acting as Matt's deputy..
This was a sequel to the previous season's "Hill Girl," with French, James and Lane Bradbury reprising their comedic roles.

472) Slocum

October 21st, 1968

Written by Ron Bishop, Directed by Arthur Penn

Guest Cast: Dub Taylor, Will Geer, James Wainwright, Ross Hagen, Lee Lambert , Mills Watson, Stephen Sandor, William Erwin

The Rikers have a nice side-line going to supplement their ranch income — they are moonshiners. When Matt gets after them, they try and fix him permanently.

473) O'Quillian

October 28th, 1968

Written by Ron Bishop, Directed by John Rich

Guest Cast: John McLiam, Anthony James, Victor French, Vaughn Taylor, Ken Drake, Steve Raines, Iron Eyes Cody, Lou Antonio, Roy Barcroft

A feisty Irishman is being tracked by a killer, but he isn't at all grateful when Matt intervenes to help him.

474) 9:12 To Dodge

November 11th, 1968

Written by Arthur Rowe, Directed by Herschel Daugherty

Guest Cast: Joanne Linville , Todd Armstrong, Robert Emhardt, Frank Martin, Johnny Hamer, Harry Lauter, Troy Melton, Fred Colby, Tom Water, Lee de Broux, Harry Harvey, Sr, William Murphy, Ed Long, Pete Kellett, Frank Marth, Johnny Raymer, Link Wyler

Matt and Doc are on the train to Dodge with a prisoner. They know that he has friends aboard who aim to free him, and are ready. What they didn't expect was a woman who is intent on prison reform to badger their tracks.

GUNSMOKE

CLIPPING FILE: DOCTOR GALEN ADAMS

Doc Adams has a mysterious past, of which he never talks. Clearly, he was a doctor before he hung his shingle up in Dodge, but where this might have been or why he left it are never subjects of conversation for him. He is a fine doctor who keeps totally up to date on new discoveries. He is also eager to train youngsters to follow after him, as he did with Newly O'Brien before Newly took up law enforcement.

Doc is somewhat snappy and cantankerous, but this covers his own good nature. In his line of business, he hates getting too close to his patients. A good number of them die on him through no fault of his own; bullet wounds often prove fatal. He is especially grumpy whenever Matt gets shot, and is constantly on his case to stop taking so many risks. In fact, he is probably Matt's only true friend, with the exception of Kitty Russell.

Doc is skittish about women, possibly due to past experiences. He accepts Kitty as a member of his friends, but has neither romantic interest nor friendly interest in any other women. With men, Doc is simply plain snippy.

Chester bears the brunt of Doc's sarcastic wit and frequent criticisms, but Chester never really listens to them. Festus later was the butt of many of Doc's snide comments and bitter words. Festus refuses to take them at all seriously. In fact, Doc likes both deputies, but would never admit to that!

It often seems Doc is never paid for his work. Many times, he is given food, trade of work or other considerations instead. This doesn't really worry him.

The only thing Doc ever seems keen on getting is as much coffee as possible for free from Chester or Festus — all the while complaining about the quality of it.

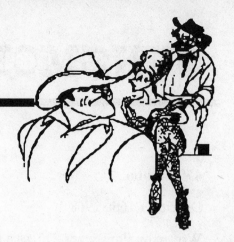

475) Abelia

November 18th, 1968

Written by Calvin Clements, Directed by Vincent McEveety

Guest Cast: Jacqueline Scott, Jeremy Slate, Tom Stern, Jack Lambert, Gregg Palmer, Mike Durkin

Festus poses as a widow's husband, in order to save her and her two children from a gang of outlaws.

476) Railroad

November 25th, 1968

Written by Arthur Rowe, Directed by Marvin Chomsky

Guest Cast: Jim Davis, Shug Fisher, Ramon Bieri, Buck Holland, Don Hanmer, James McCallion, Roy Jenson, Don Hacmer

The railroad wants to buy a farm from a homesteader to allow them to lay tracks. The man won't sell, and faces the wrath of Dodge, whose citizens want the railroad to come through.

477) The Miracle Man

December 2nd, 1968

Written by Calvin Clements, Directed by Bernard McEveety

Guest Cast: Don Chastain, Sandra Smith, William Bramley, Joey Walsh, Lisa Gerritsen, Bruce Watson, Margie de Meyer, Kevin Cooper

A traveling salesman becomes a farm hand for a wealthy widow and her three children. Festus suspects that Sullivan hopes to con money out of her.

478) Waco

December 9th, 1968

Written by Ron Bishop, Directed by Robert Totten

Guest Cast: Victor French, Harry Carey, Jr, Louise Latham, Tom Reese, Joy Fielding, Lee de Broux, Mills Watson, Lawrence Mann, Pat Thompson, Liz Marshall, Fred McDougall

Matt is taking a prisoner back to Dodge, and is being trailed by the man's gang. Then he finds a pregnant woman in need of a doctor, and events come to a head.

GUNSMOKE

479) Lobo

December 16th, 1968

Written by Jim Byrnes, Directed by Vincent McEveety

Guest Cast: Morgan Woodward, David Brian, Sheldon Allman, Sandy Kenyon, Ken Swofford, Eddie Firestone, Fred Colby, William Murphy

A rogue wolf has been attacking cattle, so Matt teams with with an old friend, mountain man Luke Brazo, to hunt the creature down.

480) Johnny Cross

December 23rd, 1968

Written by Calvin Clements, Directed by Herschel Daugherty

Guest Cast: Jeffrey Pomeranz, Kelly Jean Peters, Dean Stanton, Shug Fisher, John Crawford, Charles Thompson, Tadd Jordan

Newly gets involved with Johnny Cross, a wanted man. He claims to be innocent, but two relentless bounty hunters are on his trail.

481) The Money Store

December 30th, 1968

Written by William Blinn, Directed by Vincent McEveety

Guest Cast: Charles Aidman, Eric Shea, Pamelyn Ferdin, William Schallert, Virginia Vincent, Ralph James

When the bank refuses to loan money to help poverty-stricken Ray Jarvis on his farm, his two children decide that the best answer is to rob the bank.

482) Twisted Heritage

January 6th, 1969

Written by Arthur Rowe & Paul Savage, Story by Robert Heverly & Jack Turley, Directed by Bernard McEveety, Assistant Director Robert R. Shue, Incidental Music Leon Klatzkin

Guest Cast: John Ericson, Virginia Gregg, Lisa Gerritsen, Nora Marlowe, Conlan Carter, David McLean, Charles Kuenstle, Richard O'Brien, Joshua Bryant, Steve Raines, Robert Luster, Robert Karnes

Kitty saves Blaine Copperton's life after a stage mishap. He invites her back to his ranch, where she meets his domineering mother, and his silent daughter. When the mother decides to get revenge on squatters for causing the accident, Kitty gets involved — and kidnapped.

483) Time Of The Jackals

January 13th, 1969

Written by Paul Savage, Story by Richard Fielder, Directed by Vincent McEveety

Guest Cast: Leslie Nielsen, Beverly Garland, Edmund Hashim, Jonathan Lippe, Kip Whitman, Charles Maxwell, Robert Knapp, Sid Haig

 Jess Trevor is out to kill Leona, despite Matt protecting her. Trevor has his men attack Matt to give him a chance at the killing.

484) Mannon

January 20th, 1969

Written by Ron Bishop, Directed by Robert Butler

Guest Cast: Steve Forrest, Roy Barcroft, Michelle Breeze, Harry Bean , Pat Wines

 Will Mannon once rode with Quantrill's Raiders. He is now a gunman, and itching to prove his reputation by beating Matt in a gunfight.He shoots Festus, steals his mule and terrozies Dodge City.

485) The Gold Mine

January 27th, 1969

Written by Calvin Clements, Directed by Gunnar Hellstrom

Guest Cast: Lou Antonio, Lane Bradbury, Anthony James, Harry Davis, Kathryn Miner, Chubby Johnson, Paul Wexler, Jack Searl

 Merry Florene and her brother are back in Dodge again, this time with a complex scheme involving selling claims in an abandoned gold mine.

GUNSMOKE

486) The Mark of Cain

February 3rd, 1969

Written by Ron Bishop, Directed by Vincent McEveety

Guest Cast: Nehemiah Persoff, Louise Latham, Robert Totten, Kevin Coughlin, Robert DoQui, Stanley Clements, Olan Soule, Roy Barcroft

 Driscoll is a well-respected rancher in Dodge until Corley arrives in town — and reveals that Driscoll was a prison commandant in the Civil War, whose notorious camp killed over 700 men.

487) Reprisal

February 10th, 1969

Written by Jack Hawn, Directed by Bernard McEveety

Guest Cast: Joe Don Baker, Jack Lambert, Eunice Christopher, James Nusser, John Pickard, I. Stanford Jolley, Dennis Cross

 Doc Adams has lost babies at birth before, but the father of the latest one vows to kill him. If that isn't enough, he's also targeted when he is the only witness to a killing and the murderer becomes his patient.

488) The Long Night

February 17th, 1969

Written by Paul Savage, Story by Richard Carr

Guest Cast: Bruce Dern, Lou Antonio, Russell Johnson, Susan Silo, Robert Totten, Robert Brubaker, Tex Holman, Matt Emery

 Matt is on his way to Dodge with a prisoner worth $10,000. Three bounty hunters, wanting the money, hold Kitty, Doc, Sam and Louie captive, anto trade.
This was filmed for the previous season, but not shown at that time.

489) The Nightriders

February 24th, 1969

Written by Calvin Clements, Directed by Irving Moore

Guest Cast: Jeff Corey , Robert Pine, Bob Random, Norman Alden, Warren Vanders, Kate O'Mara, Iris Russell, Duncan Lamont, Robert Karnes, Scott Hale, Ed Bakey

While Matt is out of town and Festus is in charge, a gang of nightriders from Missouri begin terrorizing Dodge City. They are after righting wrongs begun in the Civil War, when they lost their homes and family.

490) The Intruder

March 3rd, 1969

Written by Jim Byrnes, Directed by Vincent McEveety

Guest Cast: Charles Aidman, John Kellogg, Gail Kobe, Eric Shea, Ralph James

Festus wounds a man he is after, and is forced to stop off at a ranch on the way back to Dodge in order to tend to the man. The owner was once married to his prisoner.

491) The Good Samaritans

March 10th, 1969

Written by Paul Savage, Directed by Bernard McEveety

Guest Cast: Brock Peters, Rex Ingram, L.Q. Jones, Sam Melville, Robert DoQui, Hazel Medina, Pauline Myers, Lynn Hamilton, Davis Roberts, John Brandon, Alyssia Gardner, Pepe Brown, Dan Ferrone

Matt is carrying valuable papers, and is attacked and wounded. A band of former slaves, traveling to a new home, help him. One of them, lured by greed, plans to betray him to his pursuers.

492) The Prisoner

March 17th, 1969

Written by Calvin Clements, Directed by Arthur Penn

Guest Cast: Jon Voigt, Ramon Bieri, Kenneth Tobey, Ned Glass, Paul Bryar, David Fresco, Don Happy, Mark Slade

A prisoner with a bounty saves Kitty's life. She is reluctant to turn him over to an out-of-town sheriff. To repay him, she helps him to win a poker game. It is at this point that his explosive temper shows her his true nature.

GUNSMOKE

493) Exodus 21:22

March 24th, 1969

Written by Arthur Rowe, Directed by Herschel Daugherty

Guest Cast: Steve Ihnat, Kaz Garas, Brandon Carroll, William Bramley, Lane Bradford, Sarah Hardy

Reardon is an ex-lawman, hunting the men who killed his pregnant wife. He doesn't want justice, though — simply revenge.

CLIPPING FILE:
CHESTER GOODE

Chester is an orphan, although he has a brother, Magnus. They were raised by an old man named Ben Cherry, who seems to have been somewhat simple in his tastes and ideas about raising children. He would always cook the same foods, and had a definite taste for coffee.

Chester was raised rather oddly, and this still shows. He is uncomfortable around people, though not as uncomfortable as his brother. Magnus is a fur hunter who spends months alone in the wilds.

When Ben Cherry died, Chester struck out on his own to make his way in life. He joined the Army for a while, and still has several friends in the lower ranks at Fort Dodge. Finally, he became Matt Dillon's assistant.

Chester admires Matt more than anyone else he's ever known, and happily does what he can to help out. Matt is not overly tidy, so Chester keeps the jailhouse clean, and looks after matters there. He sleeps on a cot in the office, while Matt has a small room in town.

Chester is a mean hand at brewing coffee, but his cooking isn't too good. He'd much rather eat at Delmonaco's in town.

Chester never carries a gun, but does have a rifle that he uses when on official business. He uses suspenders rather than a belt, and is not inclined to get into fights. Partly this is because of his amiable nature, and partly because of his limp. He leg is locked at the knee, though he never seems to have told anyone how this occurred. It slows him slightly, but despite the handicap, he is amazingly agile. Chester is generally pleasant and likable, but if he ever dislikes a person, he can be extremely sour and vindictive.

Chester's a pleasant and easy-going soul, simple rather than stupid. He can get very confused and confusing, and has a habit of exaggeration. His stories are frequently long, involved and wildly inaccurate. Still, he has a good heart, and will happily help out anyone in trouble. On the other hand, since he's not overly competent, the help he gives may be worse than the trouble people are in to begin with.

He always calls Matt "Mister Dillon" — he respects and admires him too much to be familiar with him. Kitty is always "Miss Kitty," and treated with equal respect. Doc, on the other hand, is the person with whom he argues. Doc delights in belittling or annoying Chester, and Chester returns the "compliments." His favorite occupation is to go fishing, as has a taste for fresh catfish.

More than anything, Chester wants to marry and settle down. The problem is that his luck with women is always bad. Either the women are conning him, or they fall for someone else. He even tried to buy a mail-order bride once, and one of the few women who genuinely loved him became a prisoner of the Comancheros. His luck ran constantly along such lines, much to his deep regret. He treats women with courtesy and considerable charm, and is very naive about them.

His biggest embarrassment is his family. He has a lot of uncles and cousins, most of whom are on the nether side of respectability and the law. None of them are particularly close to him, and he hopes that it will remain that way for the rest of his and their lives.

GUNSMOKE

Season Fifteen

September 22, 1969 through March 23rd, 1970

Produced by Joseph Dackow
Executive Producer: John Mantley
Executive Story Consultant: Calvin Clements
Director of Photography: Monroe Askins, ASC
Art Director: Joseph R. Jennings
Film Editor: Donald W. Ernst
Production Manager: Robert M. Beche
Post Production Executive: Ron Honthaner
Assistant Story Consultant: Jim Byrnes
Casting: Pam Polifroni
Music Editor: Gene Feldman
Sound Effects Editor: Jack A. Finlay
Production Sound Mixer: Andrew Gilmore
Script Supervisor: Edle Bakke
Set Decorator: Herman N. Schoenbrun
Property Master: Clem R. Widrig
Costumer: Alexander Velcoff
Makeup Artists: Glen Alden, Newton Jones
Hair Stylist: Gertrude Wheeler
Musical theme "Gunsmoke" also known as "Old Trails": Glenn Spencer and Rex Kouty

Cast:

Marshall Matt Dillon: James Arness
Doc Galen Adams: Milburn Stone
Kitty Russell: Amanda Blake
Festus Haggen: Ken Curtis
Newly O'Brien: Buck Taylor
Sam, the bartender: Glenn Strange
Louie Pheeters: James Nusser
Barney: Charles Seel
Howie: Howard Culver
Ed O'Connor: Tom Brown
Percy Crump: John Harper
Hank: Hank Patterson
Ma Smalley:Sarah Selby
Nathan Burke: Ted Jordan
Mr. Bodkin: Roy Roberts
Mr. Lathrop: Woodrow Chambliss
Halligan Charles Wagenheim

495) The Devil's Outpost

September 22nd, 1969

Written by Jim Byrnes & Robert Barbash, Story by Robert Barbash, Directed by Philip Leacock

Guest Cast:Robert Lansing, Jonathan Lippe, Karl Swenson, Sheila Larken, Val de Vargis, Ken Swofford, I. Stanford Jolley, Warren Vanders, Sam Edwards

When a gang raids a stage, Matt fights them off and captures the leader's brother. The rest of the gang are determine to get him back and kill Matt.

496) Stryker

September 29th, 1969

Written by Herman Groves, Directed by Robert Totten

Guest Cast: Morgan Woodward, Joan van Ark, Royal Dano, Andy Devine, Mills Watson, Walter Sande, Ted French

Stryker was the Marshal of Dodge before Matt. Sentenced to 15 years for murder, he is now out and aims to get revenge on Matt for the loss of his job, his freedom and his arm.

497) Coreyville

October 6th, 1969

Written by Herman Groves, Directed by Bernard McEveety

Guest Cast: Nina Foch, Ruth Roman, Kevin Coughlin, Thomas Hunter, Bruce Glover, Jo Ann Harris, James Almanzar, John Shuck, Charles Fredericks

After a saloon girl is killed in Coreyville, the leading lady frames a young cowboy to protect the real killer — her brother. Flo Watson knows the truth, but she keeps quiet for her own reasons.

498) Danny

October 13th, 1969

Written by Preston Wood, Directed by Bernard McEveety

Guest Cast: Jack Albertson, Scott Brady, Frank Marth, Vito Scotti, Rayford Barnes, Steve Raines

Danny is a con artist who is living on borrowed time. He wants to leave money for a grand funeral and wake, and to raise the money, he's taken a contract to kill Matt.

GUNSMOKE

499) Hawk

October 20th, 1969

Written by Kay Lenard & Jess Carneol, Directed by Gunnar Hellstrom

Guest Cast:Brendan Boone, Louise Latham, Michael J. Wixted, Hillarie Thompson, X Brands, Robert Brubaker, Bill Hart, Hal Needham

Festus finds an injured man on the trail and takes him to a nearby farm for help. The woman who owns the place recognizes the victim — her half-breed son, fathered by her Apache captor years ago. Her son is now a policeman on the trail of three renegades.

500) A Man Called "Smith"

October 27th, 1969

Written by Calvin Clements, Directed by Vincent McEveety

Guest Cast:Earl Holliman, Jacqueline Scott, Susan Olsen, Val Avery, Michael Durkin, William Fawcett, Margarita Cordova, Sid Haig

Abelia is not the widow that Festus believed. Her husband is an outlaw, who now returns to seek her help. This was a sequel to "Abelia" (11/18/68)

501) Charlie Noon

November 3rd, 1969

Written by Jim Byrnes, Directed by Vincent McEveety

Guest Cast: James Best, Miriam Colon, Ronny Howard, Edmund Hashim, Kip Whitman

Matt is forced to cross a terrible desert with his captive, Charlie Noon, and an Indian woman and her son. On their heels is a band of Comanches out for their blood.

502) The Still

November 10th, 1969

Written by Calvin Clements, Directed by Gunnar Hellstrom, Assistant Director Al Kraus, Incidental Music Leon Klatzkin

Guest Cast: Lane Bradbury, Anthony James, Shug Fisher, J. Edward McKinley

Once again, Merry Florene is having problems with her family. This time, they have set up an illegal still in the cellar of the schoolhouse where she is teaching. Then they steal a prize bull and try to hide that in there also...

503) A Matter Of Honor

November 17th, 1969

Written by Joy Dexter, Directed by Richard Totten

Guest Cast: John Anderson, Katherine Justice, Tom Simcox, Jack Bailey, Richard Bakalyan, Walter Sande, Dan Ferrone

A man is found murdered in Dodge City, and Louie Pheeters is dead drunk next to him. When he wakens, Louie can't recall what happened, and all the evidence points to his having committed murder.

504) The Innocent

November 24th, 1969

Written by Walter Black, Directed by Marvin Chomsky

Guest Cast: Eileen Heckart, Barry Atwater, Anthony James, Lee de Broux, Tom Nolan , Little Sky, Robert B. Williams, Manual Padilla, Jr.

A missionary employs Festus to show her the way to Cimarron territory. They are then ambushed by the Yewkers, a family of hide thieves, who dislike her and all she stands for.

505) Ring Of Darkness

December 1st, 1969

Written by Arthur Dales, Directed by Bernard McEveety

Guest Cast: Tom Drake, John Crawford, Rex Holman, Anthony Caruso, Pamela Dunlap, William Boyett

Ben Hurley's daughter, Susan, is blind. To raise money to help her, Hurley steals horses for outlaws. Newly tracks the horses to the farm, unaware that the gang trails him.

506) MacGraw

December 8th, 1969

Written by Kay Lenard & Jess Carneol, Directed by Philip Leacock

Guest Cast: J.D. Cannon, Diana Ewing, Michael Larrain, Ned Wertimer, Sid Haig, Allen Jaffe, Bobby Hall, Sam Edwards, Charles Kuenstle, Sam Melville

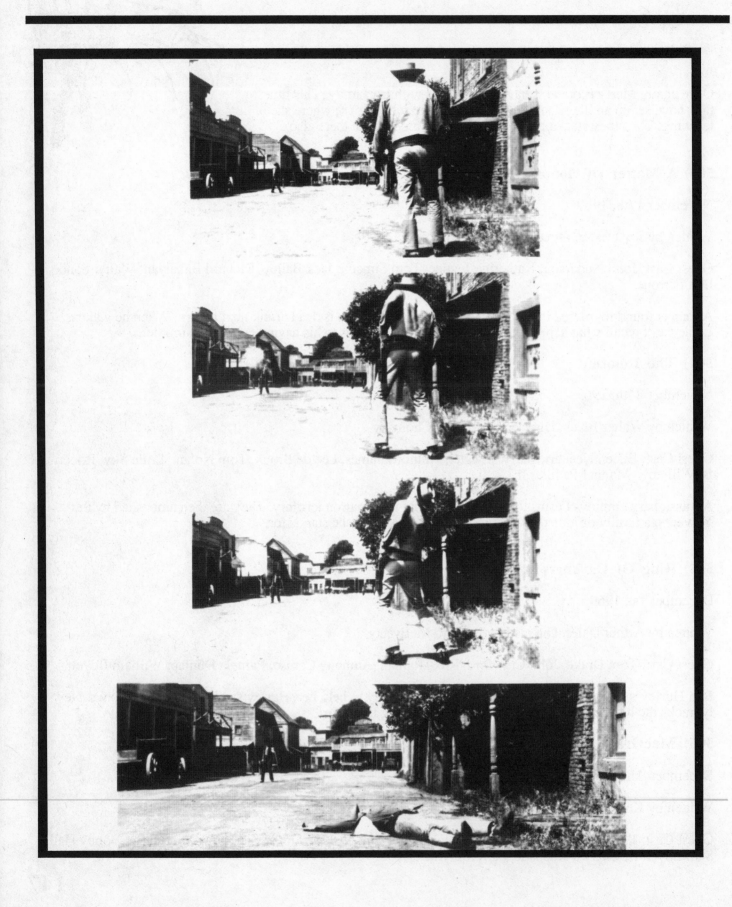

GUNSMOKE

Gunman Jake MacGraw heads for Dodge City upon his releas from prison. Everyone expects trouble, but he seems to be simply enjoying his time with a pretty girl and a cowboy. He takes a job as a piano-player at the Long Branch, but is he simply waiting for something?

507) Roots Of Fear

December 15th, 1969

Written by Arthur Browne, Directed by Philip Leacock

Guest Cast: John Anderson, Louise Latham, Warren Vanders, Cliff Osmond, Jody Foster, Walter Burke

A run on the bank forces it to close its doors to the public. The Sadler's will lose their farm without money, so they plan to rob the bank to raise the cash they need.

508) The Sisters

December 29th, 1969

Written by William Kelley, Directed by Philip Leacock

Guest Cast: Jack Elam, Lynn Hamilton, Gloria Calomee, Susan Batson, Erica Petal, Chris Hundley, CeCe Whitney

No-account Pack Landers runs into three nuns. They believe that they can reform him; he believes he can swindle them. Who will win this war of nerves?

509) The War Priest

January 5th, 1970

Written by William Kelley, Directed by Bernard McEveety

Guest Cast: Forrest Tucker, Richard Anderson, John Crawford, Richard Hale, Sam Melville, Link Wyler, Tom Sutton

Apache war priest Gregorio takes Kitty captive, so Sgt. Holly sets off on their trail.

510) The Pack Rat

January 12th, 1970

Written by Jim Byrnes & Arthur Browne, Story by Arthur Browne, Directed by Philip Leacock

Guest Cast:Manuel Padilla, Jr, William C. Watson, Loretta Swit, Heidi Vaughn, Bill Catching, Robert Rothwell, Robert Brubaker, Tom Sutton

Matt captures Sam Danton and heads back to Dodge with him in tow. Sancho, a young sneakthief, tries to rob Matt. Caught, Matt teaches him to behave and Sancho discovers a trap ahead.

511) The Judas Gun

January 19th, 1970

Written by Harry Kronman, Directed by Vincent McEveety

Guest Cast: Ron Hayes, Peter Jason, Richard X. Slattery, Laurie Mock, Sean McClory, Margarita Cordova, William Fawcett, Brad David, Ralph Neff

Two families have been feuding for years, but when one hires a killer, the affair comes to a tragic head.

512) Doctor Herman Schultz, MD

January 26th, 1970

Written by Calvin Clements, Story by Benny Rubin, Directed by Bernard McEveety

Guest Cast: Benny Rubin, Pete Kellett

Dr. Schultz is a hypnotist, supposedly using his powers for therapy. Instead, he commits robberies. Festus gets suspicious and Doc Adams determines to bring him to justice.

513) The Badge

February 2nd, 1970

Written by Jim Byrnes, Directed by Vincent McEveety

Guest Cast: Beverly Garland, Henry Jones, John Milford, Roy Jenson, Jack Lambert, William O'Connell, John Finn, Mary Angela, Fred Colby

When Matt is wounded again, Kitty puts the Long Branch up for sale and leaves town. In her new town, she finds something to disturb her deeply.

GUNSMOKE

514) Albert

February 9th, 1970

Written by Jim Byrnes, Directed by Vincent McEveety

Guest Cast: Milton Selzer, Patricia Barry, L.Q. Jones, Bob Random, William Schallert, Dorothy Neuman, Natalie Masters

Albert, an elderly bank teller about to be dismissed, foils a bank robbery. He pockets several thousand dollars, blaming it on the fleeing men. Later, they return, and demand his help to successfully rob the bank, or they will reveal the real story.

515) Kiowa

February 16th, 1970

Written by Ron Bishop, Directed by Bernard McEveety

Guest Cast: Victor French, Dub Taylor, John Beck, Lucas White, Joyce Ames, Richard Angarola, Jean Allison, Richard Lapp

Kiowa renegades strike at a ranch, kidnapping the rancher's daughter. The man's brother, a preacher and Matt set off after the raiding party.

516) Celia

February 23rd, 1970

Written by Harry Kronman, Directed by Philip Leacock

Guest Cast:Melissa Murphy, Cliff Osmond, Frank Marth, George Petrie, Walker Edmiston

Town blacksmith Ben Sommars falls for pretty Celia and refuses to believe Newly's warnings that she's simply out to fleece him.

517) Morgan

March 2nd, 1970

Written by Kay Lenard & Jess Carneol, Directed by Bernard McEveety

Guest Cast: Steve Forrest Hank Brandt, Charlotte Stewart, Ed Long, Mills Watson, Jonathan Lippe, Jack Garner, I. Stanford Jolley, Fletcher Bryant

Matt escorts a shipment of gold back to Dodge. Cole Morgan and his gang, armed with cannon, take over the town and await his arrival.

518) The Thieves

March 9th, 1970

Written by Tommy Thompson, Directed by Philip Leacock

Guest Cast: Michael Burns, Bill Callaway, Timothy Burns, Royal Dano, Daphne Field, John Schuck

Three teenaged boys, on probation from the county jail, are welcomed in Dodge City—for a while.

519) Hackett

March 16th, 1970

Written by William Kelley, Directed by Vincent McEveety

Guest Cast:Earl Holliman, Morgan Woodward, Jennifer West, Ken Swofford, Robert Totten, Bill Erwin, Allen Jung

Sargent gave up crime many years ago to settle down and farm. Now Hackett, his old partner, wants his help in a train robbery, and refuses to take no for an answer.

520) The Cage

March 23rd, 1970

Written by Calvin Clements, Directed by Bernard McEveety

Guest Cast:Steve Carson, Laura Figueroa, Jorge Moreno, Allen Jaffe, Renata Vanni, Ken Mayer, Gregg Palmer, Hank Brandt

In New Mexico, Matt and a posse hunt gold thieves. A man in the possee wants revenge on the thief that killed his brother.

GUNSMOKE

CLIPPING FILE: FESTUS HAGGEN

Festus is born of a mountain clan, who live off by themselves. They were all raised only in the family, insular and somewhat peculiar. They all verge on the lawless side, though some are more law-abiding than others.

Festus grew up in a sort of rough and tumble way. He isn't overly enthusiastic about staying clean, or shaving. He often likes to be alone to think, deeply, about matters that most folks hardly give a thought to.

Dodge City has become his home, and he enjoys being Matt's deputy. He alone calls the Marshal "Matthew," refusing to shorten the given name at all. He treats Miss Kitty with respect, but like Chester before him, he enjoys bickering with Doc. Though Festus is unused to civilized ways, he isn't naive. Civilized folks do the strangest things, to his manner of thinking.

He is an excellent tracker, and a very great assistance to Matt. He knows that he'll never make the grade as a full lawman, but sees his job of supporting the Marshal as one of great importance. Festus is happy with that.

The only thing Festus is unhappy with are the visits of any member of his family to Dodge. The Haggens are a close clan, and don't like him to be so far away. He, on the other hand, prefers it that way. Even by his own odd standards, the rest of the family are extremely peculiar.

Season Sixteen
Septermber 14th, 1970 through March 8th, 1971

Produced by Joseph Dackow
executive Producer: John Mantley
Executive Story Consultant: Calvin Clements
Director of Photography: Monroe Askins
Production Manager: Paul Nichols
Script Supervisor: Lloyd Nelson
Casting: Pam Polifroni
Post Production Executive: Ron Honthaner
Assistant Story Consultant: Paul F. Edwards
Art Director: Joseph R. Jennings
Set Decorator: Herman N. Schoenbrun
Property Master: Clem R. Widrig
Film Editor: Thomas McCarthy, ACE
Supervising Music Editor: Gene Feldman
Sound Effects Supervisor: Jerry Rosenthal
Production Sound Mixer: Ted Keep
Costumer: Alexander Velcoff
Makeup Artists: Glen Alden, Irving Pringle
Hair Stylist: Cheri Banks
Musical theme "Gunsmoke" also known as "Old Trails": Glenn Spencer and Rex Kouty

Cast:

Marshall Matt Dillon: James Arness
Doc Galen Adams: Milburn Stone
Kitty Russell: Amanda Blake
Festus Haggen: Ken Curtis
Newly O'Brien: Buck Taylor
Sam, the bartender: Glenn Strange
Louie Pheeters: James Nusser
Barney: Charles Seel
Howie: Howard Culver
Ed O'Connor: Tom Brown
Percy Crump: John Harper
Hank: Hank Patterson
Ma Smalley: Sarah Selby
Nathan Burke: Ted Jordan
Mr. Bodkin: Roy Roberts
Mr. Lathrop: Woodrow Chambliss
Halligan: Charles Wagenheim

GUNSMOKE

521) Chato

September 14th, 1970

Written by Paul Edwards, Directed by Vincent McEveety

Guest Cast:Ricardo Montalban, Miriam Colon, Peggy McKay, William Bryant, Rodolfo Hoyos, Robert Knapp, Pedro Regas, Jim Sheppard

Matt goes to New Mexico to hunt Chato, a half-breed who has vowed to kill all white men and did kill Matt's friend.

522) The Noose

September 21st, 1970

Written by Arthur Browne, Directed by Vincent McEveety

Guest Cast:Tom Skerritt, William Fawcett

A mysterious stranger kidnaps Kitty to lure Matt, Doc and Festus into a trap.

523) Stark

September 28th, 1970

Written by Don Sanford, Directed by Robert Totten

Guest Cast:Richard Kiley, Suzanne Pleshette, Henry Wilcoxon, Shelly Novak, Bob Burrows, Rusty Lane

Lewis Stark, a bounty hunter who believes that rancher John Bramley has cheated him out of money, kidnaps young Adam Bramley and holds him for ransom.

524) Sam McTavish, MD

October 5th

Written by Gerry Day & Bethel Leslie, Directed by Bernard McEveety

Guest Cast: Vera Miles, Arch Johnson, Dee Carroll, Lisa Gerritsen, Glenn Redding, Kathleen O'Malley, Amzie Strickland

Doc needs a replacement in Dodge for a while, and advertises. Sam McTavish responds. Doc is furious when he learns she is a woman, and doesn't trust her at first. She gradually wins his respect — and then his love.

525) Gentry's Law

October 12th, 1970

Written by Jack Miller, Directed by Vincent McEveety

Guest Cast: John Payne, Louise Latham, Shug Fisher, Peter Jason, Robert Pine, Don Heifer, Darlene Conley, Robert Totten, John Finn, Ron Keefer

Rich and autocratic landownerAmos Gentry refuses to turn over his two sons after they hang a squatter.

526) Snow Train (Part One)

October 19th, 1970

Written by Preston Wood, Directed by Gunnar Hellstrom

Guest Cast:Clifton James, Gene Evans, Ken Lynch, Roy Engel, Pamela Dunlap, Richard Lapp, Loretta Swit, Doreen Long, Tim Considine, Richard D. Kelton, John Milford, Dana Elcar, Ron Hayes, Ann Seymour, Eddie Applegate, X Brands

Matt travels back to Dodge by train. A band of Sioux Indians stops the train looking for the men who sold their tribe poisoned whiskey, which blinded and killed some of their tribe.
Filmed on location in the Black Hills of South Dakota.

527) Snow Train (Part Two) October 26th, 1970

Written by Preston Wood, Directed by Gunnar Hellstrom

Guest Cast:Clifton James, Gene Evans, Ken Lynch, Roy Engel, Pamela Dunlap, Richard Lapp, Loretta Swit, Doreen Long, Tim Considine, Richard D. Kelton, John Milford, Dana Elcar, Ron Hayes, Ann Seymour, Eddie Applegate, X Brands

Passengers want illegal moonshiners turned over to the Indians. Meanwhile, one of the passengers gives birth.

528) Luke

November 2nd, 1970

Written by Jack Miller, Directed by Bernard McEveety

Guest Cast: Morgan Woodward, Katherine Justice, Anthony Costello, Rex Holman, Victor Izzy

A wounded and dying old-time outlaw seeks out his long-lost daughter in Dodge City. To his disgust he finds her working as a saloon hostess.

GUNSMOKE

529) The Gun

November 9th, 1970

Written by Don Sanford, Directed by Bernard McEveety

Guest Cast: L.Q. Jones, Kevin Coughlin, Patricia Morrow, Robert Phillips, Sam Melville, Ken Mayer, Stanley Clements

A teenaged boy kills a famous gunfighter by accident. Scenting a story, a St. Louis reporter arrives to milk the lad for all he's worth.

530) The Scavengers

November 16th, 1970

Written by Jack Miller, Directed by Bernard McEveety

Guest Cast: Yaphet Kotto, Slim Pickens, Cicely Tyson, Roy Jenson, Link Wyler, Steve Patmes, Eddie Little Sky

Piney Biggs, the sole survivor of a massacred wagon train, tells Matt that Indian raiders massacred his party. A buffalo hunter, Colley, captures some of the Indians. Matt wonders if the Indians were the raiders or simply scavengers.

531) The Witness

November 23rd, 1970

Written by Shimon Wincelberg, Directed by Philip Leacock

Guest Cast: Harry Morgan, Tim O'Connor, Barry Brown, Dack Rambo, Annette O'Toole, June Dayton, I. Stanford Jolley, Roy Young, Herb Vigran, I. Stanford Jolley

Matt captures Ira Pickett, a wanted killer. His father kills the first witness against his son, then stalks the second.

532) McCabe

November 30th, 1970

Written by Jim Byrnes, Directed by Bernard McEveety

Guest Cast:Dan Kemp, Mitch Vogel, Jim Davis, David Brian, Jon Lormer, Robert Sorrells, Tani Phelps, Mills Watson, Lew Brown, Marie Cheatham, Tom Sutton

Matt captures killer McCabe after a hunt, but getting him back to Dodge for trial may be impossible. When he stops at a town, Matt finds McCabe wanted for murder there also, and slated to hang.

533) The Noon Day Devil

December 7th, 1970

Written by William Kelley, Directed by Philip Leacock, Assistant Director Martin Cohan, Incidental Music John Parker

Guest Cast: Anthony Zerbe, Ernest Sarracino, Warren Vanders, Anthony Cordova, Pepe Callahan, Natividad Vacio, Annette Cardona, Fred Coby, Tony Davis, Julio Medina, Bert Madrid, John Dullaghan, Natividad Vacio

One twin a murderer and a thief; the other a priest, each wants to win the other over to his side. It's not a predictable victory.

534) Sergeant Holly

December 14th, 1970

Written by William Kelley, Directed by Bernard McEveety

Guest Cast: Forrest Tucker, Albert Salmi, Victor Eberg, Gregg Palmer, Vito Scotti, David Renard, Med Flory, Read Morgan

Sergeant Holly returns to Dodge — this time accused of desertion and stealing an Army payroll. Proving him innocent depends on his catching the real thieves.
A sequel to the previous season's "The War Priest."

535) Jenny

December 28th, 1970

Written by Jack Miller, Directed by Robert Totten

Guest Cast: Lisa Gerritson, Steve Ihnat, Rance Howard, Steve Raines, Bob Burrows

Newly runs afoul of the law when he releases a dangerous outlaw to visit his nine-year-old daughter.

536) Captain Sligo

January 4th, 1971

Written by William Kelley, Directed by William Conrad

Guest Cast: Richard Basehart, Salome Jens, Royal Dano, Stacy Harris, Bobby Eilbacher, Geri Reischi, Royce Donnet

Captain Sligo retires from whaling to settle down in Dodge. Though he looks like an easy target, he proves very capable of repelling unwanted boarders.

537) Mirage

January 11th, 1971

Written by Jack Miller, Directed by Vincent McEveety

Guest Cast:John Anderson, Gary Wood, Mary Rings, Kevin Burchett, Harry Raybould, Robert Knapp, Daniel McWhite

Festus shoots a man in the desert. Lost, he stumbles into a ghost town.

538) Tycoon

January 25th, 1971

Written by Robert Vincent Wright, Directed by Bernard McEveety

Guest Cast:Shug Fisher, Nora Marlowe, Gwynne Gilford, John Beck, James Minotto

When Festus inherits $500, he decides to begin his own freight business. He soon discovers an unexpected hazard — a woman trying to marry off her daughter.

539) Jaekel

February 1st, 1971

Written by Calvin Clement, Story by True Boardman, Directed by Bernard McEveety

Guest Cast: Eric Braeden, Julie Gregg, Mia Bendixsen

Jaekel, a sadistic killer, is finally released from prison. He returns to Dodge to seek the woman he has been corresponding with, only to discover she did so only out of kindness.

GUNSMOKE

540) Murdock

February 8th, 1971

Written by Jack Miller, Directed by Robert Totten

Guest Cast: Jack Elam, Anthony Caruso, Jim Davis, Bob Random

Marshal Murdock uses a gold shipment as bait to draw out the notorious Carver gang — unaware that his own son belongs to the gang.

541) Cleavus

February 15th, 1971

Written by Donald Z. Koplowitz & Richard, D. Scott, Directed by Robert Totten

Guest Cast: Robert Totten, Arthur Hunnicutt, William Challee, Robert Cornthwaite, Rocky B. Williams

Cleavus is a loser of terrific proportions. His luck apparently takes a turn for the better when he finds a miner and his claim..

542) Lavery

February 22nd, 1971

Written by Don Sanford, Directed by Vincent McEveety

Guest Cast: Anthony Costello, Judi West, David Carradine, Karl Swenson, Ken Swofford, David Huddleston
Lavery saves Matt, and Matt returns the favor.

543) Pike (Part One)

March 1st, 1971

Written by Jack Miller, Directed by Bernard McEveety

Guest Cast: Jeanette Nolan, Dack Rambo, Cliff Osmond, Jim Boles, William Murphy, Ross Hagen, William Mims

Sally Fergus is a drifter and junk collector who finds a wounded outlaw and nurses him back to health. The two form an unlikely friendship.
The immensely popular story led to a spin-ff series, "Dirty Sally" (1974).

544) Pike (Part Two)

March 8th, 1971

Written by Jack Miller, Directed by Bernard McEveety

Guest Cast: Jeanette Nolan, Dack Rambo, Cliff Osmond, Jim Boles, William Murphy, Ross Hagen, William Mims

GUNSMOKE

Season Seventeen

September 13th, 1971 through March 13th, 1972

Produced by Leonard Katzman
Executive Producer: John Mantley
Executive Story Consultant: Jack Miller
Director of Photography: Monroe Askins, ASC
Art Director: Craig Smith
Set Decorator: Herman N. Schoenbrun
Property Master: Howard Cole
Film Editor: Gerard Wilson, ACE
Supervising Music Editor: Gene Feldman
Sound Effects Supervisor: Jerry Rosenthal
Production Sound Mixer: Andrew Gilmore
Production Manager: Paul Nichols
Script Supervisor: Lloyd Nelson
Associate Producer: Ron Honthaner
Casting: Pam Polifroni
Assistant Story Consultant: Paul F. Edwards
Costumer: Alexander Velcoff
Makeup Artist: Glen Alden, Irving Pringle
Hair Stylists: Gertrude Wheeler, Esperanza Corona
Musical theme "Gunsmoke" also known as "Old Trails": Glenn Spencer and Rex Kouty

Cast:

Marshall Matt Dillon: James Arness
Doc Galen Adams: Milburn Stone
Kitty Russell: Amanda Blake
Festus Haggen: Ken Curtis
Newly O'Brien: Buck Taylor
Sam, the bartender: Glenn Strange
Louie Pheeters: James Nusser
Barney: Charles Seel
Howie: Howard Culver
Ed O'Connor: Tom Brown
Percy Crump: John Harper
Hank: Hank Patterson
Ma Smalley:Sarah Selby
Nathan Burke: Ted Jordan
Mr. Bodkin: Roy Roberts
Mr. Lathrop: Woodrow Chambliss
Halligan: Charles Wagenheim
John Chapman, MD: Pat Hingle (episodes 549-555)

545) The Lost

September 13th, 1971

Written by Jack Miller, Story by Warren Vanders, Directed by Robert Totten

Guest Cast:Laurie Prange, Mercedes McCambridge, Royal Dano, Charles Kuenstle, Link Wyler, Peggy Rea, Dee Carroll, Harry Carey, Jr., Jerry Brown, Jon Jason Mantley, Maria Mantley

Kitty, lost in the desert after a stagecoach accident, depends on Girl, who has lived wild in this inhospitable land all of her young life.

546) Phoenix

September 20th, 1971

Written by Anthony Lawrence, Directed by Paul Stanley

Guest Cast:Glenn Corbett, Mariette Hartley, Gene Evans, Ramon Bieri, Frank Corsetino

An outlaw tries to earn money to begin a new life by becoming a hired gun.

547) Waste (Part One)

September 27th, 1971

Written by Jim Byrnes, Directed by Vincent McEveety

Guest Cast: Ruth Roman, Jeremy Slate, Ellen Bustyn, Johnny Whitaker, David Sheiner, Shug Fisher, Lieux Dressler, Don McGowan, George Chandler, Rex Holman, Ken Swofford, Don Keefer, Merry Anders, Lieux Dressler, Claire Brennan, Lee Pulford, Emory Parnell

Matt trails an outlaw, but constantly wastes his time. First, he runs into a wagon full of saloon women, and then into a young boy looking for his mother.
This story was filmed on location in southern Utah

548) Waste (Part Two)

October 4th, 1971

Written by Jim Byrnes, Directed by Vincent McEveety

Guest Cast: Ruth Roman, Jeremy Slate, Ellen Bustyn, Johnny Whitaker, David Sheiner, Shug Fisher, Lieux Dressler, Don McGowan, George Chandler, Rex Holman, Ken Swofford, Don Keefer, Merry Anders, Lieux Dressler, Claire Brennan, Lee Pulford, Emory Parnell

Matt and his companions confront the outlaws he searched for.

GUNSMOKE

549) New Doctor In Town

October 11th, 1971

Written by Jack Miller, Directed by Philip Leacock

Guest Cast: Lane Bradford, Jon Lormer

Doc Adams vanishes. Doctor Chapman takes his place. Festus is suspicious of him initially, while some of the patients in town won't allow him to treat them.
Pat Hingle appeared as John Chapman, taking over from Doc Adams for the next few episodes. Ostensibly, Doc Adams left town for a while, and asked his friend to fill in; in fact, actor Milburn Stone suffered a heart attack, and had to be replaced for a couple of months until he recovered.

550) Ma Colter

October 18th, 1971

Written by Calvin Clements, Jr, Directed by Philip Leacock

Guest Cast: Kim Hunter, Jan-Michael Vincent, Greg Mullavey, Richard D. Kelton, Bryan O'Byrne, Lloyd Nelson, Pat Dennis-Leigh, Victor Izay

Travis Colter wants to follow his older brothers into a life of crime. His mother, a saloon hostess, desperately tries to prevent this from happening.

551) Trafton

October 25th, 1971

Written by Ron Bishop, Directed by Bernard McEveety

Guest Cast: Victor French, Sharon Acker, Patti Cohoon, Paul Stevens, Philip Carey, Marie Windsor, Clay Tanner, Bill Catching, Fred Stromson, John Dullaghan, Mike Mazurki, John Lormer, Paul Stevens

Cold-blooded killer Trafton is shaken to the core when a priest he mortally wounds forgives him. Matt still wants to destroy the killer who has slain both the priest and the sheriff of a small Kansas town.

552) Lynott

November 1st, 1971

Written by Ron Bishop, Directed by Gunnar Hellstrom

Guest Cast: Richard Kiley, Peggy McCay, Anthony Caruso, Jonathan Lippe, William Bramley, Gregg Palmer, Ken Lynch

A one-time marshall saves Matt Dillon's life and fills in for him while he recovers from a wound.

553) Lijah

October 8th, 1971

Written by William Blinn, Directed by Irving Moore

Guest Cast:Denny Miller, Harry Townes, Erin Moran, Lane Bradford, Erin Moran, Herb Vigran

A jury tries silent mountain man Lijah for killing three people and abducting a fourth, a ten year old girl.

554) My Brother's Keeper

November 15th, 1971

Written by Arthur Dales, Directed by Paul Stanley

Guest Cast:John Dierkes Pippa Scott, Malcolm Atterbury, Ray Reinhardt, Charles McGraw, Dana Laurita

All Indian wants to die in peace; Festus wants to keep him alive. The two work for their mutually contradictory desires.

555) Drago

November 22nd, 1971

Written by Jim Byrnes, Directed by Paul Stanley

Guest Cast:Buddy Ebsen, Ben Johnson, Edward Faulkner, Michael Silverman, Rich Gates, Del Monroe, Tani Phelps Guthrie

Drago, an old Army scout, tracks down four killers of a woman who befriended him.

556) Gold Train [or The Bullet] (Part One)

November 29th, 1971

Written by Jim Byrnes, Directed by Vincent McEveety

Guest Cast: Eric Braeden, Katherine Justice, Alejandro Rey, Robert Hogan, Pepe Callahan, Sian Barbara Allen, Warren Kemmerling, Walter Sande, Harry Carey, Jr, Sam Melville, Eddie Firestone, Robert Sorrells, John Crawford, Mills Watson, Jonathan Lippe, Harry Harvey, Sr, Dan Ferrone

GUNSMOKE

Matt lies with a bullet lodged near his spine. Doc dares not attempt to operate, and takes him on a train to Denver. The train is carrying gold bullion, and outlaws aim to ambush it.

557) Gold Train [or The Bullet] (Part Two)

December 6th, 1971

Written by Jim Byrnes, Directed by Vincent McEveety

Guest Cast: Eric Braeden, Katherine Justice, Alejandro Rey, Robert Hogan, Pepe Callahan, Sian Barbara Allen, Warren Kemmerling, Walter Sande, Harry Carey, Jr, Sam Melville, Eddie Firestone, Robert Sorrells, John Crawford, Mills Watson, Jonathan Lippe, Harry Harvey, Sr, Dan Ferrone

The bandits strike and are defeated by Festus and Newly.

558) Gold Train [or The Bullet] (Part Three)

December 13th, 1971

Written by Jim Byrnes, Directed by Vincent McEveety

Guest Cast: Eric Braeden, Katherine Justice, Alejandro Rey, Robert Hogan, Pepe Callahan, Sian Barbara Allen, Warren Kemmerling, Walter Sande, Harry Carey, Jr, Sam Melville, Eddie Firestone, Robert Sorrells, John Crawford, Mills Watson, Jonathan Lippe, Harry Harvey, Sr, Dan Ferrone

Doc must operate or watch Matt die.

559) P.S., Merry Christmas

December 27th, 1971

Written by William Kelley, Directed by Herb Wallerstein

Guest Cast: Jeanette Nolan, Jack Elam, Patti Cohoon, Jodie Foster, Erin Moran, Josh Albee, Brian Morrison, Willie Aames, Todd Lookinland, Jack Collins, Herb Vigran, Maudie Prickett

This Christmas story revolves around a misunderstanding at an orphanage. The custodian and the woman in charge distrust one another, and both do what they feel is best for the children — even if it means taking the children away from the place. En route to California, seven homeless children find a Christmans they have never known.

560) No Tomorrow

January 3rd, 1972

Written by Richard Fielder, Directed by Irving Moore

Guest Cast: Sam Groom, Pamela McMyler, Henry Jones, Leo Gordon, Steve Brodie, Richard Hale, Liam Dunn, H.M. Wynant, Leo Genn, Dan Flynn

A homesteader, Ben Justin, is falsely accused of horse stealing. Imprisoned, he becomes the prime suspect when a guard is found murdered.

561) Hidalgo

January 10th, 1972

Written by Paul Edwards, Directed by Paul Stanley

Guest Cast:Alfonso Arau, Thomas Gomez, Fabian Gregory, Linda Marsh, Edward Colmans, David A. Renard, Julio Medina, Stella Garcia

Critically wounded while in Mexico, Matt relies on the help of a boy, a feeble old man and a woman to survive the inhospitable desert.

562) Tara

January 17th, 1972

Written by William Kelley, Directed by Bernard McEveety, Assistant Director Gordon Webb, Incidental Music John Parker

Guest Cast: Michele Carey, L.Q. Jones, Ken Swofford, Ken Mayer, James McCallion, Lawrence Delaney, Henry Hickox, John Dullaghan, Natalie Masters, Gene Tyburn, Don Pulford, Denny Arnold

Newly falls head over heels for Tara Hutson, not knowing she is the widow of a dead outlaw. Wanting to get hold of the missing $5,000 her dead husband stole, Tara pits Newly against a gunslinger.

563) One For The Road

January 24th, 1972

Written by Jack Miller, Directed by Bernard McEveety

Guest Cast: Jeanette Nolan, Jack Albertson, Melissa Murphy, Victor Holchak, Herb Vigran, Dorothy Neumann, Jack Perkins

GUNSMOKE

Dirty Sally is back again, and doing her best to help out the unfortunate. This time around, she stumbles across a drunkard whose daughter and her fiance are attempting to gain control of his estate.

564) The Predators

January 31st, 1972

Written by Calvin Clements, Directed by Bernard McEveety

Guest Cast: Claude Akins, Jacqueline Scott, Jodie Foster, Brian Morrison, George Murdoch

Abelia returns again, and this time she must match her wits against killer Howard Kane, and also against a killer dog.

565) Yankton

February 7th, 1972

Written by Jim Byrnes, Directed by Vincent McEveety

Guest Cast: Forrest Tucker, James Stacy, Pamela Peyton-Wright, Nancy Olson, Margaret Bacon

Yankton is a cheerful cowboy who sees marriage to wealthy Will Donavan's daughter as a ticket to the better life. Unfortunately, he can't disguise his real interest in the "romance."

566) Blindman's Bluff

February 21st, 1972

Written by Ron Honthaner, Directed by Herb Wallerstein

Guest Cast:Anne Jackson, Victor French, George Lindsey, Charles Kuenstle

A wounded mountain man, Jed Frazer, staggers into the home of spinster Phoebe, who insists on nursing him back to health and beginning a romance.

567) Alias Festus Haggen

March 6th, 1972

Written by Calvin Clements, Directed by Vincent McEveety

Guest Cast:Ramon Bieri, Lieux Dressler, Robert Totten, Jon Lormer, William Bryant, Booth Colman, Herb Vigran, Gregg Palmer, Rusty Lane

BIOGRAPHY: AMANDA BLAKE

Amanda Blake was born Beverly Louise Neill on February 20th, 1921, in Buffalo, NY. She began her career as an actress in stock theatre, including parts in such productions as "You Can't Take It With You," "George Washington Slept Here," "The Corn Is Green" and "Macbeth." Besides acting she also painted scenery. She was educated at Pomona College and when she obtained her first motion picture contract with MGM, while still in her teens, they intended for her to follow in the steps of Greer Garson. Blake played the second lead in **Stars In My Crown**, as well as parts in **Duchess of Idaho, Lili** and **The Glass Slipper** and eleven other films. Her television debut was for **Schlitz Playhouse**, in a story called "Crossroads." Recognition for the performance as well as in "Double Exposure," for the same show, was such that she was immediately cast for **Cavalcade Of America, Four Star Playhouse, Fireside Theatre** and others. She also appeared on **My Favorite Husband, Professional Father, The Red Skelton Show** and **Climax**. Finally cast in **Gunsmoke**, she stayed there for 19 of its 20 years. Since **Gunsmoke** left the air, she has appeared only in one episode of **The Quest** and one made for television movie, **The Betrayal**.

Television
Gunsmoke (1955-74)
Schlitz Playhouse Of The Stars: "Crossroads" (8/1/52)
Schlitz Playhouse Of The Stars: "Double Exposure" (8/15/52)
Cavalcade Of America: "Breakfast At Nancy's" (10/23/53)
Fireside Theatre: "Nine Quarts Of Water" (4/20/54)
Four Star Playhouse: "Vote Of Confidence" (11/11/54)
Matinee Theatre: "Sound Of Fear" (9/27/56)
Studio One: "Tide Of Corruption" (2/17/58)
GE Theatre: "Night Club" (10/11/59)
The Quest: "Day Of Outrage" (10/27/76)
My Faforite Husband
Professional Father
The Red Skelton Show
Climax

Movies
Battleground (1950)
Duchess Of Idaho (1950)
Stars In My Crown (1950)
Counterspy Meets Scotland Yard (1951)
Smuggler's Gold (1951)
Scarlet Angel (1952)
Cattle Town (1952)
Lili (1953)
Sabre Jet (1953)
Cinderella's Glass Slipper (1953)
Miss Robin Crusoe (1954)
About Mrs Leslie (1954)
The Adventures Of Hajji Baba (1954)
A Star Is Born (1954)
High Society (1955)
Betrayal (1974) TV

Gunsmoke — Return To Dodge (1987) TV

GUNSMOKE

Festus meets his look-alike, killer Frank Eaton. He stands trial before a jury that believes him to be the other man.
Both roles were played by Ken Curtis.

568) The Wedding

March 13th, 1972

Written by Harry Kronman, Directed by Bernard McEveety

Guest Cast: Morgan Woodward, Sam Elliot, Melissa Murphy, Lane Bradford, James Chandler, Fran Ryan, George Wallace, Byron Mabe, Melissa Newman

Walt Clayton disapproves of his daughter marrying Cory Soames. The youngsters gather their courage to go ahead with the wedding anyway.

Season Eighteen
September 11th, 1972 through March 5th, 1973

Produced by Leonard Katzman
Executive Producer: John Mantley
Executive Story Consultant: Jack Miller
Associate Producer: Ron Honthaner
Director of Photography: Monroe Askins, ASC
Art Director: Albert Heschong
Set Decorator: Herman N. Schoenbrun
Property Master: Earl Huntoon
Film Editor: Thomas McCarthy, ACE
Supervising Music Editor: Gene Feldman
Sound Effects Supervisor: Jack A. Finlay
Production Manager: Paul Nichols
Production Sound Mixer: Andrew Gilmore
Casting: Pam Polifroni
Assistant Story Consultant: Paul F. Edwards
Script Supervisor: Lloyd Nelson
Costumer: Alexander Velcoff
Makeup: Glen Alden, Kenneth Chase
Hair Stylist: Esperanza Corona
Musical theme "Gunsmoke" also known as "Old Trails": Glenn Spencer and Rex Kouty

Cast:

Marshall Matt Dillon: James Arness
Doc Galen Adams: Milburn Stone
Kitty Russell: Amanda Blake
Festus Haggen: Ken Curtis
Newly O'Brien: Buck Taylor
Sam, the bartender: Glenn Strange
Louie Pheeters: James Nusser
Barney: Charles Seel
Howie: Howard Culver
Ed O'Connor: Tom Brown
Percy Crump: John Harper
Hank: Hank Patterson
Ma Smalley: Sarah Selby
Nathan Burke: Ted Jordan
Mr. Bodkin: Roy Roberts
Mr. Lathrop: Woodrow Chambliss
Halligan: Charles Wagenheim

GUNSMOKE

569) The River (Part One)

September 11th, 1972

Written by Jack Miller, Directed by Herb Wallerstein

Guest Cast: Jack Elam, Miriam Colon, Slim Pickens, Patti Cohoon, Clay O'Brien, Roger Torrey, Jerry Gatlin, Red Morgan, Pete Kellett, Gene Tyburn, Jack Perkins, Maudie Prickett

Matt recovers the loot from the notorious gang led by Charlie Utter. When the gang pursues him, he leaps off a cliff into rushing water, where he is saved by the runaway Kincaid children.
Filmed on location in the Rogue River country near Grants Psas, Oregon.

570) The River (Part Two)

September 18th, 1972

Written by Jack Miller, Directed by Herb Wallerstein

Guest Cast: Jack Elam, Miriam Colon, Slim Pickens, Patti Cohoon, Clay O'Brien, Roger Torrey, Jerry Gatlin, Red Morgan, Pete Kellett, Gene Tyburn, Jack Perkins, Maudie Prickett

The gang continues to pursue, herding Matt and the children down river. Matt and the children eventually navigate the river filled with dangerous rapids— only to discover that the gang of killers is waiting for them.

571) Bohannon

September 25th, 1972

Written by William Kelley, Directed by Alf Kjellin

Guest Cast:Richard Kiley, Linda Marsh, Vincent Van Patten, Helen Kleeb, Ed Bakey, Regis Cordic

Bohannan wanders the West offering his faith healing skills until Doc exposes him as a charlatan with the help of a terminally ill boy.

572) Judgment

October 2nd, 1972

Written by Shimon Wincelberg, Directed by Philip Leacock

Guest Cast: William Windom, Ramon Bieri, Tim O'Connor, Mariette Hartley, Katherine Helmond, Richard Kelton

Musgrove, a gunman, arrives in Dodge hunting an apparently harmless derelict, Spratt. When he can't find the man, the gunman threatens to kill Gideon, a prominent Dodge citizen, if the drifter isn't produced.

573) The Drummer

October 9th, 1972

Written by Richard Fielder, Directed by Bernard McEveety

Guest Cast: Victor French, Fionnuala Flanagan, Brandon Cruz, Bruce Glover, Kiel Martin, Herb Armstrong, Paul Sorensen

Daniel Shay seems to be simply a traveling rat trap salesman, but the local bully knows something of the past he prefers to keep hidden. Shay then meets up with Jimmy Morgan and his widowed mother, and finally begins to deal with his guilty past.

574) Sarah

October 16th, 1972

Written by Calvin Clements, Directed by Gunnar Hellstrom

Guest Cast:Anne Francis, Anthony Caruso, Jonathan Lippe, Michael Lane, John Orchard, Kay E. Kuter, Rex Holman, George Keymas, Larry Duran, Ronald Manning, Alberto Rina

Sarah, one of Matt's old girl-friends, now rules a robber's roost saloon. She saves his life by passing him off as her outlaw husband. Matt is then expected to take part in an upcoming stage robbery.
Filmed on location in Old Tucson, Arizona

575) The Fugitives

October 23rd, 1972

Written by Charles Joseph Stone, Directed by Irving Moore

Guest Cast: James Olson, Darrell Larson, Vic Tayback, Russell Johnson, Troy Melton

Doc and Festus are captured by an outlaw gang. To save both of their lives, Doc must operate successfully on a critically wounded member of the gang. Manwhile Festus escapes and brings Matt and a possee.

576) Eleven Dollars

October 30th, 1972

Written by Paul Savage, Directed by Irving Moore

Guest Cast: Susan Oliver, Josh Albee, Ike Eisenmann, Diane Shalet, E.J. Andre, Roy Engle, Sam Edwards, Owen Bush, Phil Chambers, A. G. Vitanza, Jerry Brown, Gloria LeRoy, Tom Waters, Brad Trumbull

Festus is on his way to close out a small deal for eleven dollars. He runs afoul of two con men who think he's big business.

577) Milligan

November 6th, 1972

Written by Ron Bishop, Directed by Bernard McEveety

Guest Cast: Harry Morgan, Joseph Campanella, Lynn Carlin, Patti Cohoon, Sorrell Booke, Charles MacCauley, Scott Walker, Lew Brown, Read Morgan, Gene Tyburn, John Pickard

A robber, Norcross, held up the local bank. As he flees, farmer Milligan shoots him in the back. The townsfolk side with the thief, and ostracize the farmer.

578) Tatum

November 13th, 1972

Written by Jim Byrnes, Directed by Gunnar Hellstrom, Assistant Director Robert R. Shue, Incidental Music Richard Shores

Guest Cast:Gene Evans, Sandra Smith, Sheila Larken, Jay MacIntosh, Jeff Pomerantz, Ana Korita, Ken Tobey, Lloyd Nelson, Neil Summers, Robert Tindall, Duncan Inches

Trapper and ex-gunfighter Brodie Tatum is fatally mauled by a bear. With death near, his young Indian wife sends for his three grown daughters who bring him to Spearville to be buried alongside his first wife, their mother. The townfolk oppose this and Matt must intervene.
Filmed on location in Old Tucson, Arizona

579) The Sodbusters

November 20th, 1972

Written by Ron Bishop, Directed by Robert Totten

Guest Cast: Alex Cord, Morgan Woodward, Katherine Justice, Leif Garrett, Dawn Lyn, Harrison Ford, Paul Prokop, Colin Male, Richard Bull, Joe di Reda, Robert Viharo, Norman Bartold

Farmers and cattlemen square off over who has the rights to a much-needed waterhole.
Filmed on location in Old Tucson, Arizona.

BIOGRAPHY: MILBURN STONE

Milburn Stone was born in Burton, Kansas on July 5th, 1904. Stone turned down an appointment to the U.S. Naval Academy to join the act of Stone and Strain, "songs, dances and snappy chatter." The successful act was featured on network radio. Stone made his Broadway debut in 1932, in Sinclair Lewis's "The Jayhawker." Two years later he made the first of about 150 films, **Ladies Crave Excitement**, with Marie Wilson. Universal Studios put him under contract from 1942 until 1946. Milburn won an Emmy in 1967-68 for his long-running role on **Gunsmoke** as Doc Adams. He won an even more unique honor for the same role. The Kansas Medical Society gave him honorary membership for the authenticity of his performance. This made him one of only five laymen who have received the award in the Society's 100-year history. He died from a heart attack in 1980.

Television
Gunsmoke (1955-75)
Wild Bill Hickock: "The Silver Mine Protection Story" (1952)
Dragnet: "The Big Jump" (1952)
TV Reader's Digest: "A Million Dollar Story" (5/2/55)
Front Row Center: "Morals Squad" (3/11/56)
Climax!: "The Great World And Timothy Colt"

Movies
The Fighting Marines (1935)
Ladies Crave Excitement (1935)
Rendezvous (1935)
The Three Mesquiteers (1935)
The Milky Way (1936)
China Clipper (1936)
The Princess Comes Across (1936)
Two In A Crowd (1936)
A Doctor's Diary (1937)
Atlantic Flight (1937)
Federal Bullets (1937)
Wings Over Honolulu (1937)
Blazing Barriers (1937)
Music For Madame (1937)
Swing It, Professor (1937)
Youth On Parole (1937)
The Thirteenth Man (1937)
The Man In Blue (1937)
Mr. Boggs Steps Out (1937)
The Port Of Missing Girls (1938)
Crime School (1938)
Wives Under Suspicion (1938)
The Storm (1938)
Paroled From The Big House (1938)
California Frontier (1938)
Sinners In Paradise (1938)
Tail Spin (1939)
Mystery Plane/Sky Pilot (1939)
Young Mr. Lincoln (1939)
Tropic Fury (1939)
King Of The Turf (1939)
Society Smugglers (1939)
Fighting Mad (1939)
Blind Alley (1939)
Stunt Pilot (1939)
When Tomorrow Comes (1939)
Sky Patrol (1939)
Made For Each Other (1939)

Danger Flight (1939)
Crashing Through (1939)
Charlie McCarthy, Detective (1939)
Nick Carter —— Master Detective (1939)
Enemy Agent/Secret Enemy (1940)
Give Us Wings (1940)
Chasing Trouble (1940)
Johnny Apollo (1940)
An Angel From Texas (1940)
Framed (1940)
Lillian Russell (1940)
Colorado (1940)
The Great Plane Robbery (1940)
The Great Train Robbery (1941)
The Phantom Cowboy (1941)
Death Valley Outlaws (1941)
Frisco Lil (1942)
Rubber Racketeers (1942)
Eyes In The Night (1942)
Invisible Agent (1942)
Police Bullets (1942)
Pacific Rendezvous (1942)
Reap The Wild Wind (1942)
Captive Wild Woman (1943)
Keep 'em Slugging (1943)
You Can't Beat The Law (1943)
Get Going (1943)
Corvette K-225/The Nelson Touch (1943)
Sherlock Holmes Faces Death (1943)
The Mad Ghoul (1943)
Gung Ho! (1943)
The Imposter (1944)
Hi, Good Looking (1944)
Jungle Woman (1944)
The Great Alaskan Mystery (1944)
Hat Check Honey (1944)
Moon Over Las Vegas (1944)
Phantom Lady (1944)
Twilight On The Prairie (1944)
The Master Key (1945)
The Beautiful Cheat/What A Woman! (1945)
She Gets Her Man (1945)
The Frozen Ghost (1945)
The Daltons Ride Again (1945)
I'll Remember April (1945)
On Stage Everybody (1945)
Strange Confession (1945)
Sing Out, Sister (1945)

The Royal Mounted Rides Again (1945)
The Spider Woman Strikes Back (1946)
Inside Job (1946)
Danger Woman (1946)
Smooth As Silk (1946)
Little Miss Big/Baxter's Millions (1946)
Strange Conquest (1946)
Her Adventurous Night (1946)
Cass Timberlane (1947)
Killer Dill (1947)
The Michigan Kid (1947)
Headin' For Heaven (1947)
Buck Privates Come Home/Rookies Come Home (1947)
Train To Alcatraz (1948)
The Judge/The Gamblers (1948)
The Green Promise/Raging Waters (1949)
Calamity Jane And Sam Bass (1949)
Sky Dragon (1949)
No Man Of Her Own (1950)
The Fireball (1950)
Snow Dog (1950)
Branded (1951)
The Racket (1951)
Road Block (1951)
Flying Leathernecks (1951)
The Atomic City (1952)
The Savage (1952)
Behind Southern Lines (1952)
The Sun Shines Bright (1953)
Invaders From Mars (1953)
Second Chance (1953)
Pickup On South Street (1953)
Arrowhead (1953)
The Siege At Red River (1954)
Black Tuesday (1955)
The Long Gray Line (1955)
White Feather (1955)
Smoke Signal (1955)
The Private War Of Major Benson (1955)
Durango (1957)
The World Of Sport Fishing (1972) Documentary

GUNSMOKE

580) The Brothers

November 27th, 1972

Written by Calvin Clements, Directed by Gunnar Hellstrom

Guest Cast: Steve Forrest, Joe Silver, Angus Duncan, Eddie Ryder, Richard O'Brien, Regis J. Cordic, Edward Faulkner, Reid Cruikshanks

Cord Wrecken arrives in Dodge, searching for his brother's killers. The guilty parties are Beal Brown and one Miss Kitty Russell.

581) Hostage!

December 11th, 1972

Written by Paul Edwards, Directed by Gunnar Hellstrom

Guest Cast: William Smith, Geoffrey Lewis, Marco St. John, James Chandler, Nina Roman, Hal Baylor, Sandra Kent, Stafford Repp, Woordow Chambliss

The Dog Soldiers, a notorious band of marrauders, marks Matt for death for the execution of one of their members. Jude Bonner shoots Kitty down in the streets of Dodge and Matt Takes off his badge and goes hunting for Bonner.

582) Jubilee

December 18th, 1972

Written by Paul Savage, Story by Jack Freeman, Directed by Herb Wallerstein

Guest Cast:Tom Skerritt, Colin Wilcox-Horne, Scott Brady Alan Hale, Lori Rutherford, Todd Cameron

Ed Well's is a farmer who dreams of striking it rich with his horse. Festus forces the farmer to pit his horse against one owned by Dave Chaney in a match race.

583) Arizona Midnight

January 1st, 1973

Written by Dudley Bromley, Directed by Irving Moore

Guest Cast:Billy Curtis, Stanley Clements, Mills Watson, Ken Mayer, Sadye Powell

A midget cowboy calling himself Arizona arrives in town astride a giant horse. He claims that at midnight on nights with a full moon he transforms into an elephant. Disbelieving townfolks are dumbstruck when a great, lumbering elephant, wearing the midget's hat on its huge head, appears.

584) Homecoming

January 8th, 1973

Written by Calvin Clements, Directed by Gunnar Hellstrom

Guest Cast: Richard Kelton, Robert Pratt, Stuart Margolin, Lurene Tuttle, Claudia Bryar, Ivy Jones, Lynn Marta

Doc is tending Anna Wilson, who is dying on her farm. Her two sons arrive home in time to speak with her, but both have now become outlaws and hold Kitty and Doc hostage.

585) Shadler

January 15th, 1973

Written by Jim Byrnes, Directed by Arnold Laven

Guest Cast: Earl Holliman, Diana Hyland, Denver Pyle, Linda Watkins, John Davis Chandler, Alex Sharp

Shadler, an escaped convict disguised as a priest, and Newly save the town from a gang of outlaws.

586) Patricia

January 22nd, 1973

Written by Calvin Clements, Directed by Alf Kjellin

Guest Cast: Jess Walton, Ike Eisenmann, Gail Bonney, Donald Elson, Charles Waggenheim, Richard Lundin, John Baer

Patricia arrives in Dodge to marry Newly. Doc discovers Patricia suffers from a blood disease that could take her life.

587) A Quiet Day In Dodge

January 29th, 1973

Written by Jack Miller, Directed by Alf Kjellin

Guest Cast: Margaret Hamilton, Willie Aames, Leo Gordon, Shug Fisher, Douglas V. Fowley, John Fiedler, Helen Page Camp, J. Pat O'Malley, Herb Vigran, Walker Edmiston

A tough day for Matt Dillon. He returns to Dodge with a dangerous prisoner in tow, not having slept in two days and looking forward to a rest. Instead he finds a runaway boy with larcenous thoughts, a brawl at the Long Branch and a hopping mad Kitty.

GUNSMOKE

588) Whelan's Men

February 5th, 1973

Written by Ron Bishop, Directed by Paul Edwards

Guest Cast: Robert Burr, William Bramley, Harrison Ford, Noble Willingham, Frank Ramirez, Bobby Hall, Ed Craig, Gerald McRaney, Richard Hale, Seaman Glass

With Matt out of town, Whelan and his band of killers ride in and take over the town. Kitty challenges Whelan to a game of poker. The stakes: Matt's life and the fate of the town.

589) Kimbrough

February 12th, 1973

Written by Jim Byrnes, Directed by Gunnar Hellstrom

Guest Cast: John Anderson, Michael Strong, William Devane, Tom Falk, Rick Weaver, Doreen Long, Lisa Eilbacher, Wendell Baker, William Brawley, Robert Burr, Noble Willingham, Harrison Ford, Frank Ramirez, Richard Hale, Seaman Glass, Ed Craig, Bobby Hall, Gerald McRaney

Matt finds the man who taught him everything he knows, Kimbrough, a drunkard sweeping out stables. Matt recruits him to help guard a gold shipment which is ambushed by outlaws.

590) Jesse

February 19th, 1973

Written by Jim Byrnes, Directed by Bernard McEveety

Guest Cast: Brock Peters Jim Davis, Regis J. Cordic, Don Stroud, Leonard Stone, Robert Pine, Ted Gehring, Lloyd Nelson, Norman Bartold

Festus and Newly must decide whether to free Jesse Dillard when the gang he cooks for descend upon them. Jesse once called Festus friend but now walks the outlaw trail.

591) Talbot

February 26th, 1973

Written by Jim Byrnes, Directed by Vincent McEveety

Guest Cast:Anthony Zerbe, Salome Jens, Peter Jason, Bill Williams, Charles MacCauley, Chanin Hale, Robert Totten, Link Wyler, Victor Izay, Robert Donner, Gloria Dixon, Tom Sutton

Talbot lays plans to rob the Dodge bank while the town is loaded with prosperous cattlemen. Love for Katharine, the widow of a man he shot in self-defence distracts him.

592) This Golden Land

March 5th, 1973

Written by Hal Sitowitz, Directed by Gunnar Hellstrom

Guest Cast: Paul Stevens, Victor French, Richard Dreyfuss, Bettye Ackerman, Joseph Hindy, Wayne McLaren, Scott Selles, Kevin Coughlin, Stephanie Epper, Robert Nichols

Moshe Gorofsky and his family came from Russia. Moshe's devotion to the Torah is put to the test when cowboys kill one of his sons. It is tested further when one of his other sons goes after the killer with a gun.

GUNSMOKE

Season Nineteen

September 10th, 1973 through April 1st, 1974

Produced by Leonard Katzman
Executive Producer: John Mantley
Musical theme "Gunsmoke" also known as "Old Trails": Glenn Spencer and Rex Kouty

Cast:

Marshall Matt Dillon: James Arness
Doc Galen Adams: Milburn Stone
Kitty Russell: Amanda Blake
Festus Haggen: Ken Curtis
Newly O'Brien: Buck Taylor
Sam, the bartender: Glenn Strange
Louie Pheeters: James Nusser
Barney: Charles Seel
Howie: Howard Culver
Ed O'Connor: Tom Brown
Percy Crump: John Harper
Hank: Hank Patterson
Ma Smalley:Sarah Selby
Nathan Burke: Ted Jordan
Mr. Bodkin: Roy Roberts
Mr. Lathrop: Woodrow Chambliss
Halligan: Charles Wagenheim

593) Women For Sale (Part One)

September 10th, 1973

Written by Jim Byrnes, Directed by Vincent McEveety, Narrated by William Conrad

Guest Cast: James Whitmore, Shani Wallis, Nicholas Hammond, Kathleen Cody, Sally Kemp, Larry D. Mann, Dan Ferrone, Gregory Sierra, Dawn Lyn, Lieux Dressler, Robert Manning, Francesca Jervis, Gilbert Escandon, Edgar Monetathchi

Settlers and travelers captured by a band of renegade Indians and sold into white slavery.

594) Women For sale (Part Two)

September 17th, 1973

Written by Jim Byrnes, Directed by Vincent McEveety,
Narrated by William Conrad

Guest Cast: James Whitmore, Shani Wallis, Nicholas Hammond, Kathleen Cody, Sally Kemp, Larry D. Mann, Dan Ferrone, Gregory Sierra, Dawn Lyn, Lieux Dressler, Robert Manning, Francesca Jervis, Gilbert Escandon, Edgar Monetathchi

Matt rescues Stella and Marcy, now a motherless child, from their Indian captors. He then goes after Fitzpatrick, the white slaver attempting to bring his slaves to Mexico.

595) Matt's Love Story

September 24th, 1973

Written by Ron Bishop, Directed by Gunnar Hellstrom

Guest Cast: Michael Learned, Victor French, Keith Andes, Jonathan Lippe, William Schallert, Nathan Lapp, Richard Lunding, Neil Summers, S. Michael de France

When Matt loses his memory, he forgets about Kitty and falls in love with the woman tending his wounds. Then the gang that he was after catches up with him and the woman.

GUNSMOKE

596) The Boy And The Sinner

October 1st, 1973

Written by Hal Sitowitz, Directed by Bernard McEveety

Guest Cast: Ron Moody, Vincent Van Patten, Warren Vanders, John Crawford, Ken Lynch, Read Morgan, Florida Friebus, Victor Izay, Hal Baylor

Noah Beel is a drunkard of no account who falls under the spell of Colby Eaton, a farm boy who believes he can reform the old reprobate. Now Noah must choose between keeping the respect of Colby and fulfilling his promise to two hired gunmen.

597) The Widowmaker

October 8th, 1973

Written by Paul Edwards, Directed by Bernard McEveety

Guest Cast: Steve Forrest, Barra Grant, David Huddleston, Randolph Roberts, Rand Brooks, Jerry Gatlin, J.R. Clark, James Chandler

Coltrane, a gunslinger known as the widow maker, has hung up his guns to live in peace with Teresa, the girl he loves. But there are still plenty of men who want to earn a reputation by killing him.

598) Kitty's Love Affair

October 22nd, 1973

Written by Paul Savage, Story by Susan Kotar & Joan E. Gessler, Directed by Vincent McEveety

Guest Cast: Richard Kiley, Leonard Stone, Christopher Connelly, Paul Picerni, Don Keefer, Jack Perkins, Gerald McRaney, Del Monroe, Virginia Baker

A reformed gunman saves Kitty from outlaws, and then falls in love with her. She is torn between her feelings for him and for Matt.

599) The Widow And The Rogue

October 29th, 1973

Written by Paul Savage, Story by Harvey Marlowe & Paul Savage, Directed by Bernard McEveety

Guest Cast: James Stacy, Beth Brickell, Clay O'Brien, Helen Page Camp, Monika Svensson, Paul Sorensen, Richard A. Lundin, Walker Edminston, Ed McCready

Festus escorts Honigger to trial in Dodge City. When they fall in with widowed Mrs. Cunningham and her son, Honigger charms the widow. He finds himself more interested in her than he intended.
Filmed on location in Old Tucson, Arizona

600) A Game Of Death... An Act Of Love (Part One)

November 5th, 1973

Written by Paul Edwards, Directed by Gunnar Hellstrom

Guest Cast: Morgan Woodward, Donna Mills, Paul Stevens, Whitney Blake, John Pickard, Geoffrey Horne, Avan Haranjo, Michael Learned, Garry Walberg, Herb Vigran, X Brands, Peter Canon, Clay Tanner

Bear Sanderson seeks his own revenge when Indians slay his wife and burn his home. Matt suspects ta different killer, a white man.

601) A Game Of Death... An Act Of Love (Part Two)

November 12th, 1973

Written by Paul Edwards, Directed by Gunnar Hellstrom

Guest Cast: Morgan Woodward, Donna Mills, Paul Stevens, Whitney Blake, John Pickard, Geoffrey Horne, Avan Haranjo, Michael Learned, Garry Walberg, Herb Vigran, X Brands

Matt defends the Indians accused of killing Bear Sanderson's wife before a hostile jury.

602) Lynch Town

November 19th, 1973

Written by Calvin Clements, Story by Joann Carlino & Anne Snyder, Directed by Bernard McEveety

Guest Cast: David Wayne, Mitch Vogel, Scott Brady, Warren Kemmerling, Ken Swofford, Norman Alden, Julie Cobb, Nancy Jeris

Matt forces alcoholic Circuit Judge Warfield to hold an inquest into the death of a woman saloon keeper. The judge is in town boss John King's pocket until a lynching triggers a belated rebirth of conscience.

183

GUNSMOKE

KEN CURTIS

Ken Curtis entered show business as a singer, joining the Tommy Dorsey band as the replacement for Frank Sinatra. His rendition of Tumbling Tumbleweeds while a member of the Sons of the Pioneers gained Columbia Pictures's attention. They placed him in movies as a cowboy sidekick to "Big Boy" Williams for a long string of Westerns. Curtis followed that with appearances in **The Searchers, The Alamo, The Quiet Man, How The West Was Won** and **Cheyenne Autumn. The Killer Shrews, The Giant Gila Monster** and **My Dog, Buddy** found him in a different role, on the other side of the camera as producer. He has also appeared on television but his most memorable role was as Festus Haggen, a bit part that became a series regular for many years. Since **Gunsmoke** he briefly appeared in The Yellow Rose as Hoyt Coryell, a ranch hand.

Television
Gunsmoke (1964-1975)
Ripcord (1961-1963)
The Yellow Rose (1983-1984)

Movies
The Quiet Man (1952)
The Searchers (1956)
The Alamo (1960)
How The West Was Won (1962)
Cheyenne Autumn (1964)

As Producer:
The Killer Shrews
The Giant Gila Monster
My Dog, Buddy

184

603) The Hanging Of Newly O'Brien

November 26th, 1973

Written by Calvin Clements, Directed by Alf Kjellin

Guest Cast:Billy Green Bush, Jimmy Van Patten, Jessamine Milner, Jan Burrell, Rusty Lane, Deborah Dozier, Walter Scott, Billie Bird

When Newly unsuccessfully operates on a dying man in a mountain community, the vengeful family sentence him to death.

604) Susan Was Evil

December 3rd, 1973

Written by William Keys, Directed by Bernard McEveety

Guest Cast:Kathleen Nolan, Katherine Cannon, Art Lund, George di Cenzo, Henry Olek, James Gannon, Robert Brubaker

When a wounded outlaw arrives at a remote way station, the woman who runs the place and her niece have very different ideas on what to do with the man.

605) The Deadly Innocent

December 17th, 1973

Written by Calvin Clements, Directed by Bernard McEveety

Guest Cast:Russell Wiggins, Charles Dierkop, Herb Vigran, Danny Arnold, Jack Garner, William Shriver, Erica Hunton

A young retarded man is provoked to violence whenever he sees anyone hurting anything. He tries to fit into society, but is branded a menace, and demands are made that he be locked away for good.

606) A Child Between

December 24th, 1973

Written by Harry Kronman, Directed by Irving Moore

Guest Cast: Sam Groom, Sondra Morgan, John Dierkes, Eddie Little Sky, Pete Kellett, Bill Hart, Alex Sharp

Lew Harrod is married to an Indian woman. When their child gets sick, he wants to take it to a doctor. Harrod is a wanted man though, and Makesha fears that if he ventures into town, she'll lose both her baby and her husband.

185

GUNSMOKE

607) A Family Of Killers

January 14th, 1974

Written by William Keys, Directed by Gunnar Hellstrom

Guest Cast:Glenn Corbett, Anthony Caruso, Mills Watson, Morgan Paull, Zina Bethune, George Keymas, Frank Corsentino, Stuart Margolin

US Marshal Hargraves chases a family who killed one of his deputies and wounded another. The men leave a trail of violence behind them.

608) Like Old Times

January 21st, 1974

Written by Richard Fielder, Directed by Irving Moore

Guest Cast: Nehemiah Persoff, Gloria de Haven, Daniel J. Travanti, Charles Haig, Hal Bokar, Rhodie Cogan, Robert Brubaker, Victor Izay

After twelve years in prison, Ben Rando returns to Dodge to try and re-establish his life. Convincing people that he has reformed is not easy.

609) The Town Tamers

January 28th, 1974

Written by Paul Savage, Directed by Gunnar Hellstrom

Guest Cast: Jim Davis, Jean Allison, Ike Eisenmann, Leo Gordon, Rex Holman, Kay Kuter, Sean McClory, Dan McGowan, James Jeter

A lawless frontier town proves too much for one lawman. Matt joins forces with Rumbaugh to stop the lawlessness.

610) The Foundling

February 11th, 1974

Written by Jim Byrnes, Directed by Bernard McEveety

Guest Cast:Kay Lenz, Bonnie Bartlett, Donald Moffat, Dran Hamilton, Don Collier, Jerry Hardin

Maatt finds a homeless baby girl and attempts to locate new parents for the tiny child.

611) The Iron Blood Of Courage

February 18th, 1974

Written by Ron Bishop, Directed by Gunnar Hellstrom

Guest Cast: Eric Braeden, Gene Evans, Lloyd Bochner, Miriam Colon, Mariette Hartley, Patti Cohoon, John Milford, Bing Russell, Robert Karnes, John Baer

One of two ranchers disputing water rights hires a gunslinger to protect his herd.

612) The Schoolmarm

February 25th, 1974

Written by Dick Nelson, Directed by Bernard McEveety

Guest Cast: Sondra Blake, Lin McCarthy, Todd Lookinland, Scott Walker, Janet Nichols, Laura Nichols, Kevin C. McEveety, Richard A. Lundin, Charlotte Stewart, Howard Curtis

A teacher is raped. When she discovers herself pregnant, she retreats into herself, and avoids all offers of help.

613) Trail Of Bloodshed

March 4th, 1974

Written by Paul Savage, Directed by Bernard McEveety

Guest Cast: Kurt Russell, Tom Simcox, Craig Russell, Janice Baldwin, Harry Carey, Jr, Nina Roman, Read Morgan, Craig Stevens, Larry Pennell

Buck Henry hunts the man who killed his father — and finds his uncle.

614) Cowtown Hustler

March 11th, 1974

Written by Jim Byrnes, Directed by Gunnar Hellstrom

Guest Cast: Jack Albertson, Jonathan Lippe, Nellie Bellflower, John Davis Chandler, Richard O'Brien, Henry Beckman, Dabbs Greer, Lew Brown, Dabs Greer, Robert Swan, Chuck Hicks

Moses Derby, a former pool player now trying to recover his lost past, enters a high-stakes match. With him, and of somewhat uncertain help, is Dave Rope, his bodyguard.

GUNSMOKE

615) To Ride A Yellow Horse

March 18th, 1974

Written by Calvin Clements, Directed by Vincent McEveety

Guest Cast: Louise Latham, Kathleen Cody, Thomas Leopold John Reilly, Parker Stevenson, Simon Scott, Herb Vigran, Elizabeth Harrower

Joan Shepard dominates her children, whether they like it or not.

616) Disciple

April 1st, 1974

Written by Shimon Wincelberg, Directed by Gunnar Hellstrom

Guest Cast: Dennis Redfield, Frank Marth, Marco St. John, Paul Picerni, David Huddleston, R.G. Armstrong, Claire Brennan, Robert Phillips, Robert Brubaker, Bobby E. Clark

When Matt no longer feels he can maintain law and order in Dodge City, he turns in his badge.

BIOGRAPHY: BUCK TAYLOR

Born into a Hollywood show business family, Buck Taylor grew up on a
small ranch in the San Fernando Valley. He attended North Hollywood High
School and studied weekends at Chouinard Art Institute in Los Angeles, hoping to become an illustrator. He
later attended the University of Southern California, where he pursued an interest in cinema, theatre arts and
art for a year. Taylor left USC when he was activated along with the rest of his Naval Reserve Unit during
World War Two. He served two years as a U.S. Navy fire fighter in Japan. When he mustered out he entered a career doing stunt work for film and injured his should in a saddle fall from a horse on the **Rebel** series. Taylor won the first part he ever auditioned for, a one-liner as a member of a kid gang in **Episode 8**.
His later appearances, and they number no less than 100, were in shows including **Ben Casey, The Fugitive, Big Valley** and as an ugly heavy in a two-part **Gunsmoke** entitled "Vengeance," which won him his
lasting part as Newly O'Brien.

Television
Gunsmoke (1967-75)
The Monroes (1966-67)
Ben Casey
The Fugitive
Big Valley

GUNSMOKE

Season Twenty

September 9th, 1974 through March 31st, 1975

Executive Producer: John Mantley
Producer: Leonard Katzman
Musical theme "Gunsmoke" also known as "Old Trails": Glenn Spencer and Rex Kouty

Cast:

Marshall Matt Dillon: James Arness
Doc Galen Adams: Milburn Stone
Festus Haggen: Ken Curtis
Newly O'Brien: Buck Taylor
Louie Pheeters: James Nusser
Barney: Charles Seel
Howie: Howard Culver
Ed O'Connor: Tom Brown
Percy Crump: John Harper
Hank: Hank Patterson
Ma Smalley: Sarah Selby
Nathan Burke: Ted Jordan
Mr. Bodkin: Roy Roberts
Mr. Lathrop: Woodrow Chambliss
Halligan: Charles Wagenheim
Miss Hannah: Fran Ryan

617) Matt Dillon Must Die!

September 9th, 1974

Written by Ray Goldrup, Directed by Victor French

Guest Cast:Morgan Woodward, Joseph Hindy, Bill Lucking, Henry Olek, Douglas Dirkson, Frederick Herrick, Elain Fulkerson

After Matt shoots an outlaw, the man's father and four brothers hold him captive, and plan to hunt him down.

618) A Town In Chains

September 16th, 1974

Written by Ron Bishop, Directed by Bernard McEveety

Guest Cast: Ramon Bieri, Russell Wiggins, Gretchen Corbett, Ron Soble, Lance le Gault, Med Flory, John Crawford, Paul C. Thomas, Thad Halb, Don Stroud

When Dillon goes to warn a town about an invading band of outlaws, he find them in control of the town and becomes their prisoner.

619) The Guns Of Cibola Blanca (Part One)

September 23rd, 1974

Written by Paul Savage, Directed by Gunnar Hellstrom

Guest Cast: Harold Gould, Dorothy Tristan, Richard Anderson, James Luisi, Jackie Coogan, Henry Beckman, Gloria Le Roy, Shug Fisher, Rex Holman, Michael Christofer

Doc and Lyla are taken captive by Confederate officers-turned-bandits headquartered in a remote mountain fortress.

620) The Guns Of Cibola Blanca (Part Two)

September 30th, 1974

Written by Paul Savage, Directed by Gunnar Hellstrom

Guest Cast: Harold Gould, Dorothy Tristan, Richard Anderson, James Luisi, Jackie Coogan, Henry Beckman, Gloria Le Roy, Shug Fisher, Rex Holman, Michael Christofer

Matt, Festus and Newly lead a posse into Cibola Blanca, where they pose as outlaws to get in.

GUNSMOKE

621) Thirty A Month And Found

October 7th, 1974

Written by Jim Byrnes, Directed by Bernard McEveety

Guest Cast: Gene Evans, Van Williams, Nicholas Hammond, David Brian, Ford Rainey, Kim O'Brien, Victor Izay, Hal Baylor

Three drovers — Parmalee in his sixties, Quincy in his forties and Doak in his twenties — are faced with difficult decisions to make with cattle drives becoming a thing of the past.

622) The Wiving

October 14th, 1974

Written by Earl Wallace, Directed by Victor French

Guest Cast: Henry Morgan, Karen Grassle, John Reilly, Dennis Redfield, Linda Sublette, Herman Poppe, Michelle Marsh

Jed Hockett decides his three sons should be married, so he sends them off to find brides — and warns them not to come back single. The boys all kidnap unwilling women.

623) The Iron Men

October 21st, 1974

Written by John Mantley, Directed by Gunnar Hellstrom

Guest Cast: Cameron Mitchell, John Russell, Barbara Colby, Eric Olson, George Murdock, William Bryant, Marc Alaimo, Paul Gehrman, Alec Murdock

Chauncey Demon was once a fine lawman. After his family was massacred by Indians, he became a drunken saloon bum. Matt determines to get Demon back onto his feet again.

624) The Fourth Victim

November 4th, 1974

Written by Jim Byrnes, Directed by Bernard McEveety

Guest Cast:Biff McGuire, Leonard Stone, Paul Sorensen, Victor Killian, Lloyd Perryman, Frank K. Janson

A series of killings plague Dodge, all without a sound or leaving a trace. Matt fears a pattern in the murders, a path which leads to Doc.

625) The Tarnished Badge

November 11th, 1974

Written by Robert Vincent Wright, Directed by Michael O'Herlihy

Guest Cast: Victor French, Pamela McMyler, Nick Nolte, Ruth McDevitt, Garry Walberg, James Lyon, Eddie Firestone, Ross Elliot, Sam Edwards, William Kitt

Sheriff Bo Harker rules his town with an iron grip. The townsfolk appeal to Matt to save them from this dictator.

626) In Performance Of Duty

November 18th, 1974

Written by William Keys, Directed by Gunnar Hellstrom

Guest Cast: Eduard Franz, David Huddleston, Paul Koslo, Bonnie Bartlett, Rance Howard, Martin Kove, Michael MacRae

Matt is tries to convict a family of killers, but all the witnesses against the family turn up murdered. The judge won't hold the killers without sufficient evidence.

627) Island In The Desert (Part One)

December 2nd, 1974

Written by Jim Byrnes, Directed by Gunnar Hellstrom

Guest Cast: Strother Martin, William C. Watson, Regis J. Cordic, Hank Brandt

Festus is wounded whilst crossing the desert after a criminal. Ben Snow, a gold miner abandoned by his partner years back, saves his life. Ben then turns Festus into a human pack animal.

628) Island In the Desert (Part Two)

December 9th, 1974

Written by Jim Byrnes, Directed by Gunnar Hellstrom

Guest Cast: Strother Martin, William C. Watson, Regis J. Cordic, Hank Brandt

Snow plans to transport his gold back to civilization to use against his enemies.

GUNSMOKE

629) The Colonel

December 16th, 1974

Written by Arthur Dales, Directed by Bernard McEveety

Guest Cast: Lee J. Cobb, Julie Cobb, Daniel J. Travanti, Richard Ely, Todd Lookinland, Randolph Robert, Roy Jen

A once-proud military officer suddenly faces a painful and unplanned reunion with his daughter Ann..

630) The Squaw

January 6th, 1975

Written by Jim Byrnes, Directed by Gunnar Hellstrom

Guest Cast: John Saxon, Arlene Martel, Tom Reese, Morgan Paull, William Campbell, Harry Middlebrooks, X Brands

Gristy Calhoun double-crosses his outlaw partners then flees from both Matt and his ex-partners. Qanah, an Indian woman cast out by her tribe, is the only one who can help him survive in the badlands.

631) The Hiders

January 13th, 1975

Written by Paul Savage, Directed by Victor French

Guest Cast:Ned Beatty, Mitch Vogel, Lee de Broux, Sierra Bandit, Damon Douglas, Robert Donner, Ellen Blake

Festus tries to reform a young man who earns his living working with a group that skins dead cattle on the range. The hiders don't take at all kindly to his interest in the youth.

632) Larkin

January 20th, 1975

Written by Jim Byrnes, Directed by Gunnar Hellstrom

Guest Cast:Richard Jaekel, Anthony Caruso, Jack Rader, Robert Sorrells, Kathleen Cody, Michael le Clair, Elliot Lindsay, Robert Gentry, Maggie Malooly

Newly brings in a prisoner while a gang of bounty hunters get on their trail. They want the man for the reward on his head.

BIOGRAPHY:
GLENN STRANGE

Glenn was born in Carlsbad, New Mexico, and is of Irish and Cherokee blood. Work as a cowboy was the first job pursued by Glenn. He began in show business with performances for the Doug Morgan Stock Company on radio in El Paso, Texas, and in Los Angeles in the early Thirties. He appeared in a series of Westerns with Dick Foran from 1936 until 1937. As a badman in Westerns, he claims he was killed by every cowboy hero since Hoot Gibson. Strange smashed his left kneecap when a runaway stagecoach hit him in one of the Westerns. This injury may have led to his first career breakthrough, the role of the Frankenstein monster for Universal's House of Frankenstein, House of Dracula and Abbott and Costello Meet Frankenstein. He began pouring beer in the Longbranch Saloon in 1962 and didn't stop until 1974.

Television
Gunsmoke (1962-74)

Movies
House of Frankenstein
House of Dracula
Abbott and Costello Meet Frankenstein

GUNSMOKE

633) The Fires Of Ignorance

January 27th, 1975

Written by Jim Byrnes, Directed by Victor French

Guest Cast: John Vernon, Allen Garfield, Lance Kerwin, Herb Vigran, Diane Shalet, George di Cenzo

Harker doesn't think that education is important for his young son, and keeps him home to work on the farm. The boy's teacher cannot get through to Harker, and starts a fight that lands them both in court. This episode makes a strong statement in favor of compulsory education.

634) The Angry Land

February 3rd, 1975

Written by Jim Byrnes, Story by Herman Groves, Directed by Bernard McEveety

Guest Cast:Carol Vogel, Eileen McDonough, Bruce M. Fischer, Dayton Loomis

When a young girl's parents are murdered, she is taken to her aunt. The women, bitter and reclusive, refuses to take the child in.

635) Brides And Grooms

February 10th, 1975

Written by Earl Wallace, Directed by Victor French

Guest Cast: Harry Morgan, Dennis Redfield, David Soul, Amanda McBroom, Linda Sublette, Michelle Marsh, Jim Backus, Spencer Milligan, Jerry Hoffman, Ray Girardin

Finally, Jed Hockett's sons return with three prospective brides. Their problems are not over yet; it's a stormy road to a triple wedding.
This was a sequel to the earlier story "The Wiving."

636) Hard Labor

February 24th, 1975

Written by Earl Wallace, Story by Hal Sitowitz

Guest Cast: John Colicos, Hal Williams, William Smith, Kevin Coughlin, Ben Piazza, Gregory Sierra, Gerald McRaney, Don Megowan, Lloyd Nelson

Matt has been forced to kill an escaped prisoner, but he is placed on trial for this. Corrupt Judge Flood sentences Matt to life imprisonment and hard labor in the silver mine owned by the Judge.

637) I Have Promises to Keep

March 3rd, 1975

Written by Paul Savage & Earl Wallace, Story by Paul Savage (as "William Putman"), Directed by Vincent McEveety

Guest Cast: David Wayne, Tom Lacy, Ken Swofford, Ken Renard, Trini Tellez, Ed McCready

Reverend Byrne attempts to build a church for the Comanches. Neither they nor the whites want it to succeed, but Festus offers his help.

638) The Busters

March 10th, 1975

Written by Jim Byrnes, Directed by Bernard McEveety

Guest Cast: Gary Busey, John Beck, Lynn Benesch, Gregg Palmer

Two bronco busters risk their lives to raise money for a ranch in Montana, only to have the dream ruined by a wild stallion.

639) Manolo

March 17th, 1975

Written by Earl Wallace, Story by Earl Wallace and Harriet Charles, Directed by Gunnar Hellstrom

Guest Cast: Nehemiah Persoff, Robert Urich, Mark Shera, Alma Lenor Beltram, Jess Walton, Brioni James, Michael Gregory, Joe Barns

According to Basque tradition, a son must defeat his father in combat to prove his manhood. Manolo refuses to do so, and is ostracized by his family of sheep herders.

640) The Sharecroppers

March 31st, 1975

Written by Earl Wallace, Directed by Leonard Katzman

Guest Cast: Susanne Benton, Victor French, Terry Williams, Jacques Aubuchon, Bruce Boxtleitner, Lisa Eilbacher, Graham Jarvis,

Marie Pugh tries to get her family to plant a crop before the landlord runs them off the property. She ropes Festus into helping.

197

GUNSMOKE

Gunsmoke: Return To Dodge (1987) TV Movie

Produced by John Mantley
Directed by Vincent McEveety

Cast:

Matt Dillon: James Arness
Kitty Russell: Amanda Blake
Newly O'Brien: Buck Taylor
Miss Hannah: Fran Ryan
Mannon: Steve Forrest
Jake Flagg: Earl Holliman
Lt. Dexter: Ken Olandt
Digger: W. Morgan Sheppard
Bright Water: Patrice Martinez
Little Doe: Tantoo Cardinal
Oakum: Mickey Jones

Matt has retired as Marshal of Dodge. His place was taken by Newly. Twenty years have passed and Matt now lives in the mountains. Mannon returns after his release from jail, determined to get his revenge on Matt and Kitty.

This movie was filmed in Alberta, Canada, and featured clips from the series. Mannon had appeared first in "Mannon," the episode of January 20th, 1969.

This guide could not have been managed without the help of two excellent reference works on "Gunsmoke." They are:
"Gunsmoke: A Twenty Year Videography" by Kristine Fredrikkson
This was printed in several parts in "The Journal Of Popular Film And Television," beginning with the issue of Spring, 1984.
"Television Drama Series Programming" by Larry Gianakos (The Scarecrow Press)
Both works are recommended, especially the first which contains much information on the show.

BIOGRAPHY:
DENNIS WEAVER

Dennis Weaver was born on June 4th, 1924, in Joplin, Missouri. He was educated at the University of Oklahoma, where he was a track star. During the Second World War, he was a Navy pilot, and after the war he took up acting. He won an Emmy for his role as Chester in **Gunsmoke** in 1958-59. Dennis also made his directorial debut for the show. His son, Robby, is now also acting, occasionally with his father.

As Actor
Television
Gunsmoke (1955-64)
Kentucky Jones (1964-65)
Gentle Ben (1967-69)
McCloud (1970-77)
Centennial (1978-79)
Stone (1979-80)
Emerald Point, NAS (1983-84)
Buck James (1987-88)
Dragnet: "The Big Bible" (12/2/54)
Schlitz Playhouse Of The Stars: "Underground" (1/21/55)
Dragnet: "The Big Screen" (1/27/55)
Big Town: "Crime In The City Room" (5/15/56)
The Silent Service: "Two Davids And Goliath" (7/5/57)
Climax!: "Burst Of Fire" (1/30/58)
Playhouse 90: "The Dungeon" (4/10/58)
Alfred Hitchcock Presents: "Insomnia" (5/8/60)
The Twilight Zone: "Shadow Play" (5/5/61)
Dr. Kildare: "A Reverence For Life" (4/29/65)
Combat: "The Farmer" (10/12/65)
Judd, For The Defense: "The View From The Ivy Tower" (3/7/69)
The Name Of The Game: "Give Till It Hurts" (10/31/69)
The Virginian: "Train Of Darkness" (2/4/70)
The Hardy Boys And Nancy Drew:
"The Mystery Of The Hollywood Phantom"

Movies
Horizons West (1952)
The Lawless Breed (1952)
The Raiders (1952)
The Mississippi Gambler (1953)
War Arrow (1954)
Dangerous Mission (1954)
The Bridges At Toko-Ri (1955)
Seven Angry Men (1955)
Storm Fear (1955)
Touch Of Evil (1958)
The Gallant Hours (1960)
Duel At Diablo (1966)

Way, Way Out (1966)
Gentle Giant (1967)
Mission Batangas (1968)
A Man Called Sledge (1971)
What's The Matter With Helen? (1971)
The Forgotten Man (1971) TV
Duel (1971) TV
Rolling Man (1972) TV
Female Artillery (1973) TV
The Great Man's Whiskers (1973) TV [Filmed 1969]
Terror On the Beach (1973) TV
Intimate Strangers (1977) TV
The Islander (1978) TV
Pearl (1978) TV
Ishi: The Last Of His Tribe (1978) TV
The Ordeal Of Patty Hearst (1979) TV
Amber Waves (1980) TV
The Ordeal Of Dr. Mudd (1980) TV
The Day The Loving Stopped (1981) TV
Don't Go To Sleep (1982) TV
Cocaine: One Man's Seduction (1983) TV

As Director
Television
Gunsmoke: "Marry Me" (12/23/61)

199

GUNSMOKE

AWARDS THE SERIES WON

Radio Daily's Annual All-American Poll::
1/15/57-4th place under Best Filmed Series
1/20/58-tied with **Wagon Train** for 1st place under Western Show of Year for TV
1/19/59-1st place under Western Show of Year for TV
1/29/60-3rd place under Western Show of Year for TV
1/29/62-2nd place under Western Show of Year for TV
2/25/63-2nd place under under Best Western on TV
1/28/64-2nd place under under Best Western of Year for TV
1/26/65-2nd place place under under Best Western of Year for TV
(Radio-Television Daily is no longer published)

Motion Picture Daily Annual Television Poll:
1/15/60-1st place in Best Western Series
1/16/61-2nd place in Best Western Series
1/18/62-2nd place in Best Western Series
1/21/63-2nd place in Best Western Series
1/20/64-2nd place in Best Western Series
1/25/65-2nd place in Best Western Series
1/24/66-2nd place in Best Western Series
1/23/67-2nd place in Best Western Series
1/22/68-2nd place in Best Western Series
1/22/69-2nd place in Best Western Series
1/21/70-2nd place in Best Western Series
2/10/71-2nd place in Best Western Series
1/21/72-2nd place in Best Western Series

Academy of Television Arts and Sciences (Emmy):
4/15/58-Best dramatic series with continuing characters.
Emmy to Mike Pozen for best TV film editing in "How to Kill a Woman"

5/6/59-Emmy to Dennis Weaver for best supporting actor
    (continuing character) in a dramatic series
5/19/68-Emmy to Milburn Stone for outstanding continu
    ing performance by an actor in a supporting role
    in a drama
5/18/70-Emmys to Richard E. Raderman and Norman Karlin for outstanding
    achievement in film sound editing in "Charlie Noon"

TV-Radio Mirror Poll:
May, 1958-Favorite TV Western Program
May, 1959-Favorite half hour TV dramatic program

Look Television Poll:
12/30/58-Voted Best Action Series "For the series that most effectively presented
    Western, mystery or other adventure stories"

Reno Chamber of Commerce:
5/28/60-Silver Spurs Award to James Arness as outstanding Western actor of the
    year

National Headliner Award:
8/27/64-Award to Kathleen Hits for her scripts

National Cowboy Hall of Fame and Western Heritage Center:
4/14/67-Wrangler Trophy for episode aired 1/8/66-Calvin Clements, writer; Mark
    Tydell, director; Philip Leacock, producer; and, John Mantley, associate
    producer
1968-Amanda Blake, the first woman and first living person inducted into the Hall
    of Fame of Great Westen Performers, National Cowboy Hall of Fame
4/24/71-Wrangler Award to John Mantley (executive producer) and John Parker
    (composer-conductor) for two-part "Show Train"
4/22/72-Wrangler Award to John Mantley (executive producer), Leonard Katzman
    (producer), Jack Miller (writer), Jeanette Nolan and Dack Rambo (guest
    cast) and all regular cast for two-part "Pike"

GUNSMOKE

Western Writers of America:

6/17/71-Golden Spur Award to Paul Edwards (writer) and to **Gunsmoke** for
   "Cahto" as Best Western Teleplay for the 1970-1971 season

6/22/72-Golden Spur Award to Jack Miller (executive story consultant and writer)
   and to **Gunsmoke** for two-part "Pike" as Best Western Teleplay for the
   1971-1972 season

Nebraskaland Days:

6/21/72-Buffalo Bill Cody Award to Amanda Blake, the first woman to receive it
for outstanding contributions to quality family entertainment

International Broadcasting Awards:

3/20/73-James Arness was honored as Man of the Year by the industry leaders
attending a banquet in Hollywood for the International Broadcasting awards

203